Advance Praise for
A Bird in Flight Leaves No Trace

"Although not often highlighted in popular Buddhist books, Korean Zen teachers have played a crucial role in the preservation, continuation, and reinterpretation of the Chinese Zen tradition since medieval times. This commentary on the teachings of the great Chan master Huangbo (d. 850) by an eminent contemporary Korean Seon master introduces Western readers and practitioners not only to that vital role but also to the vitality of the contemporary Korean Zen tradition. Seon (Zen) Master Subul is a preeminent teacher of *ganhwa Seon*, 'the Zen of examining meditative topics,' and he orients his approach to Huangbo's text around this technique, thus combining the best of medieval Chinese Zen and contemporary Korean Zen. This book should be inspiring to serious practitioners of Zen in particular, but also to all Buddhist practitioners."
—Mu Soeng, resident scholar at the Barre Center for Buddhist Studies

"How wonderful to have a clear new translation of the Zen teachings of Huangbo, one of the greatest masters of Zen's golden era. Korean Seon Master Subul's commentary is a marvelous addition to the original text, adding refinement to the meaning. Strongly suggested reading for all practitioners."
—Richard Shrobe, guiding teacher, Chogye International Zen Center of New York

"This meticulous and beautiful translation of a contemporary Korean Zen master's commentary on a Chinese Buddhist classic will benefit countless readers on their journey to spiritual awakening."
—Hwansoo Ilmee Kim, associate professor, Department of Religious Studies at Yale University

A Bird in Flight Leaves No Trace

The Zen Teachings of Huangbo with a Modern Commentary

Seon Master Subul

TRANSLATED BY

ROBERT E. BUSWELL JR.

AND

SEONG-UK KIM

Wisdom

Wisdom Publications
199 Elm Street
Somerville, MA 02144 USA
wisdompubs.org

흔적 없이 나는 새
By Subul Sunim

English translation by Seong-Uk Kim and Robert E. Buswell, Jr.

Library of Congress Cataloging-in-Publication Data

Names: Subul, 1953– author. | Buswell, Robert E., Jr., 1953– translator. | Kim, Seong-Uk, translator.
Title: A bird in flight leaves no trace: the Zen teachings of Huangbo with a modern commentary / Seon Master Subul; translated by Robert E. Buswell, Jr. and Seong-Uk Kim.
Other titles: Hunjok opsi nanun sae. English
Description: Somerville, MA, USA: Wisdom Publications, [2018] | Includes bibliographical references and index. |
Identifiers: LCCN 2018023674 (print) | LCCN 2018038874 (ebook) | ISBN 9781614295525 (e-book) | ISBN 9781614295303 (hard cover: alk. paper)
Subjects: LCSH: Buddhism—Korea. | Zen Buddhism—Korea. | Huangbo, –850.
Classification: LCC BQ656 (ebook) | LCC BQ656 .S8313 2018 (print) | DDC 294.309519—dc23
LC record available at https://lccn.loc.gov/2018023674
ISBN 978-1-61429-530-3 ebook ISBN 978-1-61429-552-5

23 22 21 20 19 5 4 3 2 1

Cover design by Phil Pascuzzo. Interior design by Tony Lulek. Set in DPG 11/14.1.

Wisdom Publications' books are printed on acid-free paper and meet the guidelines for permanence and durability of the Production Guidelines for Book Longevity of the Council on Library Resources.

♻ This book was produced with environmental mindfulness. For more information, please visit wisdompubs.org/wisdom-environment.

Printed in the United States of America.

Contents

Part II

The Wanling Record

(Wanling lu)

Translators' Introduction

Robert E. Buswell Jr.

SEON MASTER SUBUL SUNIM is a renowned contemporary teacher of Seon, the Korean analog of the Chinese Chan 禪 school, what we in the West call Zen, following the Japanese pronunciation. The clarion call of the Seon, or "Meditation," school of East Asian Buddhism is that it is "a separate transmission distinct from the scriptural teachings of Buddhism, which does not rely on words and letters; instead, it points directly to the human mind, so that we may see the nature and achieve buddhahood."[1] What is this nature that, if seen, enables us to achieve buddhahood? And if all living creatures are endowed with this nature and innately have this capacity to be enlightened, as Seon claims, what role remains for religious practice? In other words, if enlightenment is something inherent to the mind rather than a byproduct of practice, what then must people do to claim their true destiny as buddhas?

Subul Sunim draws on one of the masterpieces of the classical Chan tradition to answer such questions. *Essentials of Transmitting the Mind-Dharma* (Chinese *Chuanxinfayao,* Korean *Jeonsimbeopyo* 傳心法要) was composed by Huangbo Xiyun 黃檗希運 (d. 850), a Chinese master in an incipient Chan lineage that later evolved into the Linji 臨濟 line. The answer of both Subul Sunim and Huangbo is deceptively simple: just stop thinking there is something we need to practice. Then the enlightenment inherent to the mind manifests itself naturally, and we spontaneously receive the transmission of the mind-dharma. In this way, religious practice is perfected through, and simultaneously with, enlightenment itself. This is the quintessential "sudden awakening accompanied by sudden cultivation" (Chinese *dunwu dunxiu*, Korean *dono donsu* 頓悟頓修) approach that has inspired Seon practice throughout much of its history.

Subul Sunim (b. 1953) is the Seon master at the Anguk Seonwon 安國禪院 in Busan, one of the largest lay centers of Buddhist practice in Korea today; we will give a brief biography of him below. Subul Sunim lectures frequently on the *Essentials of Transmitting the Mind-Dharma*, for in his experience the text inspires Buddhist practitioners to want to understand the true nature of their minds and to seek a sudden awakening to that nature. But Subul Sunim is especially well known in Korea for his innovations in training both monks and laity in meditation. His meditation teaching focuses on an intensive method of questioning that is known in Korean as *ganhwa* Seon 看話禪, "the Seon of examining meditative topics."[2] We in the West usually know this technique through its later Japanese analogues in kōan (Chinese *gong'an* / Korean *gongan* 公案) training.[3] Although this type of meditation developed in the East Asian Seon tradition long after Huangbo's time, Subul Sunim places Huangbo's text explicitly in the context of ganhwa Seon practice.

Ganhwa Seon involves examining one of these enigmatic Seon questions, or "topics" (*huatou/hwadu* 話頭), such as "what was your original face before your parents conceived you?" or "who is dragging around this corpse?" You put all of your effort into examining this question until a deep sense of inquiry or questioning arises. This questioning is what the Seon tradition technically calls "doubt" (*yixin/uisim* 疑心). Once it arises, you are to focus exclusively on this doubt until it utterly suffuses your mind. Eventually the pressure created in your mind by this doubt becomes so intense that conscious thought will seem as if blocked, no matter which avenue of inquiry you pursue. Subul Sunim explains that these ingeniously contrived topics push meditators "into a dead end, where they are forced to solve the fundamental problem for themselves" (part I, chap. 3). In this dead end, such topics can no longer be confronted according to your usual ways of thinking but only from a new, nonreferential perspective. This experience initiates the transformation from the deluded persons we ordinarily perceive ourselves to be to our inherent status as enlightened buddhas. The reader will see Seon Master Subul referring frequently to the term *experience* (*tiyan/cheheom* 體驗) in the course of his commentary; by "experience," he is referring specifically to this distinctive breakthrough or release that is generated through questioning meditation.

Ganhwa Seon is widely practiced in Korea today and remains the primary focus of contemplation for most monks and nuns meditating full-time in Seon training halls around the country. Typically in Korea, monks and nuns would take up one of these hwadu, or meditative topics, for the entire three months of a summer or winter retreat, working on their hwadu for ten and often many more hours every day during that period. Most meditators continue their practice during the three-month free seasons of spring and autumn as well, and the most ardent and committed adepts expect to spend many years in such practice before having a breakthrough into awakening.

After Subul Sunim's own awakening, earnest laypeople began to ask him to teach ganhwa Seon to them so that they too would have the opportunity for such an experience. Since very few laypeople had the time to devote to three-month retreats, Master Subul fashioned a one-week intensive for them during which he taught them in the traditional Korean fashion, having them repeat the meditative topic over and over in an attempt to raise a sense of questioning. But despite their dedicated practice, these laypeople were not progressing as he hoped. Subul Sunim ultimately recognized that they were not generating a sufficient depth of inquiry, or doubt, over a week's time to make much progress. Monks or nuns with their whole lives ahead of them to practice might not have a particular urgency about generating this doubt; for them, repeating the question continually until the doubt finally arises might be an appropriate approach. But laypeople did not have the luxury of time; this one-week retreat might be their only chance to gain such an experience. Subul Sunim therefore began to develop an expedient style of ganhwa Seon that dispensed with the preliminary recitation of one of the traditional meditative topics. Instead, he performs a simple gesture and then asks, "What makes me do this?" This is Subul Sunim's variation on the most basic of all Korean hwadus: "What is it?" (*imwotko*).[4] Seon Master Subul alludes to this same question at the very end of his commentary: "If you know what makes your mouth chew, you will be able to digest the meaning of these words 'to chew without chewing anything.' But if you don't, you will face a sheer precipice. It is not the mouth that chews; it is not I that chews; it is not that there is no chewing. You must directly awaken to this matter for yourself. But if you approach it intellectually, you will never be able to escape the endless cycle of birth and death" (part II, chap. 44).

Once students have heard his question "What makes me do this?" Seon Master Subul tells them to set the question itself aside and just search for the answer to the hwadu, thus moving directly to the stage of intense inquiry. To discourage thinking about the question, Subul Sunim advises students to examine the hwadu with their "whole body" (*onmon euro*); he sometimes describes this technique as meditating from the neck down. In this way, rather than just thinking about the question in their heads, meditators feel the doubt as a palpable physical sensation that pervades their entire bodies. Because this inquiry can generate intense sensations and emotions, there can be strong physiological reactions to the inquiry, as if they were blocked on all fronts by a "silver mountain and iron wall that are right before their eyes" (part I, chap. 1), or choking on the "spiky burr of a chestnut" that they can't spit out or swallow.[5] At this point, the sensation of doubt becomes so stifling that it coalesces into the "mass, or ball, of doubt" (*yituan/uidan* 疑團), which completely entraps the student. Because these strong physiological reactions may accompany his style of ganhwa Seon, Seon Master Subul strongly discourages laypeople from attempting this practice on their own; he recommends that they try it only in a formal retreat and under the guidance of an experienced teacher.

Once the doubt becomes so intense that the meditator can no longer bear the pressure it creates, the "silver mountain and iron wall" collapse, and the meditator has an "experience" of breakthrough and release, when "the body feels lighter than a feather, and the mind is completely empty, as if there were no beginning or end. All is cool and refreshing."[6] This is the moment of sudden awakening, the goal of ganhwa Seon training.

So that students will focus all their energies on their personal practice during the short period of the retreat, Master Subul Sunim also dispenses with much of the formality of the traditional Korean meditation hall. He is not concerned with whether his retreatants maintain correct meditative posture or move occasionally during their sitting practice; he only asks that they keep searching for the answer to the hwadu "What makes me do this?" His retreats are thus noted for their freestyle practice, where meditators are encouraged to practice in whatever way best suits them. The only expectation is that his retreatants devote themselves wholeheartedly to their inquiry for the entire week of the retreat. In similar fashion, Subul Sunim discourages his meditators from spending their brief time during the retreat trying to control their distracted thoughts before focusing on the hwadu, as many Seon masters teach. Instead, if they will just keep returning to the sensation of doubt, such distractions will fade away on their own.

Deploying this approach to practice, Master Subul Sunim found that laypeople were gaining an authentic experience of ganwha Seon and this was profoundly transformative for them. Throughout his subsequent career, Subul Sunim has especially targeted laypeople for his retreats, and over twenty-five thousand laypeople and monks around Korea and elsewhere around the world have responded enthusiastically to his teachings and found success in his retreats. They have helped support Master Subul Sunim's continuing efforts to bring ganhwa Seon out of the monastic meditation hall and into the lives of ordinary people. The support he received led to the establishment of the Anguk Seonwon in the southern Korean city of Busan, which has subsequently grown into a worldwide organization. His success in helping ganhwa Seon students quickly raise what he considers an authentic sense of doubt has become so widely known in Korea that scores of monks and nuns have also now attended his retreats in order to gain a solid foundation going forward for their lifelong practice of this form of meditation. Subul Sunim has gone on to serve as abbot of Beomeo Monastery 梵魚寺 and to become an influential monk in the Jogye Order of Korean Buddhism (Daehan Bulgyo Jogyejong 大韓佛敎曹溪宗), but he continues to focus much of his energies on propagating the practice of ganhwa Seon among laypeople and younger monks and nuns.

Ganhwa Seon and Huangbo's Text

Based on his own experience in teaching ganhwa Seon, as we have described above, Master Subul Sunim advocates that this technique is best suited for short bursts of intensive meditation under the guidance of an experienced teacher. In his rendition, this practice is not intended to calm the mind and reduce stress. Just the opposite often occurs, in fact: faced with the realization that we don't know the most fundamental thing about our existence—how we are able to make even the simplest of gestures—meditators are left frustrated and obsessed with "seeking the answer." The reactions to ganhwa Seon are intended to be cathartic, shaking students out of their complacency so they are forced to look for their true natures.

After catalyzing such a breakthrough, however, Subul Sunim's view is that the hwadu has served its purpose. There is no need to go back to his question or to try another topic. As he often says, after putting yourself through such an intense, and even traumatic, experience, why would you want to start over and do it all again? Ganhwa Seon practice, as he envisions it, is specifically intended for a short-term, intensive period of meditation and is not suitable for intermittent use during an active life in the world. At the end of the retreat, those who have not had a breakthrough are firmly warned to stop the inquiry and not to try to continue with it on their own during daily life; if they wish to try it again, they should enter another retreat later. But even for those who have had a breakthrough or release experience, there is no need to examine other hwadus. All hwadu are designed to generate questioning, and the doubt generated by one hwadu is the same as the doubt generated by all; it would be redundant to restart the process of inquiry.

Still, after finishing their retreats, his retreatants are often eager for instruction on what to do next. What about starting another practice like insight meditation, or mindfulness training, or visualization? Subul Sunim chides them for wanting to sample this or that technique, comparing this desire to a kid in a candy store eager to try this and that morsel. The pursuit of more practice and spiritual experiences is just another sort of attachment, which can become a hindrance in its own right.

So what, his students then ask, should we do after having this "experience" in ganhwa Seon? Master Subul Sunim's answer is cryptic: "Live well." The usual reaction: what do you mean by "living well"? This is where Master Subul turns to Huangbo's *Essentials of Transmitting the Mind-Dharma*. As Huangbo reiterates time and again throughout his text, we are already enlightened. We don't need to do anything in order to develop our enlightenment, whether that is making merit, mastering the six perfections of the bodhisattva, or practicing different styles of meditation. There is, Huangbo says in his opening section, "not the slightest dharma that you need to attain, for this mind is in fact a genuine buddha" (part I, chap. 1).

Master Subul draws on Huangbo's message to help wean his more advanced students in particular from their attachment to their "experience" and even to meditation itself: just stop thinking there is something more you need to do, and all will be perfectly clear in and of itself. Subul Sunim therefore recommends the *Essentials* as offering an ideal guide on how to "live well." As Master Subul says, "The Way is already fully revealed. There is nothing that needs to be eliminated or sought. After having an 'experience' through your meditation practice, there is nothing you need to do but pass the time by going along with the flow of causes and conditions" (part I, chap. 8). Commenting on Huangbo's statement, "This mind is in fact the buddha. There is no other buddha and no other mind" (part I, chap. 1), Subul Sunim also notes,

> Once you have a breakthrough in your training, you will be able to believe these words and leave things just as they are. Whether things go your way or not, if you let things take their natural course, one day everything will be revealed accordingly. As time passes, things mature and naturally reveal themselves. If you have already recognized the original quiescence inherent in your mind, what more is there for you to be concerned about?

Pei Xiu 裴休 (787/797–870), the eminent Buddhist layman and senior government official who serves as the interlocutor throughout the *Essentials of Transmitting the Mind-Dharma*, was himself a devout Buddhist and experienced practitioner, much like the laypeople Master Subul himself is teaching. Subul Sunim notes at several points in his commentary how fortunate we are to have a record of Pei Xiu's questions, because the kinds of questions he asked twelve centuries ago are exactly the kind of questions practitioners today often ask him. This relevance for contemporary lay Buddhists is another reason the *Essentials* has figured prominently in Subul Sunim's lectures. After working through the text multiple times with his advanced disciples, Subul Sunim eventually developed a comprehensive Seon commentary to every passage in the text. He delivered an extended set of lectures on the *Essentials of Transmitting the Mind-Dharma* in 2010 at the Anguk Seonwon branch in Seoul and subsequently compiled these lectures in the book *Heunjeok eopsi naneun sae*.[7] It is this book that we translate here. Subul Sunim embeds in his commentary the original Chinese text of Huangbo's records along with a modern Korean translation. Our English translation of the *Essentials of Transmitting the Mind-Dharma* is made from this same Chinese text, which we reproduce in the main body of the book.[8]

There are different editions of *Essentials* in varying lengths. The order, numbering, and titles of the chapters of the text also vary slightly among the different editions. The shortest version of the text, but by far the best known, is titled *Essentials of Transmitting the Mind-Dharma* (*Chuanxinfayao*), which comprises part I of our translation here. This part was compiled in 842 and purports to offer Pei Xiu's own transcript of his exchanges with Huangbo on the meaning of Chan. Longer editions of the text add to this eponymous part I a second part, the *Wanling Record* (*Wanling lu*). The *Wanling Record* was compiled in 848 and is named after Wanling, the capital of Anhui province; it includes additional exchanges between Huangbo and Pei Xiu. Since this *Wanling Record* designates Pei Xiu by his honorific government title of Grand Councilor, it is sometimes presumed that much of it may have been recorded and compiled not by Pei Xiu himself but by Huangbo's disciples who were in attendance during the discussions between the two men. The longest edition of the text appends to the *Wanling Record* a so-called "Account of Activities" (*Xingzhuang*), a traditional biographical genre that is often compiled soon after an eminent teacher's death by his closest disciples. Here, this "Account" consists almost entirely of additional exchanges between Huangbo and his students, exchanges that are in the emblematic encounter-dialogue format of the classical Chan tradition. Therefore the *Essentials of Transmitting the Mind-Dharma* designates part I of the collection, but it also lends its name to the entire collection.[9]

The Translation

Huangbo's text has received several renderings into English. In 1958, the pioneering scholar of Buddhism and Chinese religions John Blofeld published the first complete rendering of the *Essentials of Transmitting the Mind-Dharma*.[10] His rendering offers some brilliantly intuitive readings of the Chinese, which are always creative and often insightful. For someone working during the incipiency of Zen studies in the West, his rendering is genuinely inspired, which is why it has stood the test of time and remains in print still today. But at too many places, Blofeld's renderings are obsolete, especially in the second half of the *Wanling Record*, the "Account of Activities," where his translation of Huangbo's Seon encounter dialogues did not have the benefit of more recent advances in our understanding of medieval colloquial Chinese, a central feature of this encounter-dialogue genre of Buddhist literature. His approach to the text is also heavily beholden to D. T. Suzuki's account of Zen, which is now long outmoded.

In 2005, John McRae published in the Bukkyō Dendō Kyōkai English Tripiṭaka series a much more accurate and literal rendering of the text, which follows closely Iriya Yoshitaka's Japanese translation and study.[11] McRae's rendering is a major improvement over Blofeld's; but McRae translates only the first part of the text, the eponymous *Chuanxinfayao*. (Iriya Yoshitaka's Japanese translation team also does not translate the "Account of Activities" section of the *Wanling Record*.) Additionally, because of the restrictions of the series in which his translation appeared, McRae was not able to include any annotation to the text. Our new version is therefore the first complete English translation in fifty years of the full Chinese text of Huangbo's *Essentials of Transmitting the Mind-Dharma*, and the first one ever to include extensive annotation to Huangbo's sources. Subul Sunim's Seon commentary to the entire text, translated from the Korean, also enhances the significance of Huangbo's work for modern readers.

Blofeld translated the title of Huangbo's *Chuanxinfayao* quite freely as *The Zen Teaching of Huang Po on the Transmission of Mind*; McRae's rendering is *Essentials of the Transmission of Mind*. We have chosen to translate the title more strictly, as "Essentials (*yao*) of Transmitting (*chuan*) the Mind-Dharma (*xinfa*)." Our rendering follows Huangbo's own guidance on how to parse the title:

> When people of this world hear it said that all the buddhas transmit the mind-dharma, they assume that there is a discrete dharma that can be realized and acquired with reference to the mind. They thereupon seek that dharma with the mind, not knowing that the mind is nothing but that dharma and that dharma is nothing but the mind. You cannot seek the mind with the mind. . . . Therefore, it is said that, once there are neither dharmas nor the original mind, you will understand the mind that is the "mind-dharma" (part I, chap. 3, and part II, chap. 29).

We have also attempted in this translation to trace the many quotations and allusions that Huangbo employs in his text. These are important to show the range and breadth of influences on Huangbo's presentation of Seon Buddhism. Master Subul Sunim's commentary refers to some of these sources, though without precise citations. We have consulted the Japanese translation of Professor Iriya Yoshitaka and his team for additional leads on sources and have used the tools of modern digital Buddhist studies to track still more. We believe we have succeeded in ferreting out many of the sources Huangbo used in his teachings that were previously unidentified.

About Seon Master Subul Sunim

Subul Sunim (b. 1953) is the Seon master at the Anguk Seonwon in Korea. (Sunim 스님 is the Korean honorific used to refer to ordained monks and nuns; it is also seen transcribed as Seunim or Sŭnim.) The Anguk Seonwon has its main center in the city of Busan but also has branches in Seoul and, more recently, the United States. Subul Sunim was ordained under Jiyu Sunim 知有 (1931–), the Seon master at Beomeosa 梵魚寺, as a novice monk, or *śramaṇera*, in 1975, and as a fully ordained monk, or *bhikṣu*, two years later, under Goam Sunim 高庵 (1899–1988). After completing seminary study at Beomeosa in 1978, he "relinquished doctrine and entered Seon" (*shejiao ruchan / sagyo ipseon* 捨教入禪), as the Koreans say, and spent three years in intensive ganhwa Seon practice in meditation halls around the country. In 1981, during a conversation with Jiyu Sunim, he had an awakening experience that was sanctioned by his teacher. Jiyu Sunim then gave him the dharma name Subul 修弗, which means literally "cultivating 'not,'" implying that Jiyu Sunim considered his student had nothing further he needed to practice.

Subul Sunim remained in seclusion for the next several years before deciding to dedicate himself to popularizing ganhwa Seon among the laity. This aspiration led in 1989 to the founding of the Anguk Seonwon in Busan and the Seoul branch in 1996. Over three thousand lay Buddhists regularly attend events held at his two centers in Korea. Subul Sunim has also led over three hundred week-long ganhwa Seon retreats in Korea and throughout the world, including the United States, China, India, and New Zealand. Over twenty-five thousand monks and laypeople over the years have gained experience in ganhwa Seon through these retreats. As the Anguk Seonwon organization grew, Subul Sunim simultaneously held numerous administrative positions in the Jogye Order and the Korean Buddhist ecclesia. In the last few years, Subul Sunim has served as the abbot of Beomeosa and the Seon master at the International Meditation Center at Dongguk University, and was one of the two finalists for the position of administrative head of the Jogye Order in the most recent ecclesiastical balloting.

We are honored to have this opportunity to offer to a new generation of readers a translation of the complete text of Huangbo's *Essentials of Transmitting the Mind-Dharma*, together with an illuminating commentary by one of the most influential Seon masters in contemporary Korean Buddhism.

Preface by Seon Master Subul Sunim

WITH THE DEVELOPMENT of information technologies, exchanges of intellectual culture between the East and the West are taking place today at a rapid pace. Accordingly, the universal intellect of humankind has awakened throughout the world. As that awakening expands, we may expect that the human intellect, including the fields of science and technology, will experience revolutionary changes. It is evident to me that the cross-cultural exchanges are moving humanity in a direction that accords with more objective and universal values. As the collective intellect of the human race comes to be awakened just like the shining of the sun, we therefore have reason to hope that obsolete mental values that are blind and materialistic will inevitably die out.

Seon, which the Chinese know as Chan and the Japanese as Zen, is one of humankind's most noble mental and cultural heritages. Its goal is to reveal the ultimate truth of existence exactly as it is. Even though this primordial truth clearly manifests itself right in front of our eyes, it is hard for ordinary people to recognize it. Seon directly points to absolute truth, which it calls an "open secret." However, most people today, entangled in the complexities of daily life and myriad stereotypical ideas, cannot see this reality.

The veracity of Seon Buddhism has been verified by luminaries as numerous as the stars in the sky. Throughout its history, people in both East and West have taken an interest in Seon. Furthermore, more than a few have tasted the truth of Seon directly for themselves through meditation. Such people attest that Seon is the fastest, most exact, and the easiest teaching by which to ward off the mind's darkness and restore its brightness. Fortunately, this precious approach is in fact very close to us all.

Seon training to restore the mind's intrinsic brightness is a task we would all do well to undertake. Ordinary people have accustomed themselves to wandering around in the dark, running in circles with their busy routines, not realizing that this truth is there to be rediscovered. This is all the more reason why it is so urgent to share the insights of Seon with the people of the world.

Two pioneers zealously tackled this very issue in a series of dialogues about twelve hundred years ago. The questioner was Grand Councilor Pei Xiu (791–870) of the Tang dynasty, who was a renowned literatus and public intellectual. His counterpart was Huangbo Xiyun (d. 850), a pioneering Seon master who had personally realized the truth. The *Essentials of Transmitting the Mind-Dharma* (*Chuanxinfayao*) records their exchanges, with Huangbo answering questions posed by Pei Xiu regarding the true nature of reality.

Pei Xiu was a Confucian scholar and high-ranking government official, but he was also well versed in Buddhist doctrine. His mind opened immediately after he met Master Huangbo. In order to perfect his study of the truth, he repeatedly invited Huangbo to visit him so that he could ask questions about the dharma.

Because ultimate truth is absolute, it always transcends the relative. Because discriminative knowledge is generated in the dichotomous realm of the relative, it cannot digest the absolute dharma of nonduality, which transcends all dichotomies. Therefore one can realize the nondual dharma only by attaining true wisdom.

Pei Xiu was a scholar who always sought the truth. Due to his habitual dichotomizing tendencies, he asked about the truth of existence. In response, the master Huangbo revealed the absolute from the transcendent standpoint of the nondual dharma. Pei Xiu kept asking about the dharma from the standpoint of the relative, while his counterpart answered consistently from the standpoint of the absolute. Since people today are used to the dichotomies in the realm of relative truth, they will feel as if Pei Xiu's questions are their own.

For the most part, Seon masters deflect questions that arise from delusory conceptions. However, Master Huangbo, perhaps foreseeing the future value of this record that Pei Xiu would leave, sincerely and tolerantly answered each and every question, even when a question was foolish. This is the reason why the *Essentials of Transmitting the Mind-Dharma* is regarded in both East and West as a rare masterpiece that expresses absolute truth by using relative language.

One may *know* relative knowledge, but one must *realize* the wisdom of the absolute. When a student earnestly asks an unresolved question about the fundamental truth, a master directly points to the place of the absolute. At that moment, a student with affinities to the master will align with the absolute through the master's words and will attain awakening.

This Seon principle of "attaining sudden awakening through seeing the nature" was articulated by Bodhidharma (late fourth–early fifth centuries), the First Patriarch of Seon, on the basis of the Buddha's teachings. It reached greatness thanks to the Sixth Patriarch Huineng 慧能 (638–713). In this way, all the Seon patriarchs and teachers, generation after generation, led their students to obtain the true dharma-eye by revealing directly to them the absolute nature with which all sentient beings are endowed. This special practice is called Patriarchal Seon (zushi Chan / josa Seon 祖師禪).

Korean Seon Buddhism succeeds the Yangqi/Yanggi 楊岐 collateral line of the Linji/Imje 臨濟 school from among the Five Houses and Seven Schools (Wujia Qizong / Oga Chiljong 五家七宗) of the mature Chinese Chan tradition. The master Dahui Zonggao 大慧宗杲 (1089–1163), a successor in the Yangqi lineage, established the *kanhua* Chan technique, which the Korean tradition knows as *ganhwa* Seon, the "Seon of examining meditative topics." This technique is the official practice of the contemporary Korean Jogye Buddhist Order.

The Linji school compiled the *Recorded Sayings of the Four Houses* in order to promote the lineage of Mazu Daoyi 馬祖道一 (709–88) → Baizhang Huaihai 百丈懷海 (749–814) → Huangbo Xiyun → Linji Yixuan 臨濟義玄 (d. 867). The eleventh century, about the time of the production of that text, can be regarded as the golden age of Patriarchal Seon.[12]

Among those recorded sayings, the *Essentials of Transmitting the Mind-Dharma*, which is the recorded sayings of master Huangbo, was well received within the Seon tradition because its straightforward rhetoric logically revealed the principle of Seon. Thanks to the merit Pei Xiu had made in his previous lives, as soon as he heard Huangbo's words, he understood their profound meaning. Nonetheless, when we examine the questions he posed to the master, Pei Xiu's queries still seem to be trapped in dualistic thought.

Therefore, rather than being the simple record of questions and answers between a student and his master, the *Essentials* is also a record of the process through which a bright-eyed master guides his student along the path that leads upward toward enlightenment.

Despite Pei Xiu's experience of "sudden awakening" (*dunwu/dono* 頓悟), he still held to the position of "gradual cultivation" (*jianxiu/jeomsu* 漸修). In this text, we should pay careful attention to the ways in which Huangbo disabuses his student of this position and reveals to him the right path of "sudden cultivation" (*dunxiu/donsu* 頓修).

Pei Xiu's experience is not his alone. People experience a real change at the moment of their initial awakening thanks to the correct affinities they have for opening their eyes. Even so, they may continue to be yanked around by the karma that ceaselessly arises from their habituations without even recognizing it. When these tendencies persist, it is easy to be caught up again in delusion. Those who find themselves in this situation will be able to resolve any doubts that may remain about their practice by carefully reading *Essentials of Transmitting the Mind-Dharma*.

Part I

Essentials of Transmitting the Mind-Dharma

(*Chuanxinfayao* 傳心法要)

Pei Xiu's Preface

There was a great Seon master whose dharma name was Xiyun. He resided at the base of Vulture Peak on Mount Huangbo, in Gao'an county of Hongzhou prefecture. He was a legitimate descendant of the Sixth Patriarch of Caoxi, a [dharma] son of Baizhang, and a dharma nephew of Xitang.

有大禪師 法諱希運 住洪州高安縣黃蘗山鷲峰下 乃曹溪六祖之嫡孫 百丈之子 西堂之法姪.

Hongzhou prefecture is located in present-day Nanchang in Jiangxi province. The monastery of Huangbosi on Mount Huangbo is located in Liping in that same province. Most Seon temples are located in small valleys deep in the mountains, where people can also farm. Huangbosi is no exception. When I visited the monastery a few years ago, it looked like a shabby storehouse. Its old dharma hall had already collapsed. It is said that people in nearby villages had built the temple just like a storehouse in order to escape the ravages of the Red Guards during the Chinese Cultural Revolution of the 1960s and 70s.

Inside the dharma hall, the floor was dirt. A large plaque with the words *Chuanxinfayao* carved on it hung on the front wall. In the wide courtyard in front of the dharma hall, the construction of a huge main Buddha hall had commenced. It has probably been completed by now. Although this main hall is large in size, it was built in a hurry, so it will take time for it to be instilled with the dignity of a religious structure.

I still cannot forget the hospitality I was shown by the abbot Xinkong 心空, who had the look of an old country man in his mid sixties, and the Buddhist laypeople of Huangbo village. I thanked Master Huangbo for his kindness in teaching the *Essentials of Transmitting the Mind-Dharma* when I paid my respects to his memorial stūpa, which was located in the bamboo forest at the foot of the mountains near the rice paddies. That site is still fresh in my memory.

Huangbo was a fourth-generation master in a descent line from the Sixth Patriarch Huineng. The patriarch's dharma was transmitted to Mazu Daoyi (709–88) through Nanyue Huirang (677–744). Among Mazu's many disciples, Xitang Zhizang 西堂智藏 (735–814), Baizhang Huaihai (749–814), and Nanquan Puyuan 南泉普願 (748–835) were particularly renowned, sometimes referred to as the "three great gentlemen" (*sandashi* 三大士). Most of the Nine Mountain Seon schools (Gusan Seonmun 九山禪門) of Korea were founded by monks who received dharma transmission in the Mazu lineage. In particular, the state preceptor Doui 道義 (d. 825), who is honored as the putative founder of the Jogye Order of Korean Buddhism, transmitted the dharma of Xitang Zhizang, Mazu's eldest disciple, to Korea, and it became one of the antecedents of today's Jogye order.

It is said that the Seon master Baizhang sighed, saying, "The Seon lineage of Jiangxi (i.e., Mazu) has come to the Country to the East (Dongguk 東國, i.e., Korea)!" The direct line from Xitang formed Hongcheok's 洪陟 (fl. ca. 826) Silsangsan 實相山 school at the monastery of Silsangsa 實相寺 in Namwon, Hyecheol's 惠哲 (785–861) Dongnisan 桐裡山 school at the monastery of Taeansa 泰安寺 in Goseong, and Doui's eldest dharma grandson Chejing's 體澄 (804–80) Gajisan 迦智山 school at the monastery of Borimsa 寶林寺 in Jangheung.

Mazu's Recorded Sayings reports the following episode:

> Xitang, Baizhang, and Nanquan were viewing the moon with the master Mazu. The master asked, "At this very moment, what is the right thing to do?"
>
> Xitang replied, "It's perfect for making offerings."
>
> Baizhang answered, "It's perfect for practicing."
>
> Nanquan shook his sleeves and left.
>
> Mazu said, "The Buddhist scriptures have come to Xitang. Seon has returned to Baizhang. Only Nanquan surpasses all standards!"[13]

[The master himself] just esteemed the stamp of the Supreme Vehicle, which stayed far removed from words and letters. He transmitted only the one mind; there was no other dharma. The essence of mind is also empty, and the myriad conditions are all quiescent. It is like the great orb of the sun that rises in the sky: its radiance shines brightly, and it is clear without the slightest trace of dust.

獨佩最上乘離文字之印 唯傳一心 更無別法 心體亦空 萬緣俱寂 如大日輪 昇虛空中 光明照曜 淨無纖埃.

"Supreme Vehicle" (Zuishangsheng/Choesangseung 最上乘) is both the essence of the Buddhadharma that Bodhidharma himself transmitted, as well as the orthodox Seon that has been transmitted through the authentic lineage of the Jogye order. More concretely, it refers to the teaching of sudden awakening of the Southern school of Seon. From the First Patriarch, Bodhidharma, down to the present, Seon has transmitted just the one mind and nothing else. This is because the true characteristic of all the realms in the universe, which all enlightened beings perceive, is simply the one mind.

To those who have realized it, there is nothing new or old, shallow or deep. Those who preach it do not engage in intellectual knowledge and understanding; they do not establish teachers; they do not open the doors or windows [of a school]. Just like that, here it is. If you start to think, then you will be far off the mark. Only after [you understand this] will you attain your original buddhahood.

For this reason, his words are simple and his principle straightforward. His Way is lofty and his acts are aloof from others. Students and disciples from the four quarters rushed to his mountain and awakened as they looked upon his visage. There were always about a thousand people in his congregation, [which was as vast as] the sea.

When I governed the district of Zhongling during the second year of the Huichang reign-era (842 CE), I invited him

down from the mountain to come to the district and stay at Longxing Monastery. There, day and night, I asked him about the Way. When I was in charge of [the district of] Wanling in the second year of the Dazhong reign-era (848 CE), I again respectfully welcomed him to my district office and had him dwell at Kaiyuan Monastery, where day and night I received the dharma. As soon as he left, I tried to record everything [I had heard, but could remember only] one or two [episodes] out of ten. These I esteemed as a mind-stamp (*xinyin/simin* 心印) but was reluctant to distribute them. Now, fearing that [these teachings], which are suffused with the essential meaning of the spirit, might not be heard by future [generations], I have handed [my manuscript] over to the monks Dazhou and Fajian. I have requested that they return to Guangtang Monastery on the old mountain [of Huangbo] and ask the senior monks and the dharma congregation there to check whether [my manuscript] is consistent with or different from what they had regularly heard before.

Preface written on the eighth day of the tenth month in the eleventh year of the Tang dynasty's Dazhong reign-era (October 29, 857).

證之者無新舊無淺深 說之者不立義解 不立宗主 不開戶牖 直下便是 動念即乖 然後為本佛 故其言簡其理直 其道峻其行孤 四方學徒 望山而趨 睹相而悟 往來海衆常千餘人 予會昌二年廉于鍾陵 自山迎至州 憩龍興寺 旦夕問道 大中二年 廉于宛陵 復去禮迎至所部 安居開元寺 旦夕受法 退而紀之 十得一二 佩為心印 不敢發揚 今恐入神精義不聞於未來 遂出之授門下僧大舟法建 歸舊山之廣唐寺 問長老法衆與往日常所親聞 同異如何也.

唐大中十一年十月初八日序

1. Realize the One Mind and You Will Be a Buddha

The master said to me, [Pei] Xiu:

All the buddhas and sentient beings are only the one mind; there is no other dharma. Since time immemorial, this mind has never been produced or extinguished. It is neither green nor yellow; it has neither form nor characteristics (*lakṣaṇa*). It does not belong to the categories of either existence or nonexistence. It cannot be measured in terms of new or old, long or short, large or small. It transcends all limits, measures, names, traces, and comparisons. What is right in front of you—that is it. But if you start to think, you will be far off the mark.

師謂休曰 諸佛與一切眾生 唯是一心 更無別法 此心無始已來 不曾生不曾滅 不青不黃 無形無相 不屬有無 不計新舊 非長非短 非大非小 超過一切限量名言縱跡對待 當體便是 動念即乖.

There is just this one mind; there is no other dharma. This is the middle way between two extremes. If there were in fact two extremes, there would also have to be a middle. If you realize the principle that does not involve either these extremes or a middle, you will have no impediment in achieving liberation from the cycle of birth and death. Master Huangbo spoke of the middle way when he said, "This mind has never been produced or extinguished."

If you start to think, then you will be far off the mark. In other words, if you arouse your thoughts to try to figure out what this mind really is, images begin appearing in your mind, and you end up losing your original mind. The true pleasure you can enjoy by residing in the original place cannot be compared to the lesser worldly pleasures, which inevitably entail suffering. You should live your life knowing the mind and going with the flow of causes and conditions. Avoid wasting your life in the constant indulgence of worldly pleasures.

[The one mind] is like empty space. It has no boundaries and cannot be measured.

猶如虛空 無有邊際 不可測度.

It is really hard to know where and when the mind originates, for it has no boundaries by which it can be measured. It cannot be said, therefore, that the mind is either limitless or limited.

In that case, what on earth is this mind? Everyone can know this mind once they turn one thought around and look into themselves. Ignorant people mislead themselves by clinging to logical thought and generating an attachment to it. They deceive only themselves with this foolish behavior.

Only this one mind is the buddha. There is utterly no difference between the buddha and sentient beings.

唯此一心 即是佛 佛與衆生 更無別異.

The statement "Only this one mind is the buddha" is proclaimed from the level of sudden awakening to one's mind being in fact the buddha, thus transcending intellectual understanding.

Master Huangbo made this claim presuming that Pei Xiu had already experienced sudden awakening. Through these words, therefore, the master directly revealed the original nature of the mind.

Pei Xiu had already acquired significant knowledge of Buddhist doctrine thanks to his relationship with the Chan and Huayan thinker Guifeng Zongmi 圭峰宗密 (780–841), but Pei Xiu did not experience enlightenment until his first encounter with Master Huangbo. Pei Xiu then took refuge in the master and requested his guidance.

When we read the *Essentials of Transmitting the Mind-Dharma*, it is helpful to understand the circumstances in which the master delivered these precious lectures.

Sentient beings are attached to appearances and seek outside [for the buddha]; but in seeking the buddha, they lose the buddha. They make a buddha look for a buddha and use the mind to grasp the mind. Even though they exhaust themselves until the end of the eon, they will never be able to get it.

但是眾生 著相外求 求之轉失 使佛覓佛 將心捉心 窮劫盡形終不能得.

Most people are attached to outward appearances and thereby distinguish between various phenomena. However, our eyes cannot see the real characteristic of things. This very mind that looks for the buddha is the buddha. Wouldn't it be futile to make a buddha seek a buddha?

They do not know that, once they stop thinking and forget their pondering, a buddha will appear right in front of them.

不知息念忘慮 佛自現前.

If they just turn one thought around, they will naturally give up discriminative thinking and empty their minds. When they don't know this fact, people presume they need to seek something and end up entangled in all kinds of discriminative thoughts.

But also they should not try to intentionally remove the thoughts that are arising in their minds or stop working away at their practice, misunderstanding the words "stop thinking and forget their pondering." That would not only be foolish, it would also show disdain for the instructions of their spiritual mentors (*kalyāṇamitra*).

This mind is in fact the buddha. The buddha is in fact sentient beings. When it is in sentient beings, this mind is not

diminished. When it is in all the buddhas, this mind is not augmented.

此心即是佛 佛即是眾生 為眾生時 此心不減 為諸佛時 此心不添.

The mind is never diminished or augmented. Whether a buddha or a sentient being, the mind is always simply there. It is not something that exists in fact, and it cannot be described as having certain characteristics. It is just "mind." As a saying goes, "If you awaken to the mind, you are a buddha; if you are deluded, you are a sentient being." Only enlightened people can testify to this matter. Those who do not realize this matter seek the answer using logic, clinging to the words. But they can never reach the source by clinging to words.

[This mind] is inherently endowed with even the six perfections and myriad [bodhisattva] practices, along with merit as abundant as the sands of the Ganges (Gaṅgānadīvālukā). One need not try to cultivate still more.

乃至六度萬行 河沙功德 本自具足 不假修添.

Since our minds possess inherently the six perfections (*pāramitā*) and myriad practices of the bodhisattvas as well as all kinds of merit, we do not need to create any further merit.

Once you have awakened for yourself, you will know the joy of dharma and the bliss of meditation—the joy of dharma that makes you say, "Ah! So this is what it is!" If you taste even a tiny bit of this joy, you will become more relaxed and satisfied in living your life. If not, you will fall into birth and death's sea of suffering, which is right before your eyes, and flounder in its perilous waters.

When you encounter the [appropriate] conditions, act; when those conditions dissipate, remain quiescent. If, without definitive faith in the fact that this [mind] is a buddha, you

want to seek merit through practice that is attached to characteristics, you will stay mired in deluded conceptions and will deviate from the Way.

遇緣即施 緣息即寂 若不決定信此是佛 而欲著相修行 以求功用 皆是妄想 與道相乖.

Do not generate discriminative thoughts, being tossed and turned by what you see and hear. If you realize the Way, conviction will arise naturally and you will let go of everything. In fact, you will realize that there is in fact nothing to release. Ordinary people are always seeking something, even unconsciously, and so we use the expressions "let go of" or "empty your mind" provisionally. But if you work to empty what is inherently already empty, you will be far from the training that realizes the true characteristic of things.

This mind is in fact the buddha. There is no other buddha and no other mind.

此心即是佛 更無別佛 亦無別心.

Once you have a breakthrough in your training, you will be able to believe these words and leave things just as they are. Whether things go your way or not, if you allow things to follow their own natural course, one day everything will be revealed accordingly. As time passes, things mature and naturally reveal themselves. If you have already recognized the original quiescence inherent in your mind, what else is there to be concerned about?

This mind is bright and clear like empty space; it has not even the slightest mark or appearance.

此心明淨 猶如虛空 無一點相貌.

Wise people awaken to the fact that the original mind is not separate from themselves and, without hesitation, stop wandering around. However, ignorant people perform meaningless tasks, swayed by the deluded mirages that emerge from within themselves.

Arousing your mind and starting to think deviates from the essence of the dharma and creates an attachment to characteristics. Since time immemorial, no buddhas have clung to characteristics.

舉心動念 即乖法體 即為著相 無始已來 無著相佛.

The moment the ignorant arouse even a single thought, they become entrapped in the cycle of birth and death. Each and every thought that sentient beings have is the cycle of production and cessation. Enveloped in ignorance, they lose the essence. This hasn't taken place in this lifetime alone; it has occurred in all previous lifetimes.

Sentient beings also mistakenly believe that if they train themselves properly, they can achieve whatever they want without any obstacles. This ignores causes and conditions. A floating ladle will move when the water moves and remain still when the water is still. If a certain result arises due to a corresponding cause, accept the flow of causality and allow yourself to go with that flow, just like that ladle.

We cannot see the buddhas if we look for the buddhas in external appearances. Just like empty space, this mind is clear, transparent, and formless. The samādhi of no-thought, which nothing can sway, is the true appearance of the buddhas. Because a buddha has no external appearances, bear in mind that a buddha neither discriminates between things nor treats all things as equivalent.

If you pursue buddhahood by cultivating the six perfections and myriad practices, this involves a sequence [of practices]. Since time immemorial, no buddhas have followed a sequential approach.

修六度萬行 欲求成佛 即是次第 無始已來 無次第佛.

The six perfections, or *pāramitās*, are the practices of perfect generosity, morality, forbearance, effort, meditative absorption, and wisdom. Becoming a buddha by cultivating these six perfections suggests there are sequential steps in practice. Were that the case, then there would be distinctions between those who have cultivated all the perfections and those who have cultivated only some of them. This deviates from the mind of a buddha, where there is nothing to cultivate because it is originally empty.

It is not absurd to imply that one becomes a buddha after mastering a set of arduous and difficult practices, but you should know that such instructions are intended as expedients. Faith may be aroused in practitioners by outlining steps that lead upward to enlightenment. But such a teaching is simply a means to ensure they will realize their original buddhahood by turning one thought around when the time is right.

If you merely awaken to this one mind, there will not be the slightest dharma that you need to attain, for this one mind is in fact a genuine buddha.

但悟一心 更無少法可得 此即真佛.

Only those who practice Seon can digest these words. However, these words do not apply to those not yet awakened. Unawakened people should first examine a *hwadu*, or meditative topic, raise the sensation of doubt, and break through the silver mountain and iron wall[14] that are right before their eyes.

Since buddhas and sentient beings are the one mind, they are not different. Like empty space, that mind is free from admixture or deterioration. It is like the great orb of the sun that shines over all four quarters of the world.

佛與衆生一心無異 猶如虛空 無雜無壞 如大日輪 照四天下.

Because empty space is clear and transparent, there are neither separate quarters of north, south, east, and west nor separate time periods of past, present, and future. Although empty space is originally formless, differently shaped clouds arise in it, in accordance with causes and conditions. If you become attached to those shapes, you will mistakenly believe that those differently shaped clouds are real entities. But if you know that they are mere shapes and not fixed entities, and you let go of your attachment, then that's it. Out of delusion, however, you cling to your attachment, even though there is originally no attachment to let go of. I tell you, just let it go!

When the sun rises, its light shines over the entire world, but empty space has never been illuminated. When the sun sets, darkness pervades the entire world, but empty space has never been darkened.

日升之時 明遍天下 虛空不曾明 日沒之時 暗遍天下 虛空不曾暗.

Just as empty space is itself never illuminated or darkened, so too the mind has nothing to do with illumination or darkness. In accordance with causes and conditions, when dawn comes, it gets light; when sunset comes, it gets dark. There is no need to try to sustain or become attached to brightness, because the mind encompasses both brightness and darkness, while remaining unaffected by them.

The realms of light and dark alternate, but the nature of empty space is expansive and invariable. The minds of both buddhas and sentient beings are also like this.

明暗之境 自相凌奪 虛空之性 廓然不變 佛及衆生 心亦如此.

The *Flower Garland Sūtra* says, "The mind, the buddha, and sentient beings—there is no distinction among these three."[15] These three are given the names "buddha," "sentient beings," and "mind" so that we may distinguish them. Those who are awakened never distinguish among identical things that have become entangled with one another.

Although empty space accommodates differently shaped clouds, its original appearance has never changed. Although buddhas and sentient beings cast different shadows, their essence is nondual.

> **Say one observes buddhas as having the characteristics of purity, radiance, and liberation or observes sentient beings as having the characteristics of foulness, darkness, and birth and death. One who generates such an understanding will not be able to attain bodhi [enlightenment] even after kalpas [eons] as numerous as the sands of the Ganges, because one is attached to characteristics. There is only this one mind; there is not another dharma, even as small as a mote of dust, to be attained. The mind is the buddha. Those who train in the Way these days do not awaken to the essence of this mind. They then give rise to mental states overlaying this mind, seek the buddha externally, and practice while being attached to characteristics. All these are harmful techniques, not the path to bodhi.**
>
> 若觀佛 作清淨光明解脫之相 觀眾生 作垢濁暗昧生死之相 作此解者 歷河沙劫 終不得菩提 為著相故 唯此一心 更無微塵許法可得 即心是佛 如今學道人 不悟此心體 便於心上生心 向外求佛 著相修行 皆是惡法 非菩提道.

The difference between buddhas and sentient beings is that those who attain awakening for themselves are buddhas while those who do not are sentient beings. The difference between the two is that simple. If people know that they are originally buddhas, they will act like buddhas. But because they presume they are ignorant, they become sentient beings, who suffer and discriminate.

People should be able to realize that "this is it" by turning one thought around and letting go of all discriminative thoughts, without any lingering attachment. Not knowing this, they become greedy, looking left and right. How could they not but lose their original mind?

2. No-Mind

Making offerings to all the buddhas of the ten directions is not as good as making offerings to an individual practitioner of the Way who maintains no-mind.

供養十方諸佛 不如供養一個無心道人

As the *Diamond Sūtra* says, making offerings to all the buddhas in the trichiliocosm is not as good as making offerings to a single practitioner of the Way who is in a state of no-mind.[16] This statement could be confusing to ordinary Buddhists who earnestly offer donations and prayers to the Buddha. But to those who have turned one thought around and achieved awakening, it is not incomprehensible. Those with lesser spiritual capacities end up trying to evaluate whether this statement is right or wrong, helpful or unhelpful. As the ocean accepts waters from all the rivers of the earth, Buddhists too should have the expansive type of understanding that accepts any type of teaching.

Why is this? No-mind means that there are no mental states at all.

何故 無心者 無一切心也.

This is really a sublime statement. It is incorrect to say that there is either mind or no-mind. You should be able to digest any sort of description. A master may demand, "Leave behind the tetralemma and the hundred negations, which reject all sorts of right or wrong arguments, and just say one word!" Right at that moment, you should be able to answer him. Only then can you know the meaning of this statement.

The essence of suchness is internally like wood or stone, which does not move or sway; externally, it is like empty space, which has no boundaries or obstructions. It has no subject or object, no direction or locus. It has no characteristics or shapes, and nothing to gain or lose. Those who pursue it are wary of accessing this dharma, for they are afraid of falling into voidness where there is no place to roost; therefore, they retreat as if staring at a sheer precipice. All of them are seeking everywhere for intellectual understanding. This is why those seeking intellectual understanding are [as common as] fur, while those who have awakened to the Way are [as rare as] a horn.

如如之體 內如木石不動不搖 外如虛空不塞不礙 無能所無方所 無相貌無得失 趨者不敢入此法 恐落空無棲泊處 故望崖而退 例皆廣求知見 所以 求知見者 如毛 悟道者 如角.

The phrase, "Like wood or stone, which does not move or sway," directly expresses the level of a person who maintains no-mind. When people have not the slightest understanding of Buddhist training, they have nothing to be afraid of. However, when people who have opened heir eyes retain subtle lingering delusions, they may continue to be seized by fear.

People can handle what they can understand. But when they come across something incomprehensible, they become puzzled and feel pushed to the edge of a precipice. At that moment, they become eager to secure rational understanding without being aware they are doing so. However, when you let all things go, you no longer care whether a certain thought arises or not. This is because nothing affects a practitioner who experiences no-thought.

Mañjuśrī corresponds to principle. Samantabhadra corresponds to practice. "Principle" is the principle of true emptiness, which is free from obstructions. "Practice" is the practice that transcends characteristics and is inexhaustible.

文殊當理 普賢當行 理者真空無礙之理 行者 離相無盡之行.

The Buddhadharma assumes there are no fixed characteristics. You should practice the Buddhadharma with discerning eyes. Only when you open your eyes will you be able to understand the bodhisattvas Mañjuśrī and Samantabhadra and to practice Buddhism. The moment you say, "These are the myriad practices of Samantabhadra," that is nothing more than a sound you utter based on what you have learned and understood intellectually.

You cannot understand the true practices of the bodhisattva Samantabhadra without realizing them yourself. Those who have developed the power of looking at their original perfect endowments by opening their discerning eyes always act and speak just like Mañjuśrī and Samantabhadra. However, if you do not attain awakening, you may cultivate the six perfections and Samantabhadra's myriad practices all day long, but that will be nothing but hypocrisy, because you will not have transcended characteristics. Saying "do" or "do not" to those who have attained the power to transcend this level is like telling college students to answer questions meant for elementary-school students.

Avalokiteśvara represents great loving-kindness. Mahāsthāmaprāpta represents great wisdom. Vimalakīrti means "pure name": "pure" refers to the nature while "name" refers to characteristics.

觀音當大慈 勢至當大智 維摩者淨名也 淨者性也 名者相也

Bodhisattvas, in fact, are free from characteristics. In order to indicate to the world what functions without characteristics, the ancient masters revealed these functions through such designations as Avalokiteśvara or Mahāsthāmaprāpta. In order to understand why, you must open the correct eye of the Buddhadharma. If you do not open that eye, you will simply display your intellectual understanding, not believing in what has actual value.

Compassion, wisdom, and purity do not exist separately. They are all inherent in your original nature.

Since nature and characteristics are not different, [Vimalakīrti] is called "pure name." The qualities represented by all the great bodhisattvas are inherent in all human beings. They are not separate from the one mind. If one awakens to it, they will be right there.

性相不異故 號淨名 諸大菩薩所表者 人皆有之 不離一心 悟之即是

Avalokiteśvara, Mañjuśrī, Samantabhadra, and Vimalakīrti are simply manifestations of the nature. In accordance with conditions created from appearances that are free from appearances, in which beginning and end are simultaneous, the nature becomes Avalokiteśvara, Mañjuśrī, Samantabhadra, or Vimalakīrti. Although the nature may take various forms, all these appearances are not separate from the nature.

If people know why this is, they will simply accept it as it is. If they don't know why, they will then seek it out. You may think, "I will have a vision of Avalokiteśvara" or "I will achieve everything by relying on the power of Avalokiteśvara through sincere recitations or prayers." In fact, your own discrimination creates such thoughts. These types of instructions, which of course do appear in Buddhist scriptures, are intended as an expedient for strengthening beginners' faith. People misunderstand these words as being ultimate expressions of truth because they do not know the true meaning of the scriptural teachings.

Awakening means that you turn one thought around and recognize the place of the nature, which is originally thus. Whatever appearances are reflected in it, they are all simply reflections of that nature. If you know this, you can calmly accept them.

All sentient beings possess the same nature, so you should cherish your relationships with each of them. You should use your mind to help other people and live diligently; but better than trying to live diligently is living spontaneously. Then your mind transforms into Avalokiteśvara's power, Samantabhadra's vow, and Mañjuśrī's wisdom, so that you become able to benefit all sentient beings.

These days, practitioners of the Way do not seek awakening within their own minds. Instead, they look outside their minds, clinging to characteristics and holding on to external objects, turning their backs on the Way.

今學道人 不向自心中悟 乃於心外 著相取境 皆與道背.

If you do not attain awakening, then even while calling on the buddhas and bodhisattvas, you turn your back on the buddhas without even knowing it. The moment you turn one thought around and realize the true form of the nature, which is originally thus, you realize that you have been generating defilements and clinging to false appearances throughout your life, without even being aware of doing so.

Regarding "the sands of the Ganges," the Buddha said, "Even when all the buddhas and bodhisattvas, as well as Indra, Brahmā, and all the divinities, walk along those sands, those sands do not rejoice; even when oxen, sheep, ants, and insects tread along those sands, those sands are not enraged. Whether precious jewels or fragrant scents, those sands do not crave them; whether shit, urine, stench, or filth, those sands are not repelled by them." This mind means the mind of no-mind. Since they are in this way far removed from all characteristics, sentient beings and all the buddhas have utterly no differences between them. If one is able to experience no-mind, this is then indeed the ultimate realm. If practitioners of the Way do not straightaway experience no-mind, they may train for numerous kalpas but never achieve the Way. As long as they are entangled in the meritorious practices of the three vehicles, they will be unable to attain liberation.

恒河沙者 佛說是沙 諸佛菩薩 釋梵諸天 步履而過 沙亦不喜 牛羊蟲蟻 踐踏而行 沙亦不怒. 珍寶馨香 沙亦不貪 糞尿臭穢 沙亦不惡. 此心即無心之心 離一切相. 眾生諸佛 更無差別. 但能無心 便是究竟. 學道人 若不直下無心 累劫修行終不成道. 被三乘功行拘繫 不得解脫.

The nature is originally no-mind. No-mind refers to the perfect state in which you are able to accept and embrace everything. If you do not realize no-mind, you cannot achieve the Way, even though you train yourself for years on end.

Mazu Daoyi said, "The everyday mind is the Way."[17] However, if you create or seek out this everyday mind, you have already deviated from it. The mind that you originally possess, the mind that is untainted, uncontaminated, and pure, is in fact everyday mind, no-mind, the original face, and the source of the nature. The conditions that derive from this mind create all different kinds of perceptual objects. Turning one thought around, you realize that you and all the buddhas and patriarchs are originally endowed with this same nature.

It may be that you are able to practice by following a sequence of steps. However, do not cling to this way as the sole right way; for without realizing no-mind, you will simply compound your ignorance.

Nevertheless, in realizing this mind, there is slow and fast.

然證此心 有遲疾.

"I am ignorant. How is it possible I am not even slightly different from a buddha?" This wrong view comes from your attachment to your body. You must believe that, from the standpoint of absolute truth, there is no distinction between you and a buddha. Since you do not believe what you should believe and follow something ineffectual instead, you become demonic and fooled by ghosts. Here I am talking only about the nature. Whether different perceptual objects appear or not, you need only follow that original nature; you need not be attracted any longer by perceptual objects that arise in dependence on conditions.

There are those who, on hearing the dharma, attain no-mind in a single moment of thought. But there are also those who attain no-mind after progressing through [the extended bodhisattva path, that is] the ten faiths, ten abodes, ten practices, and ten dedications; there are even those others who

> **attain no-mind only after arriving at the ten stages (*bhūmi*) [the culmination of the bodhisattva path]. Whether long or short, if you achieve no-mind, then it will be right there; there is nothing more you need to practice or realize. In reality, there is nothing to attain—this is true, not false.**[18]
>
> 有聞法 一念 便得無心者. 有至十信十住十行十迴向 乃得無心者. 有至十地 乃得無心者. 長短得無心 乃住 更無可修可證. 實無所得 真實不虛.

If you conclusively realize the innate no-mind, you will know already that you have relied on your nature; consequently, you will not delude yourself into thinking there is something else you need to attain.

> **Whether you attain it in a single moment of thought or only after mastering the ten stages, both approaches are equally effective. There is no distinction in their depth or shallowness; [prolonging practice] merely entails sequential kalpas of needless bitterness and hardship.**
>
> 一念而得 與十地而得者 功用恰齊 更無深淺. 秖是歷劫 枉受辛勤耳.

When facing a problem, some people can solve it at once while others solve it only after numerous trials and errors. However, whether you solve a problem all at once or through a series of steps, the solution is the same.

Those who toil for a long time are dimwitted. If you can attain a great awakening all at once, that is all you need to do. If you attempt to gain still greater awakening through more training, you cannot but be called foolish. "What I realized first was shallow. But after further realizations, I have gone still deeper." This statement appears to make sense, but it is flawed. Those who have awakened in this manner are clinging to a sequence of steps, and they teach their students to follow the same approach.

Engaging in evil deeds or good deeds involves clinging to characteristics. If you cling to characteristics and perform evil deeds, you needlessly subject yourself to the cycle of saṃsāra. If you cling to characteristics and perform good deeds, you needlessly subject yourself to toil and drudgery.

造惡造善 皆是著相. 著相造惡 枉受輪迴. 著相造善 枉受勞苦.

Once a distinction is made between you and me, the discriminative mind is inevitably generated. Master Huangbo made Pei Xiu awaken right away through the Seon of the patriarchs, without following a sequential series of steps. The moment Pei Xiu turned one thought around and saw what he in fact possessed innately, his transformation was complete.

However, even after you achieve a breakthrough, if you arouse the thought that you want to become a buddha or bodhisattva, you delude yourself, regress from your achievement, and ignore the instructions of spiritual mentors.

Neither is equal to achieving direct realization of the original dharma for oneself through the words [of a master]. This dharma is the mind; outside the mind, there is no dharma. This mind is the dharma; outside the dharma, there is no mind. The mind is itself no-mind, but it is also free from no-mind.

總不如言下 便自認取本法. 此法即心 心外無法. 此心即法 法外無心. 心自無心 亦無無心者.

From the standpoint of absolute truth, nothing can be named or described. The masters of old called it "mind" to have a way of referring to it. But those who have already seen it have only to firmly embrace it. When it is time to eat, you eat; when it is time to sleep, you sleep. This is the sublime and mysterious function that is just as it is.

If you presume the mind is no-mind, your mind will instead turn into something existent.

將心無心 心却成有.

Everything has originally been revealed, so what is there to remove? To cling to the practice of trying to stop your thoughts from arising is all wrong. When you realize that nothing has been aroused though you rouse thoughts all day long, you simply let your thoughts flow freely. Neither cling to nor reject those thoughts.

Just silently accord with it and let all discursive and conceptual thought come to an end. This is why it is said, "The pathways of words and speech are eradicated, and the sphere of compounded things (*saṃskāra*) is extinguished."[19] This mind is the buddha whose original source is pristine. All human beings possess it. Since even wriggling worms possess numinosity, they are but one single substance with all the buddhas and bodhisattvas, without an iota of difference. It is merely due to delusory thoughts and discrimination that they generate various karmic fruitions.

默契而已 絕諸思議故 曰言語道斷 心行處滅. 此心是本源清淨佛 人皆有之. 蠢動含靈與諸佛菩薩 一體不異. 秖為妄想分別 造種種業果.

If you attain a great awakening to the truth, you will naturally realize that you are not different from the buddhas and will understand what has brought about this presumption of difference.

The buddhas appear in the world to reveal the path. The patriarchs and teachers have carried on this work in subsequent generations. Otherwise, how would we have come to know about this path? We should be grateful to them all.

3. The Mind That Is Originally Pure

For the primordial buddha, there is in reality not a single thing. He is just void, pervasive, quiescent, and serene; bright, sublime, peaceful, and blissful.

本佛上實無一物. 虛通寂靜 明妙安樂而已.

When light comes, the mind is bright; when darkness comes, the mind is dark. Although it is in fact neither light nor dark, the mind is the brightest of the bright and the darkest of the dark.

If you yourself enter deeply into awakening, just like that, here it is. It is perfect and complete, without the slightest deficiency.

深自悟入 直下便是. 圓滿具足 更無所欠.

Whether you have awakened or not, you are endowed with the original nature. You live, but without knowing your true origin. Fortunately, you have encountered the Buddha's teachings and achieved a spiritual breakthrough. However, since you still are subject to past habituations, you may ask yourself, "I have cultivated Buddhism for so long; why are delusions still arising?" Nonetheless, do not try to get rid of or chase after that thought.

You may practice strenuously for three infinite [eons] and progress sequentially through all the stages and levels; even so, when in a single moment of thought you finally attain

realization, you will just realize that you are intrinsically a buddha yourself.

縱使三秖精進修行 歷諸地位. 及一念證時 秖證元來自佛.

What we realize after many years of practice is the simple fact that we are originally buddhas. We should not mistakenly believe that only a particular action is the correct practice. We practice at this present moment because we recognize the fact that we created karma in the past. Therefore it is ignorant to think that we need to practice; but it is even more ignorant to say that we do not need to practice. How, then, should we practice?

Above all, nothing further can be added to that one thing.

向上 更不添得一物.

The nature, "that one thing," can be neither diminished nor augmented. When it changes, it may become a buddha, bodhisattva, śrāvaka, or pratyekabuddha. It may take a specific form or no form at all. Even though it appears anywhere and anytime in various forms, it does not lose its original face, which is always the same. The moment you realize this, let it go and cling to nothing else. There may be occasional traces of you wasting time or falling into stupidity, but the nature remains unaffected and is always just the same.

If you look back on your efforts over successive kalpas, all are illusory actions that took place in a dream. Therefore the Tathāgata says, "I indeed attained nothing from *anuttara[samyaksaṃ]bodhi* [supreme, perfect enlightenment]. Were I to have attained something, then the Buddha Dīpaṃkara would not have given me this prophecy."[20] He also said, "This dharma is equal [in every sentient being]; there is no superior or inferior. This is called bodhi."[21]

却觀歷劫功用 總是夢中妄為. 故如來云 我於阿耨菩提 實無所得. 若有所得 然燈佛 則不與我授記. 又云 是法平等無有高下. 是名菩提.

The Buddha Dīpaṃkara offered the prophecy of Śākyamuni Buddha's future buddhahood because Śākyamuni demonstated in his previous lifetimes the ability to manifest the nature in various ways. He was able to become a buddha not because he had cultivated the full range of practices that would lead to buddhahood—meaning, he did not receive that prophecy because he practiced. Rather, he received this prophecy of his future buddhahood from the Buddha Dīpaṃkara as a token gesture when the time was right. The making and receiving of the prophecy reveal that the Buddha and all sentient beings are one and the same.

If you cower as if you are facing a sheer precipice, thinking, "Since achieving buddhahood would take eons of practice, it is irrelevant to me," this is wrong. There is no near or far regarding the original nature. You have lived your life turning your back on your original face and never caring about enlightenment. Now, change your way of thinking and believe that enlightenment has always been innate to you. At first, when you listen to all kinds of explanations, you cannot understand them and may become confused about whether you will be able to practice correctly. However, as you recollect the teachings of the Buddha and the patriarchs, you become convinced about the truth of your original nature.

This pure mind, the original fount—whether in sentient beings or all the buddhas, whether in the mountains or rivers of this world, whether endowed with characteristics or free of characteristics—in all cases, it pervades all realms in the ten directions. Utterly equanimous, it has no characteristics of self or other.

即此本源清淨心 與衆生諸佛 世界山河 有相無相 遍十方界 一切平等 無彼我相.

Everything in the past, present, and future originates from the sea of the nature. Nothing has existed except this one thing. Practitioners who have not yet opened their eyes require no further explanation. Instead, they should be pushed into a dead end, where they are forced to solve the fundamental problem for themselves.

> **This pure mind, the original fount, is always itself perfectly bright, its radiance illuminating everywhere. Since people of this world are not awakened, they just recognize their seeing, hearing, sensing, and knowing as their minds. Since they are blinded by seeing, hearing, sensing, and knowing, they do not perceive their original essence, which is seminal and bright.**
>
> 此本源清淨心 常自圓明遍照 世人不悟 秖認見聞覺知為心 為見聞覺知所覆 所以不覩精明本體.

Here, the fount is nothing but our own minds. This clear and bright mind, which illuminates everything and discerns the myriad things, is the nature. Since our minds are blinded by our own seeing, hearing, sensing, and knowing, we miss what makes seeing, hearing, sensing, and knowing possible.

This explanation is very subtle, but the difference between knowing and not knowing is huge. There is no way to proceed except by finding a way out of that blindness for yourself.

> **If right here and now you simply maintain no-mind, the original essence manifests of itself, like the great orb of the sun that rises in the sky and shines throughout the ten directions without obstructions. Therefore, if practitioners of the Way acknowledge only what they see, hear, sense, and know, and act accordingly, then when they are emptied of what they see, hear, sense, and know, their mental pathways will be cut off, and there will be no point of access.**
>
> 但直下無心 本體自現. 如大日輪 昇於虛空 遍照十方 更無障礙. 故學道人 唯認見聞覺知施為動作 空却見聞覺知 即心路絕 無入處.

If you maintain a state of no-mind, the essence will be immediately revealed to you. However, people turn their backs on the original mind and presume that what sees, hears, senses, and knows is the mind. Strive instead to identify the moment the mind begins to function—that is, the moment before a thought arises and the moment when this thought first arises. If the conditions are right, the wall collapses in that moment. Being "emptied" does not mean that we are emptied by doing something. Because the mind is originally empty, we only need to let it be, just as it is.

You may have tasted the flavor of Buddhist practice, but this still may not be easy to do. "Let it be, just as it is" means that you neither swallow it nor spit it out. As you practice, this will begin to make sense. But after you finish practicing, it will mean something totally different.

You might say that these words are difficult to digest. However, the thing that says this is difficult—let go of that thing. Say someone asks you, "How am I supposed to let go?" If you answer, "I've no idea; do whatever you want," people would likely call you irresponsible. But this is not being irresponsible; it is instead directly pointing out the way forward from a standpoint of ultimate responsibility.

You only recognize the original mind at the sites where you see, hear, sense, and know. Even so, the original mind does not involve seeing, hearing, sensing, and knowing, and it is also not separate from seeing, hearing, sensing, and knowing. To put it simply, do not try to understand intellectually what you see, hear, sense, and know; do not develop thoughts regarding what you see, hear, sense, and know; do not seek the mind separate from what you see, hear, sense, and know; and do not cling to the dharma while abandoning what you see, hear, sense, and know. It is neither identical nor discrete, neither abiding nor attached. It is completely autonomous both spatially and temporally,[22] so there is nowhere that is not the site of enlightenment.

但於見聞覺知處 認本心 然本心不屬見聞覺知 亦不離見聞覺知 但莫於見聞覺知上 起見解 亦莫於見聞覺知上 動念

亦莫離見聞覺知覓心 亦莫捨見聞覺知取法 不即不離 不住不著 縱橫自在 無非道場.

This mind is the buddha. If you seek the buddha somewhere else, you are wrong. The pristine site of enlightenment (*bodhimaṇḍa*) is that which is not different from the nature anytime or anywhere. Do not make the mistake of seeking this site while turning your back on it.

When people of this world hear that all the buddhas transmit the mind-dharma, they assume there is a discrete dharma that can be realized and acquired with reference to the mind. They then seek that dharma with the mind, not knowing that the mind is nothing but that dharma and that dharma is nothing but the mind. You cannot seek the mind with the mind. [If you try,] the day of your attainment will never come, even after millions of kalpas.

世人聞道 諸佛皆傳心法 將謂心上 別有一法 可證可取. 遂將心覓法 不知心即是法. 法即是心 不可將心更求於心 歷千萬劫 終無得日.

If people would just recognize that what sees, hears, senses, and knows is the mind, their practice would be far easier. Not knowing what the mind is, they seek it without understanding what they are doing. They do not grasp that the mind has been with them since time immemorial and will be with them forever. Or perhaps they know intellectually this is the mind, but until they truly realize it, they will inevitably continue wandering.

It is better to maintain no-mind here and now; this is the original dharma. It is like a wrestler unaware that there is a jewel on his forehead who looks everywhere for it outside; even though he travels throughout the ten directions [in search of it], he is never able to find it. But as soon as a wise man points to it, he sees for himself that the jewel was there the entire time. Therefore, if you practitioners of the Way are deluded about your

own original mind and don't recognize that it is the buddha, you will seek it outside and engage in a variety of practices, relying on a graduated process of realization. Even if you diligently look for it in this manner over successive kalpas, you will never achieve the Way. It is better to maintain no-mind here and now.

不如當下無心 便是本法 如力士 迷額內珠 向外求覓 周行十方 終不能得. 智者指之當時 自見本珠如故. 故學道人 迷自本心 不認為佛. 遂向外求覓 起功用行 依次第證. 歷劫勤求 永不成道 不如當下無心.

The Lesser Vehicle teaches a sequence of stages and steps leading to enlightenment, ones that are adapted to the śrāvakas' mental capacities. Since the Great Vehicle and the Supreme Vehicle know that such steps are just provisional expedients, they dispense with stages of practice and instead reveal directly the original state of no-mind. If you attain awakening in one moment of thought, you see the nature directly and achieve the goal without having to master a series of stages. If this sudden approach seems too difficult, though, you might find yourself thinking, "I should just go as far as I can as a first step. How could I possibly reach the end all at once?" People have this view because they have not encountered the right conditions; whether they are "going" or "not going," they are always using the original mind.

If somebody who already knows this truth helps you open your eyes to the fact that what is here right now is the mind, you can open yourself to that truth. But sometimes you may fail to accept it even though your eyes have been opened. Some confused people say their progress in practice feels constrained even though it appears to be taking effect. Such people may eventually turn their backs on Buddhist training and end up going in a different direction.

The "Tathāgata's Nature" chapter of the *Mahāparinirvāṇa Sūtra*[23] tells a story about a wrestler, an attendant in the royal court, who had a diamond on his forehead between his eyebrows. One day, during a wrestling match, his opponent bumped his forehead and, as a result, the diamond he was so proud of was pushed under his skin so he couldn't see it. Thinking that he had lost it, he began to search for it everywhere. Later, a wise doctor informed him that the diamond had been there on his forehead the entire time. At that moment, the wrestler realized the inconceivable principle. This story tells us that all sentient beings originally possess the buddha nature, but they sometimes need guidance from a spiritual mentor in order to see it.

Know with certainty that all dharmas originally are nonexistent and unascertainable. There is nothing on which to rely and nothing in which to abide; there is no subject and no object. If you do not arouse deluded thoughts, you will realize bodhi.

決定知一切法 本無所有 亦無所得. 無依無住 無能無所. 不動妄念 便證菩提.

Delusions may arise, but if you allow yourself to be dragged around by them, you will end up turning your back on enlightenment. If you keep your mind clear and notice how those delusions arise, you can allow them to flow freely and no longer be dragged around by them. This becomes the perfection of the vow, one of the ten perfections (*pāramitā*).[24] When you perfect for yourself the vow to save all sentient beings, you can draw on that aspiration in your actions in the ordinary world, but you have to be careful not to create unnecessary mirages that you then wander around within, saying that you are helping others when you are not even saving yourself.

Speaking of cultivating the prefections, adherents of other religions may be just as good as Buddhists at practicing them. They may also labor without sparing themselves in order to help others. However, such practices bring only temporary relief. This relief does not compare to the well-being you experience when you discover the cause of suffering and realize that there are originally no delusions.

It is correct to say that if you do not arouse delusion, you will realize wisdom right away. However, depending on your spiritual maturity, this claim might be confusing. If you are in the position to arouse faith based on your vow, this statement could expel all mirages. But if you try to remove delusions intentionally, you are creating problems for yourself. You do not enter into enlightenment by getting rid of delusions. Whether there are delusions or no delusions, if you recognize this fact, you will no longer be swayed by the arising of delusions, and they will simply vanish.

When you realize the Way, you simply realize the buddha that is your original mind. Your efforts over successive kalpas will all have been needless practice. It is just as when the wrestler discovered the jewel, he only found the jewel that had been there all along on his forehead; it had nothing to do with all the efforts he had made looking for it outside. The Buddha said, "I in fact gained nothing from *anuttara[samyak]sambodhi*."[25] Because he was afraid that people would not believe him, he demonstrated it by drawing on what is seen with the five types of eyes and what is spoken of through the five types of speech. This is true, not false; it is absolute truth (*paramārthasatya*).

及證道時 秖證本心佛 歷劫功用 並是虛修 如力士得珠時 秖得本額珠 不關向外求覓之力故 佛言 我於阿耨菩提 實無所得 恐人不信故 引五眼所見 五語所言 真實不虛是 第一義諦

If you want to teach, teach those who are wise. If you teach those who are ignorant, they will be unable to digest what you impart, and to make matters worse, they might even make the mistake of understanding your teaching in their own ways. Therefore do not speak recklessly! Buddhist practitioners who listen to this type of instruction will find peace of mind. Nonpractitioners, on the other hand, seek only the intellectual pleasure that comes from satisfying their own curiosity and thereby miss the genuine pleasure that comes from liberation.

The Buddha's statement here comes from the *Diamond Sūtra*, where he speaks of the five eyes and five types of speech.[26] The five eyes refer to the physical eye, divine eye, wisdom eye, dharma eye, and buddha eye; the five types of speech mean speaking the truth, speaking in accordance with reality, speaking of things as they are, speaking without deception, and speaking without prejudice.

4. Wise Nourishment

Practitioners of the Way, have no doubt that the four great elements constitute the body, that these four great elements have no self, and that the self has no master.

學道人莫疑 四大為身 四大無我 我亦無主.

The four great elements of earth, water, fire, and wind, which constitute materiality, temporarily coalesce to form the body. However, there is no basis for presuming a self controls this body. Even though there is no self, Seon teachers tell you to find the "master" or "owner" (*zhurengong/juin'gong* 主人公) because you would otherwise not attempt to solve the fundamental problem of existence. While considering this issue, however, it is problematic if you simply memorize the words or repeat the question "Who is the master?" without actually rectifying your thoughts. Do not just memorize the words without being evaluated by someone who has real insight.

Open your eyes to that root, the true characteristic of things, so that you firmly grasp the unchanging fundamental reality of your life, a life in which everything else is otherwise changing. Only then will you not be deluded, and at the same time will you not delude others.

Know that this body has no self and no master. The five aggregates are mind, but the five aggregates have no self and no master.

故知此身 無我亦無主 五陰為心 五陰 無我亦無主.

This body seems to be ours, but it really isn't. There is nothing there that can be called a "self." The five aggregates (*skandha*) of material form, sensations, perception, volitional factors, and consciousness are the mind, but none of those constitute a "self."

What, then, makes you move? Seon masters encourage you to raise the question "Who is dragging around this corpse?" in order to push you to see your original form for yourself. If you only inquire into this question intellectually, you will continue to analyze it and end up living a benighted life, spending your whole life searching in vain for the answer.

What I explain here is Master Linji's teaching of the three phrases, the mysterious gates of the "mystery in the essence," "mystery in the word," and "mystery in the mystery." It is said that you cannot even save yourself if you realize only the first of the three phrases. This is because the first phrase is only concerned with doctrinal concepts and intellectual thinking. When you move on to the live word of the meditative topic (*huatou*/*hwadu*) and realize the second phrase, the mystery in the word—that is, such hwadus as "Who is dragging around this corpse?"—you can become a master of both humans and divinities. However, when, thanks to a master's blows and shouts, your whole body and mind become one with your doubt on the hwadu, it can be said that you have now opened your eyes to the third phrase, the mystery in the mystery.[27]

When someone asks, "Without using your mouth, describe the ineffable fundamental reality that has no beginning and no end," only those who have no further traces of attachment to speech will be able to digest this question and answer it. Others will just be confused, with no clue about what is what.

Know therefore that this mind has no self and no master. The six sense bases, six sense objects, and six sense consciousnesses come into contact with each other and become subject to production and cessation, so this is also the case with them as well. Since these eighteen elements of cognition are empty, everything is empty. There is only the original mind, which is serene and pure.

故知此心 無我亦無主 六根六塵六識 和合生滅 亦復如是 十八界既空 一切皆空 唯有本心 蕩然清淨.

"No" here in "no self" and "no master" is different from "no" as we usually understand it. Since purity and cleanliness in general are different from their religious counterparts, even though the word may be the same, this "no" is totally different in content. If you understand this difference, then you probably understand Zhaozhou Congshen's 趙州從諗 (778–897) "no" (*wu/mu* 無), one of the most widely used hwadus in the Seon tradition.

If you turn one thought around, you will realize that the eighteen elements of cognition (*dhātu*), which consist of the six sense organs (eye, ear, nose, tongue, body, and mind), the six sense objects (forms, sounds, smells, tastes, tactile objects, and mental phenomena), and the six sense consciousnesses (visual, auditory, olfactory, gustatory, tactile, and mental) are all mirages. They are originally empty.

There is the nutriment of consciousness and the nutriment of wisdom.[28] The body consisting of the four great elements is tormented by hunger and disease. Nurturing this body with only what it needs, without generating greed and craving, is called the nutriment of wisdom. Self-indulgently clinging to what is tasty, mistakenly giving rise to discrimination, seeking out only what pleases your taste buds, and without generating any sense of loathing—this is called the nutriment of consciousness.

Śrāvakas are called "auditors" because they attain awakening by hearing [the dharma].

有識食有智食 四大之身 飢瘡為患 隨順給養 不生貪著 謂之智食 恣情取味 妄生分別 惟求適口 不生厭離 謂之識食.

聲聞者 因聲得悟故 謂之聲聞.

Śrāvakas and pratyekabuddhas belong to the Lesser Vehicle, the Hīnayāna. They are awakened by practicing for their own salvation, and they enjoy enlightenment for themselves. You should instead strive to become a bodhisattva of the Great Vehicle, the Mahāyāna, who helps others attain enlightenment; such a bodhisattva has the capacity to save others. Bodhisattvas, in particular, excel in applying expedients thanks to their vows. Their expedients are as different from those of śrāvakas and pratyekabuddhas as heaven is from earth.

Therefore, although you open your own eyes, if you spend your time practicing the Great Vehicle so that you develop a firm foundation for helping others attain awakening, you cannot help but advance in your training.

If you become a bodhisattva, you will have the power to share your merit, even though you may inadvertently resist doing so. If you intentionally try to share your merit with others, you will merely end up generating more karma. We can find this kind of sharing everywhere around us. We see people who do not fear self-sacrifice, donating funds, and performing charitable activities. But sharing the path to liberation is superior to sharing material goods. From a soteriological perspective, you should transform your very foundation in order to be better able to share benefits with others.

> **But [śrāvakas] are unable to comprehend their own minds, so they generate understanding by listening to the teachings. Due to supernatural powers in some cases, due to auspicious signs, language, or actions in other cases, they hear about there being bodhi and nirvāṇa, and after three asaṃkhyeya kalpas [incalculable eons], their practice leads to the attainment of the path to buddhahood. But since they are all still involved with the śrāvaka path, so they are called śrāvaka buddhas.**
>
> 但不了自心 於聲教上 起解 或因神通 或因瑞相言語運動 聞有菩提涅槃 三僧秖劫修成佛道 皆屬聲聞道 謂之聲聞佛.

Śrāvakas keep practicing in order to draw on the power of that practice, thinking there is always something more to be developed. But however much one practices and however much karma one creates, one's original nature remains ever the same; it simply appears in various forms according to the functioning of consciousness.

Once you realize this fact, you have only to let everything follow its own natural flow. Śrāvakas think that they have to remove the conceptualizing consciousness through practice. But intentionally trying to do so merely reveals their own misunderstanding.

If you suddenly realize right here and now that your own mind is originally a buddha, there is no dharma that needs to be attained and no practice that needs to be cultivated. This is the unsurpassed Way. This is the buddha of true suchness.

唯直下 頓了自心 本來是佛 無一法可得 無一行可修 此是無上道 此是真如佛.

Although the waves on the ocean of the Buddhadharma take various forms, their nature has never changed. The buddha's wisdom, which is like a great round mirror, reflects everything just as it is.

There is nothing to remove from or add to the mind. Because the conceptualizing consciousness arises, it is said that the mind is tainted, but it is, in fact, a misunderstanding to presume that the mind is tainted; it has never been tainted. Mirages unwittingly appear and coalesce. Beings seem to repeatedly live through the cycle of birth and death, but in fact they have never been born.

If you are deluded by the appearances of rebirth, you become an ignorant sentient being. If you open your eyes to the true reality of the original cessation that is nirvāṇa, you will realize that you have never been born, and you will live undaunted even in this chaotic world.

You practitioners of the Way need only fear the existence of a single thought—that is what it means to become estranged from the Way. Thought after thought remaining free from characteristics and thought after thought remaining uncompounded—that is buddhahood.

學道人 秖怕一念有 即與道隔矣 念念無相 念念無為 即是佛.

You never think, though you think all day long, because the original place transcends causes and conditions. There is no trace of anything that can be called causes or conditions. There, a breeze suddenly arises and creates a form. This is how space and time appear. We create a cause and receive a consequent karmic fruit. We repeat this process over and over again, appearing and disappearing in a constant cycle of birth and death.

There is no exception but one. The buddha realizes this one single exception and reveals it to us in a way that we can understand easily. This is the sublime dharma. The teaching of this sublime dharma has been revealed in its entirety. Since you do not know it yet, you mistake it to be something esoteric. To those who do not yet know, it seems wondrous; but to those who do know, there is nothing wondrous about it, since they continually possess and draw on it.

> **If you practitioners of the Way wish to attain buddhahood, you need not study any teachings of the Buddha. You need only learn to be free from seeking and clinging. If you are free from seeking, then the mind will not be produced. If you are free from clinging, then the mind will not cease. Neither production nor cessation—that is buddhahood.**
>
> 學道人 若欲得成佛 一切佛法 總不用學 唯學無求無著 無求即心不生 無著即心不滅 不生不滅即是佛.

If you stop seeking, abiding, and clinging, you will always be associated with what is unchanging. The concept of "stop seeking" is difficult to explain and digest. If you understand this to mean "do not do anything," then you will fall into a state of blankness. In order for students to avoid this state, masters say, "do everything while doing nothing," or "do not abide or cling to anything."

5. The Dharma Body Is Like Empty Space

The 84,000 dharma gates that counter the 84,000 defilements are just gates intended to edify and guide. Originally, there are no such dharmas. Relinquishment is in fact the dharma, and those who know relinquishment are buddhas.

八萬四千法門 對八萬四千煩惱. 秪是教化接引門 本無一切法 離即是法 知離者是佛.

Originally, there is not a single dharma that has been established, but the 84,000 dharma gates have been opened as expedients for saving deluded people. You may reference those dharma gates all day long, but none of them can actually be referenced. Although clouds may billow up one after another, no source can be found from which they are generated. In the same way, dharmas have no fixed characteristics. Although worldly dharmas are dharmas intended to be guarded, in this passage, "dharmas" means something that should be neither guarded nor relinquished.

If you simply abandon all defilements, there will be no dharmas that can be ascertained.

但離一切煩惱 是無法可得.

If you hear this sort of statement, you may keep trying to relinquish all defilements. But dharmas and defilements are identical from the start and, at the same time, dharmas are able to transform or overcome defilements. However, neither dharmas nor defilements have any fixed basis, so even though defilements may arise all day long, none has ever truly been generated.

Has empty space ever changed in past, present, or future? While space may not change, the shapes of clouds appear and disappear in the sky, just coming and going.

> **If you practitioners of the Way want to know the essential acroamata [for attaining enlightenment], simply add not a single thing to the mind. The statement "The true dharma body of the buddha is like empty space" is an analogy for this.**[29]
>
> 學道人 若欲得知要訣 但莫於心上 著一物. 言佛真法身 猶若虛空 此是喻.

Do not cling to these words either. You must awaken to verify these words. Do not get stuck at the level of understanding this statement conceptually. From a worldly perspective, you may be considered smart if you have exceptional knowledge and learning. But though you may convince others and satisfy their intellectual curiosity, it cannot be said that you know the real characteristic of things.

Empty space that embraces all appearances is similar to the dharma body (*dharmakāya*). This dharma body has no fixed form. The "dharma body" is that which is able to assume various forms while simultaneously assuming no form at all and embracing everything.

> **The dharma body is empty space; empty space is the dharma body. People always say that the dharma body pervades empty space and empty space subsumes the dharma body. They are not aware that the dharma body is empty space and empty space is the dharma body.**
>
> 法身即虛空 虛空即法身 常人謂法身 遍虛空處 虛空中 含容法身 不知法身即虛空 虛空即法身也.

The descriptions "alertness and quiescence" (*xingxing jiji / seongseong jeokjeok* 惺惺寂寂) and "void and quiescent numinous awareness" (*kongji lingzhi / gongjeok yeongji* 空寂靈知) are often deployed to depict the dharma body. Forms may be empty space, but empty space does not feel warmth and cold; it is the dharma body that feels warmth and cold.

If you definitively claim that empty space exists, then empty space is not the dharma body. If you definitively claim that the dharma body exists, then the dharma body is not empty space. Do not develop an intellectual understanding of empty space: empty space is the dharma body. Do not develop an intellectual understanding of the dharma body: the dharma body is empty space. Empty space and the dharma body do not have different characteristics. The buddhas and sentient beings do not have different characteristics. Birth and death do not have different characteristics. Saṃsāra and nirvāṇa do not have different characteristics. Defilements and bodhi do not have different characteristics. Leaving far behind all characteristics—that is buddhahood.

若定言有虛空 虛空不是法身 若定言有法身 法身不是虛空 但莫作虛空解 虛空即法身 莫作法身解 法身即虛空 虛空與法身無異相 佛與衆生無異相 生死與涅槃無異相 煩惱與菩提無異相 離一切相即是佛.

Among all the characteristics, the sublime dharma of true characteristics leaves all characteristics far behind. It is not that true characteristics appear when false characteristics are removed; true characteristics and false characteristics exist together. If you seek true characteristics by trying to remove false characteristics, this will be misguided. Know that false characteristics are nothing but true characteristics.

Ordinary people cling to sense objects; practitioners of the Way cling to the mind. To forget both the mind and sense objects is the true dharma.

凡夫取境 道人取心 心境雙忘 乃是真法.

You should be able to let go not only of sense objects but also of the mind. You should know that, even though you let go, there has never been anything to let go of, whether you let go of it or not. If you try to let go selectively, that will be a big mistake!

It is relatively easy to forget sense objects but extremely difficult to forget the mind. People do not dare to forget the mind because they fear that they will fall into emptiness, where there will be nothing to hold onto. They do not understand that emptiness is originally not empty: it is simply the one true dharma realm, that's all.

忘境猶易 忘心至難 人不敢忘心 恐落空無撈摸處 不知空本無空 唯一真法界耳.

It is more difficult to abandon the subjective mind than objective sensory experiences. This is because people think that they will die if the subjective mind vanishes. Since people tend to think egocentrically, it is really hard for them to let go of this subjective sense of "I."

Once both subject and object fall away, you will realize that they are indeed the one true dharma realm just as they are.

Since time immemorial, this numinous enlightened nature has been as old as empty space. It has never been produced and has never been extinguished. It has never been existent and never been nonexistent.

此靈覺性 無始已來 與虛空同壽 未曾生未曾滅 未曾有未曾無.

True emptiness is neither existent nor nonexistent. It has no boundaries. It is neither created nor destroyed.

Religions, like philosophy, do not claim that something "exists"; rather, they seek to explain what makes existence or activity possible. This focus is expressed, for example, in such terms as buddha, mind, nirvāṇa, or buddha nature.

> **It has never been either tainted or pure, clamorous or quiet, young or old. It has neither direction nor locus, neither inside nor outside, neither size nor form, neither color nor sound. It cannot be sought or pursued, comprehended through wisdom, expressed in language, contacted through sense objects, or reached through meritorious practices.**
>
> 未曾穢未曾淨 未曾喧未曾寂 未曾少未曾老 無方所無內外 無數量無形相 無色像無音聲 不可覓不可求 不可以智慧識 不可以言語取 不可以境物會 不可以功用到.

This enlightened nature cannot be reached by wisdom because even wisdom is an obstacle. Wisdom is a medication that is temporarily used to treat defilements. There is originally neither medication nor malady. Mirages originally do not exist; but since people mistakenly presume they are something real, a temporary remedy for resolving this mistaken perception is administered.

Although people are then given a chance to discard those temporary remedies after the mirages are removed, they cannot let go of them easily. This is the state in which they may have abandoned the sense fields but they still cling to the mind.

> **All buddhas and bodhisattvas, together with all wriggling creatures who are endowed with numinosity, possess this great nirvāṇa nature. The nature is the mind, the mind is the buddha, and the buddha is the dharma. Any single thought that is separate from this truth is a delusory conception. You cannot use the mind to seek the mind, the buddha to seek the buddha, or the dharma to seek the dharma. Therefore you practitioners of the Way, right here and now, should remain in a state of no-mind and silently conform with it. If you put the mind to use, it will all go wrong!**

諸佛菩薩 與一切蠢動含靈 同此大涅槃性 性即是心 心即是佛 佛即是法 一念離真 皆為妄想 不可以心 更求于心 不可以佛 更求於佛 不可以法 更求於法 故學道人 直下無心 默契而已 擬心即差.

If you understand intuitively, you will naturally accord with the Way. If you do not so understand and try to do so intentionally, this will only create ignorance. Not knowing what you need to do in order to understand, you approach the matter conceptually, you act as if you understand, and accordingly you end up getting stuck there.

To transmit the mind with the mind—this is right view. You must refrain from looking outside and pursuing sense objects. Mistaking sense objects for the mind is "mistaking a thief for one's son."[30]

以心傳心 此為正見 慎勿向外逐境 認境為心 是認賊為子.

The mind-to-mind transmission does not mean that there is something to give and to take. "To give" the transmission means to give something that cannot be given; "to take" it means to take something that cannot be taken. This sort of giving and taking cannot be seen with the eyes. Digest all of this from the standpoint of absolute equality, in which all connections are severed.

Since greed, hatred, and delusion exist, we establish morality, concentration, and wisdom. If originally there were no defilements, then what need would there be for bodhi?

為有貪嗔癡 即立戒定慧 本無煩惱 焉有菩提.

The three poisons of greed, hatred, and delusion are in fact the counterparts of the three trainings in morality, concentration, and wisdom. Although there are originally no forms that need to be saved, these words are uttered from the relative standpoint that there is something that needs to be saved.

Since expedients are used to assist with this process of salvation, various steps are established provisionally to resolve the fundamental problem of birth and death.

About this, a patriarch said,

The Buddha taught all dharmas
in order to eliminate all states of mind.
Since I retain no states of mind,
what need is there for all dharmas?[31]

Do not add a single thing to the buddha, whose original source is pristine.

故祖師云 佛說一切法 為除一切心 我無一切心 何用一切法
本源清淨佛上 更不著一物.

No matter how often they are told not to attribute anything to the buddha, sentient beings unwittingly keep attributing things to him. Whether they attribute anything to him or not, if they can simply reach a point of digesting everything and moving on, they then will be able to embrace any thing and any change, just as does empty space.

As it is, although they may only have a splinter in their finger, sentient beings find the pain unbearable and flail in agony. You must cultivate Buddhist practice together with other practitioners under the guidance of a spiritual mentor.

It is like empty space: even were empty space adorned with countless precious jewels, they would never stay in place. Buddha nature is the same as empty space: even were it adorned with immeasurable wisdom and merit, those would never stay in place. They would simply delude the original nature and obscure it, that's all.

譬如虛空 雖以無量珍寶莊嚴 終不能住 佛性同虛空 雖以無量功德智慧莊嚴 終不能住 但迷本性 轉不見耳.

Our inability to add a single thing to the originally pristine mind is like our inability to hang a jewel, no matter how precious, in empty space. If we focus on the jewel, we will become even more deceived, because we will miss seeing the true nature of empty space.

The so-called "dharma gate of the mind ground"[32] means that the myriad dharmas are all established in reliance on this mind: they come into existence when they encounter sense objects and vanish when those objects vanish. You must not turn this pure nature into a sensory experience. The so-called "reflective function of meditation and wisdom" refers to the clear tranquility and alertness of one's seeing, hearing, sensing, and knowing. But these are all understandings that occur at the level of the perceptual environment. These are provisional explanations offered to those of middling or inferior spiritual faculties. If you wish to intimately experience realization for yourself, do not generate these sorts of views and interpretations.

所謂心地法門 萬法皆依此心建立 遇境即有 無境即無 不可於淨性上 轉作境解 所言定慧鑑用 歷歷 寂寂惺惺 見聞覺知 皆是境上作解 暫為中下根人說 即得 若欲親證 皆不可作如此見解.

The "dharma gate of the mind ground" means that the mind is the source of the myriad dharmas. All dharmas are produced from the mind ground, just as the myriad things are produced from the great earth. Since this mind is originally pristine, you need not add any conceptual understanding to it.

If you are not awakened, do not create obstacles for your practice by generating such concepts as "quiescence and alertness" or "seeing, hearing, sensing, and knowing."

> **These are all perceptual dharmas. If you presume there is place where [these dharmas] perish, then they will perish at that ground where they are presumed to exist. Not generating a view of existence or nonexistence in regard to all dharmas—this is seeing the dharma.**
>
> 盡是境法 有沒處 沒於有地 但於一切法 不作有無見 即見法也.

The true dharma does not belong to the categories of existence or nonexistence, for it transcends all dichotomies. If you transcend these two extreme views, the dharma will soon be made manifest.

6. The Mind and Sense Objects Are One and the Same

On the first day of the ninth month, the master said to me, Pei Xiu:

Since the great master Bodhidharma arrived in China, he taught only the one mind and transmitted only the one dharma. He transmitted the buddha by means of the buddha and never spoke of any other buddha. He transmitted the dharma by means of the dharma and never spoke of any other dharma. The dharma is the ineffable dharma, and the buddha is the intangible buddha. This is the pure mind, which is the original fount. Only this one matter is genuine; all others are fake.

九月一日師謂休曰 自達摩大師到中國 唯說一心 唯傳一法 以佛傳佛不說餘佛 以法傳法不說餘法 法即不可說之法 佛即不可取之佛 乃是本源清淨心也 唯此一事實 餘二則非真.

Only the mind, the dharma, and the buddha are genuine. They all refer to the original pristine mind. All other concepts are fake. You should clearly understand that the dharma transmitted by all the buddhas and patriarchs from generation to generation is only this mind.

Prajñā is wisdom. This wisdom is the original mind that is free from characteristics. Ordinary people do not pursue the Way. Indulging only in their six senses, they journey among the six rebirth destinies.

般若為慧 此慧即無相本心也 凡夫不趣道 唯恣六情乃行六道.

The power that enables people to see the source is called *prajñā*. Unenlightened sentient beings only increase their ignorance by seeing, hearing, sensing, and knowing in accordance with the causes and conditions that derive from their eyes, ears, nose, tongue, body, and mind. As a result, they end up taking rebirth within the six destinies (*gati*) of heavenly beings, humans, demigods, animals, hungry ghosts, and denizens of the hells.

Practitioners of the Way, if a single thought presumes there is birth and death, you fall into Māra's path. If a single thought generates all different kinds of views, you fall into non-Buddhist paths. If you perceive that things are produced and pursue their cessation, you fall into the śrāvaka path. If you do not perceive that things are produced and only perceive that things cease, you fall into the pratyekabuddha path.

學道人一念計生死即落魔道 一念起諸見即落外道 見有生趣其滅 即落聲聞道 不見有生唯見有滅 即落緣覺道.

If you presume there is a single thought involving production and cessation, you fall into the path of the śrāvakas. When you are told to contemplate production and cessation, you easily end up generating attachment, because you assume that Buddhist practice entails observing your thoughts constantly arising and ceasing. This is falling into the path of śrāvakas.

This does not negate the value of insight meditation (*vipaśyanā*); it just means you should not abide in, or cling to, that method. Such meditations as counting the breaths, generating compassion, or contemplating the foulness of the body (*aśubhabhāvanā*) are all provisional means intended to lead people to authentic practice. But if you cling to these means, you will not be able to open your eyes to the Great Vehicle.

Dharmas originally are unproduced, and now they are also not extinguished. Do not arouse such dualistic views as revulsion

or delight. All dharmas are just this one mind; subsequently, this [insight] becomes the Buddha Vehicle. Ordinary people, generating thoughts about sense objects, pursue delights and revulsions with their minds. To be free from objects, they must forget their minds. If their minds are forgotten, sense objects will become void. If sense objects become void, the mind will be extinguished.

法本不生今亦無滅 不起二見不厭不欣 一切諸法唯是一心 然後乃為佛乘也 凡夫皆逐境生心 心遂欣厭 若欲無境當忘其心 心忘即境空 境空即心滅.

According to the "Universal Vision Bodhisattva" chapter of the *Sūtra of Consummate Enlightenment*, "When an illusory body disappears, an illusory mind also disappears; when the illusory mind disappears, illusory sense objects also disappear; when illusory sense objects disappear, that illusory disappearance also disappears; when that illusory disappearance disappears, that which is not illusory does not disappear."[33]

If you become immersed in these types of explanations and generate discrimination, thinking "this mind is the same as that mind, so there is no other mind that I can use," you will end up remaining at the level of pratyekabuddhas. You may attain a small realization, but you will not be able to attain great enlightenment. Therefore you should be careful!

If you just want to remove sense objects without forgetting the mind, you will not be able to remove sense objects but will only increase your bewilderment and agitation. Thus the myriad dharmas are just the mind. But as the mind also cannot be ascertained, what more do you seek?

若不忘心而但除境 境不可除 秖益紛擾 故萬法唯心 心亦不可得 復何求哉.

The myriad dharmas are created through mental causes and conditions; nothing is created apart from the mind.

If you accord with this mind, just as gears mesh together smoothly, you will realize that nothing is originally ascertainable or unascertainable. Even if you realize this, if you are not fully certain of it, or if you cling to sense objects, your training will be disrupted. However, such disruption may also occur precisely because you are engaged in Buddhist training.

> **Those who train in prajñā see not a single dharma that can be ascertained. They stop conceiving that there are three vehicles. There is only the one genuine reality, which cannot be realized or attained. To claim, "I have had realization and attainment," is the height of conceit.**
>
> 學般若人不見有一法可得 絕意三乘 唯一真實 不可證得 謂我能證能得 皆增上慢人.

Some claim to have attained awakening even though they have simply glimpsed that state. Such people are extremely arrogant. Practitioners of the Way should not abide in something of little worth. Let go of all sense of achievement, no matter how valuable it may seem to be. If you practice like that, you will naturally be free to embrace any change.

Do not generate futile thoughts about the need for changes. It is especially dangerous to try to teach another with your own tiny achievement, not being mindful of your relationship with that person.

For students of Seon, this is especially discouraged. If, based on immense faith, you let go and embrace changes, you will over time be able to benefit others without even trying.

> **In the *Lotus* assembly, all those who flapped their garments and left were such adherents.**
>
> 法華會上 拂衣而去者 皆斯徒也

In the *Lotus Sūtra*, those who digested the Buddha's words on Vulture Peak felt blissful and remained in the assembly, while those five-thousand Lesser Vehicle adherents who did not just left in a huff. Those latter people had encountered such a valuable opportunity, but they were not ready to make use of it. Had those śrāvakas had eyes to absorb the Buddhadharma, they would have remained in the assembly. They did not open their eyes, however, and thus they chose to signal their displeasure by leaving in a huff.

Therefore, the Buddha said, "There was in reality nothing for me to attain through bodhi."[34] He just silently conformed with it, that's all.

故佛言 我於菩提 實無所得 默契而已.

If you reach this level, it means that you have digested such expressions as "original nirvāṇa," "original no-mind," and "everyday mind is the Way." If you understand this correctly, you are told that you have opened your eyes to the right view of the middle way. If you attain sudden awakening, you will easily be able to understand this.

Ordinary people who are about to die should just perceive that the five aggregates are all empty and the four great elements are not the self. The true mind is signless; it neither goes nor comes. At the moment of birth, the nature does not come, and at the moment of death, the nature does not go; placid, it remains perfectly quiescent. The mind and sense objects are one and the same. If you can simply attain sudden understanding right here and now in this manner, you will not be bound by past, present, or future. You will then be a person who has transcended the world.

凡人臨欲終時 但觀五蘊皆空 四大無我 真心無相 不去不來 生時性亦不來 死時性亦不去 湛然圓寂 心境一如 但能如是 直下頓了 不為三世所拘繫 便是出世人也.

The five aggregates and the four material elements are like clouds that come and go in accordance with causes and conditions. However, the nature is like empty space, which is not produced when clouds appear and does not perish when clouds disappear. It is always placid, perfectly still, neither produced nor extinguished. Those who have transcended the mundane world should be able to have a penetrating insight into the buddha nature. Then they will not deceive or be deceived by others.

You should not have even the slightest inclination [toward another rebirth].

切不得有分毫趣向.

Since the nature is perfect in and of itself, it has no fixed locus. "You have to go in some direction" is a phrase that applies only to deluded people. If you understand that there is neither subject nor object, you will exert yourself without leaving any trace, and there clearly will be only the one mind.

If you perceive such auspicious signs as all the buddhas coming to welcome you and various other [bodhisattvas and deities] manifesting themselves before you, do not think of following after them. If you perceive horrific signs manifesting themselves before you, do not think of fearing them. If you just forget the mind and become the same as the dharma body, you will gain complete autonomy. This is the essential point.

若見善相 諸佛來迎及種種現前 亦無心隨去 若見惡相種種現前 亦無心怖畏 但自忘心 同於法界 便得自在 此即是要節也.

Whatever shapes clouds may take, if you understand that their foundation is simply empty space, you will never be deceived by their shapes again.

In this passage, "complete autonomy" refers not to the kind of supernatural ability in which ignorant people people believe; in fact, all people are endowed with this faculty. People who think that they need to develop this faculty end up generating an attachment to it.

When people are treated with deference by others, they typically feel flattered or even arrogant, as did the Buddha's cousin Devadatta, who showed off his supernatural powers, trying to prove that he was superior to the Buddha.[35] Śrāvaka disciples who did not understand the profound meaning of the Buddhadharma were unwittingly swayed and deceived by Devadatta. In this way, it is possible both to deceive and be deceived by others.

7. The True Dharma of the One Vehicle

On the eighth day of the tenth month, the master said to me, Pei Xiu:

十月八日 師謂休曰.

Pei Xiu seems to have visited Master Huangbo about once a month. Although he was a high-ranking Chinese official, he visited the master out of his deep faith to ask about the dharma and receive his teachings. Thanks to Pei Xiu, we today have access to Master Huangbo's teachings and can benefit from them.

The "conjured city" [described in the *Lotus Sūtra*] refers to the two vehicles, and to the ten stages, virtual enlightenment, and sublime enlightenment. All of these teachings are established provisionally to guide [sentient beings]; they all comprise the conjured city.[36]

言化城者 二乘及十地等覺妙覺 皆是權立接引之教 並為化城.

The two vehicles of śrāvakas and pratyekabuddhas, as well as Mahāyāna tenth-stage bodhisattvas and the virtual enlightenment and sublime enlightenment of the buddhas, are all manifestations of the dharma body. Thus short of having attained that consummate status of great enlightenment, you do not reach true nirvāṇa.

The "treasury" refers to the original buddha of the true mind or the treasure of one's own nature. Its treasures do not involve ratiocination, for nothing can be established there.

言寶所者 乃真心本佛 自性之寶 此寶不屬情量 不可建立.

The dharma is neither produced nor extinguished. Since it is originally perfect in and of itself, when you try to establish something, it will dissipate. It is just like empty space, in which nothing can be established.

There are neither buddhas nor sentient beings; there is neither subject nor object. So where is that city? If you ask, "We have already reached the conjured city; so where is the treasury?" that treasury cannot be pointed to. If it could be pointed to, it would have a fixed locus and thus would not be a genuine treasury. This is why it is said, "It's close at hand." It is impossible to pin down its exact location. If you just comprehend it here and now, then that's it.

無佛無衆生 無能無所 何處有城 若問 此既是化城 何處為寶所 寶所不可指 指即有方所 非真寶所也 故云 在近而已 不可定量言之 但當體會契之即是.

Although the treasury is said to be close at hand, it is neither close at hand nor far away, and it is also simultaneously close at hand and far away. When it is far away, it is farther away than the ends of the universe; when it is close at hand, it is closer than your own eyes. If you hear that it is within you but do not realize it, you will unwittingly look around for it everywhere.

If you know this perfectly established fact, this fact is not about whether you find it or not. Not understanding this, you will commit the foolish act of seeking it out.

***Icchantikas* [incorrigibles] are those whose faith is inadequate. All sentient beings in the six rebirth destinies, including even the two-vehicle adherents, lack faith that they possess the**

> **fruition of buddhahood; they are all called *icchantikas* whose wholesome roots have been eradicated.**
>
> 言闡提者 信不具也 一切六道眾生乃至二乘不信有佛果 皆謂之斷善根闡提.

It is claimed in some Buddhist schools that icchantikas cannot attain buddhahood, but the *Mahāparnirvāṇa Sūtra* asserts that they can.[37] The icchantikas do not believe in causality, so they say, "No matter how hard we try, we will never be able to become buddhas!" The belief that everyone has the potential to become a buddha should be developed through thorough understanding, but the icchantikas do not have such faith.

> **Bodhisattvas have profound faith in the Buddhadharma and do not discriminate between the Great and Lesser Vehicles. They also believe that buddhas and sentient beings have the same identical dharma nature. Therefore they are called "icchantikas who have wholesome roots." Those who for the most part attain awakening by hearing the teachings are called "śrāvakas." Those who attain awakening by contemplating causes and conditions are called "pratyekabuddhas." Even though you reach the attainment of buddhahood, if that does not derive from awakening to your own mind, you would also be called a "śrāvaka buddha." Many of you practitioners of the Way awaken to the doctrinal teachings but have not awakened to the mind dharma. Even if you practice in this way for successive kalpas, this will never be the original buddha.**
>
> 菩薩者 深信有佛法 不見有大乘小乘 佛與眾生同一法性 乃謂之善根闡提 大抵因聲教而悟者 謂之聲聞 觀因緣而悟者 謂之緣覺 若不向自心中悟 雖至成佛 亦謂之聲聞佛. 學道人多於教法上悟 不於心法上悟 雖歷劫修行 終不是本佛.

No matter how many dharmas you understand, if you do not realize this mind with which you are inherently endowed, you will inevitably chase something outside. A buddha does not need to practice; if he does, he is not a buddha.

If you do not awaken to the mind and only awaken to the doctrinal teachings, you belittle the mind while prioritizing doctrine. You thus become [a dog] chasing a dirt clod because you forget the original mind. If you simply conform to the original mind, you do not need to seek the dharma, for the mind is in fact the dharma.

若不於心悟 乃至於教法上悟 即輕心重教 遂成逐塊 忘於本心故 但契本心 不用求法 心即法也.

The moment you attain sudden awakening, you simply realize, "This is it!" It is like a fully ripe fruit, which falls from a branch if you touch it at just the right time. However, people rush the process and tug at fruit that is not fully ripe. Therefore they always leave a trace—a fruit with a broken branch attached to it.

As a saying goes, "A hunting dog chases the dirt clod; a lion bites the person [who threw it]."[38]

Most ordinary people allow the perceptual environment to obstruct their minds and [emphemeral] phenomena to obstruct the [unchanging] principle. They always seek to flee phenomena in order to pacify their minds and to reject phenomena in order to preserve the principle.

凡人多為境礙心 事礙理 常欲逃境以安心 屏事以存理.

People usually think, "Since everything before my eyes is a mirage that obstructs my mind, my mind will only become peaceful if I let go of discriminative thought." When you start to think this way, try instead to use it as an opportunity to reflect on yourself. Simply examine the fact that such mirages still remain within you. That's it!

People tend to think, "If my practice were mature, I would be able to set thoughts aside as they arise rather than being dragged around by them." Or, "If I cannot remove those thoughts however hard I try, my practice must not be mature." People generate this kind of discrimination quite often. Whether thoughts arise or not, you should just let them go, but you unwittingly let your thoughts leave traces in your mind. All these traces are imbued with the fundamental ignorance, which in turn ensnares you in the cycle of rebirth.

> **They do not know that it is in fact the mind that obstructs the perceptual environment and principle that obstructs phenomena. When you just empty your mind, the perceptual environment naturally becomes empty of itself. If you allow the principle to remain tranquil, phenomena will become tranquil naturally. Do not use the mind in the opposite way!**
>
> 不知乃是心礙境理礙事 但令心空境自空 但令理寂事自寂 勿倒用心也.

If those whose practice is still immature listen to these words, they will focus only on removing their thoughts and will not try to attain sudden awakening. Those whose practice is mature do not try to remove or empty their thoughts.

> **Ordinary people by and large are unwilling to empty their minds for fear that they will fall into emptiness. They don't realize that their own minds are originally empty. Ignorant people eliminate phenomena but don't eliminate the mind. The wise eliminate the mind but don't eliminate phenomena. Bodhisattvas' minds are like empty space: they relinquish everything and do not cling greedily to the merit they have made.**
>
> 凡人多不肯空心 恐落於空 不知自心本空 愚人除事不除心 智者除心 不除事 菩薩心如虛空 一切俱捨 所作福德 皆不貪著.

Since bodhisattvas advance to the level of signlessness, they know how to relinquish both phenomena and mind. If you do not know the Buddhadharma, you cannot even glimpse this quality of bodhisattva practice.

Therefore, in the *Lotus Sūtra*, it says only buddhas and bodhisattvas can hear the Buddha's sermon. Even the śrāvaka disciples whose wisdom eyes are open cannot perceive it until they also open their dharma eyes.[39] If your conceptualizing consciousness is weak but your faith is strong, then the moment you hear the Buddha's teachings, you are able to understand them and practice what you hear. If not, you simply start thinking and become confused, presuming you need to do something.

There are three levels of relinquishment. Relinquish everything inside and outside, both physical and mental. Like empty space, cling to nothing; afterward, respond to sentient beings according to their situation while forgetting both subject and object. This is "great relinquishment."

If, from one standpoint, you practice the Way and disseminate merit, but from another standpoint, you have let go of hopes and aspirations, this is "medium relinquishment."

If you pursue vast practices of wholesome acts, hold on to hopes and aspirations, and when listening to dharma understand emptiness and in turn become free from clinging, this is "small relinquishment."

Great relinquishment is like a blazing torch right in front of you: there is no further delusion or awakening. Medium relinquishment is like a blazing torch at your side: sometimes it is light and sometimes dark. Small relinquishment is like a blazing torch behind you: you can't see a hole or a pit [in the path ahead].

Therefore bodhisattvas' minds are like empty space that relinquishes everything. Their minds in the past were unascertainable, so this is relinquishment of the past; their minds in the present are unascertainable, so this is relinquishment of the present; their minds in the future are unascertainable, so this is relinquishment of the future. This is what is called relinquishment of everything in the three time periods.

然捨有三等 內外身心一切俱捨 猶如虛空 無所取著 然後隨方應物 能所皆忘 是為大捨 若一邊行道布德 一邊旋捨 無希望心 是為中捨 若廣修眾善 有所希望 聞法知空 遂乃不著 是為小捨 大捨如火燭在前 更無迷悟 中捨如火燭在傍 或明或暗 小捨如火燭在後 不見坑穽 故菩薩心如虛空 一切俱捨 過去心不可得 是過去捨 現在心不可得 是現在捨 未來心不可得 是未來捨 所謂三世俱捨.

Relinquishing doesn't mean that you actively seek to relinquish anything; it just means that you stop clinging. If you let go of both clinging and relinquishing, what will there be either to cling to or to relinquish? By elaborating different levels of relinquishment, this account encourages you to move toward the fundamental place of neither clinging nor relinquishing—the state where you relinquish everything while relinquishing nothing.

From the moment the Tathāgata entrusted the Dharma to Mahākāśyapa, he stamped the mind [of Mahākāśyapa] with the mind [of the Buddha], but their minds were not different from one other.

自如來付法迦葉已來 以心印心 心心不異.

Even though it is said that the dharma has been transmitted from mind to mind, nothing has been transmitted. For something to be transmitted, it must have shape or form. The dharma is nothing like this. Nonetheless, it cannot be said that there is nothing. The Buddha clearly understood this paradox. Mahākāśyapa was entrusted with the dharma because he also clearly understood this truth after he met the Buddha and awakened. This transmission took place through the exchange we call "holding up a flower and smiling subtly."[40] When the Buddha held up a flower, Mahākāśyapa smiled subtly. But if you cling to this story, you'll just be chasing an unnecessary detail.

People are born and die for a reason, but if you don't understand why this happens, you will be confused. If you fully realize that there is not the slightest distinction between you and the buddhas, it can be said that the transmission of mind has occurred.

By stamping empty space, that stamp could not be expressed in written texts; by stamping a thing, that stamp could not complete the dharma. Therefore he stamped the mind with the mind, but their minds are not different from one another.

印著空即印不成文 印著物即印不成法 故以心印心 心心不異.

It is not that a stamp is not able to stamp: the mind may be stamped, but it is stamped on the air. Therefore it accepts something unchanging during the ceaseless process of change. It cannot be said that it changes or does not change.

Although the Buddha's mind and our mind are not different, they function differently because of their different karma. But regardless of their karma, each of those minds is always the same ultimately. Therefore, even though you may accumulate karma as high as Mount Sumeru, the moment you turn one thought around, the Buddha will be right there with you.

Just as a bird in flight all day long leaves no traces in the sky, you let everything go when you attain a penetrating awakening. But still, it's hard to do. It is like a turtle that brushes away its tracks with its tail but inevitably leaves traces behind.

Since it is difficult to match the stamping subject and the stamped object, few have achieved it.

能印所印 俱難契會 故得者少.

There is in fact nothing that is matched. However many clouds appear, change, or disappear, all go through this process in the sky. Clouds have never left and will never leave the sky.

Nevertheless, mind means no-mind and attainment means there is nothing to attain.

然心即無心 得即無得.

Everyone speaks of "mind," but there is nothing that can be called "mind." Since nothing can be called "mind," nothing is to be attained. Therefore, the *Heart Sūtra* says, "There is nothing to be attained."[41] When you turn back to the original characteristic of truth, there is originally neither a subject nor an object that you can say you have attained. Although your discriminative thought creates the mind that likes attaining and dislikes losing, the nature is originally not something that you attain or lose. By thoroughly understanding this, you are not dragged around by delusive thought.

A buddha has three bodies. The *dharma body* preaches the dharma of the pervasiveness of the self-nature. The *reward body* preaches the dharma of everything being pure. The *transformation body* preaches the dharma of the six perfections and the myriad practices.

佛有三身 法身說自性虛通法 報身說一切清淨法 化身說六度萬行法.

From the perspective of realizing the primary statement (*yiju/ilgu* 一句), even the word *buddha* is used merely as an expedient. The three bodies and four wisdoms of a buddha are in reality false. The dharma body (*dharmakāya*), reward body (*saṃbhogakāya*), and transformation body (*nirmāṇakāya*) are typically compared to the moon, the moonlight, and the shadows cast by the moon.

The form of the original characteristic of truth pervades the entire dharma realm. Since that form involves nothing that is either redundant or deficient, when you illustrate it by drawing the moon, you should not misunderstand that that drawing is its actual form.

The dharma body's preaching of the dharma cannot be sought in language, sound, characteristics, or writing. Nothing is preached and nothing is realized. The self-nature is empty and pervasive, that's all.

法身說法 不可以言語音聲形相文字而求 無所說 無所證 自性虛通而已.

Even though the dharma body fully reveals itself, it is just so. Even though it disappears, it is just so. It has been just so in the past and present, and will remain just so in the future. While it is just so, motion suddenly appears and it is displayed in different forms.

Therefore, "The fact that there is no dharma to be preached is called 'preaching the dharma.'"[42]

故曰 無法可說 是名說法.

The entire dharma realm is preaching the dharma. Since the true buddha's preaching of the dharma is like an activity that suddenly arises in the place of the pristine dharma body, there is nothing that can be called "preaching the dharma." However, since the ignorant think that verbal preaching with the mouth is the only true preaching, the true buddha sometimes assumes a physical form in order to preach. Even though a buddha opens his mouth to remove mirages, this in fact creates other mirages.

Since the wise know that every mirage manifesting at the site of the dharma body of the pristine Vairocana Buddha is preaching the dharma, they make dharma offerings to the buddha everywhere and at all times.

The reward body and transformation body respond and display [their teachings] according to spiritual capacity. The dharmas they preach accord with circumstances and respond to spiritual capacity in order to help and edify [their audiences]. But these are not the true dharma. Therefore, it is said,

The reward and transformation bodies are not the true buddha.
They are also not the ones who preach the dharma.[43]

報身化身皆隨機感現 所說法亦隨事應根以為攝化 皆非真法 故曰 報化非真佛 亦非說法者.

After Huangbo helped Pei Xiu first arouse faith through the expedient teaching of the three bodies of a buddha, the master affirmed the reality only of the dharma body, saying that the reward body and transformation body are not a buddha's true form. The reference to the pristine Vairocana Buddha is nothing but a name that is given tentatively.

When you have the power to see the transformations occurring in the sea of the nature, you will understand what the dharma body indicates.

There is the phrase "in similar fashion, this one seminal brightness divides into six that combine together."[44]

所言 同是一精明 分為六和合.

Your six sense faculties of eye, ear, nose, tongue, body, and mind, which derive from a single source, are divided into these six when you are ignorant. But once you know, they return to the nondual site of the nature. Not knowing this, you unwittingly become subject to rebirth, discriminating these six faculties as being your home.

The "one seminal brightness" is the one mind. The "six that combine together" are the six sense organs. These six sense organs combine, respectively, with the six sense objects: the eyes combine with forms, the ears combine with sounds, the nose combines with smells, the tongue combines with tastes, the body combines with touch, and the mind combines with mental objects. Between them, six sense consciousnesses arise. Together, these make up the eighteen elements of cognition.

一精明者 一心也 六和合者 六根也 此六根各與塵合 眼與色合 耳與聲合 鼻與香合 舌與味合 身與觸合 意與法合 中間生六識為十八界.

Since the mirages that are generated by the pristine dharma body in response to conditions create the eighteen elements of cognition, everything is empty. If you return to the time before everything is generated, you will be able to find out what causes everything. When you realize true form prior to the creation of causes and conditions, you will know the one seminal brightness.

If you understand that the eighteen elements of cognition have no objective reality, then these six will combine together into the one seminal brightness. This one seminal brightness is nothing but the mind. All practitioners of the Way know this. They simply cannot avoid creating conceptual understanding of this one seminal brightness and these six combinations. Eventually, these practitioners are bound by dharmas and do not conform with the original mind.

若了十八界無所有 東六和合為一精明 一精明者 即心也 學道人皆知此 但不能免作一精明六和合解 遂被法縛不契本心.

Although those with dualistic thoughts may understand doctrine, they cannot accord with the truth. Something in their minds is completely unable to be digested. But if they turn one thought around and experience the principle of signlessness, they will digest both what has signs and what is signless and will be bound by nothing.

The Tathāgata appeared in the world, wanting to preach the true dharma of the one vehicle. But sentient beings lacked faith; they slandered him and drowned in the sea of suffering.

如來現世 欲說一乘真法 則衆生不信興謗 沒於苦海.

Even though you praise Śākyamuni Buddha's six years of ascetic practices and forty-nine years of ceaseless preaching, if you do not solve your own fundamental issue, you are slandering the Buddha and drowning yourself in the sea of suffering.

Neither cling to the appearance of the Buddha bestowing his great compassion nor arouse the extreme arrogance that you never cling to such an appearance. If you are a true Buddhist practitioner, the more you practice, the more humble you become, because you recognize your shortcomings.

Had [the Buddha] not preached at all, he would have been stingy by not widely disseminating the sublime Way to sentient beings. Therefore he adopted expedient explanations and preached that there were three vehicles.

若都不說 則墮慳貪 不為衆生溥捨妙道 遂設方便 說有三乘.

Since people did not understand the one vehicle, the Buddha had no choice but to espouse three vehicles in accord with sentient beings' spiritual capacities. He presented various expedients so that sentient beings could proceed toward the sublime dharma of the one vehicle, preaching diverse teachings to sentient beings with diverse spiritual capacities.

Vehicles may be greater or lesser, and attainments may be shallow and profound, but none of these is the original dharma.

乘有大小 得有淺深 皆非本法.

It is not that there are distinctions in enlightenment; rather, people's spiritual capacities are superior and inferior. However, if you attain perfect enlightenment, you will transcend even the Supreme Vehicle. You alone will be honored. If you do not realize this principle thoroughly, you will be unable to digest these words.

Therefore, [the Buddha] said,

> **There is only the one-vehicle path.**
> **The other two are not genuine.**[45]

Because [the Buddha] ultimately could not reveal publicly the one-mind dharma, he invited Mahākāśyapa to share his dharma seat,[46] specifically entrusting the one mind to him. This was the ineffable preaching of the dharma that transcends language.

故云 唯有一乘道 餘二則非真 然終未能顯一心法 故召迦葉同法座 別付一心 離言說法.

The Buddha and Mahākāśyapa transmitted and received something that is invisible. You cannot even glimpse it. When you attain enlightenment yourself, however, you will know naturally what they transmitted and received.

This one branch of the dharma was to be separately practiced. If you are able to conform with it and awaken, you will reach the stage of buddhahood.

此一枝法令別行 若能契悟者 便至佛地矣.

This dharma has been separately transmitted; it does not appear anywhere in the Buddha's scriptural teachings. Right here and now, the moment you realize your nature, you will be a buddha.

8. Cultivating the Way

It is meaningless to say you are "cultivating the Way" when your eyes are wide open. Since the Way has no form, it cannot be cultivated. Nevertheless, masters tell those who do not know much yet about Buddhist practice to "cultivate the Way." Practitioners of the Way should be able to digest all kinds of words. They need eyes that can perceive both the mundane and the supramundane.

Mazu's line "everyday mind is the Way" can be understood as meaning that all sentient beings possess the buddha nature. If you mistakenly understand that the everyday mind is separate from the buddha nature and thereby arouse discriminative thought, you will be even more confused.

> **[Pei Xiu] asked, "What is the Way? How should I cultivate it?"**
>
> **The master responded, "What is this supposed Way that you want to cultivate?"**
>
> **Pei Xiu asked, "Why is it that eminent masters everywhere have investigated Chan and studied the Way generation after generation?"**
>
> **The master answered, "Those are words meant to entice people of dull spiritual faculties; they cannot be relied on."**
>
> 問 如何是道 如何修行 師云 道是何物 汝欲修行 問 諸方宗師 相承參禪學道如何 師云 引接鈍根人語 未可依憑.

Pei Xiu was enlightened to the Way but still had a concern. He may have already had a sudden awakening when he met Master Huangbo, but he did not know what to do after that, so he asked the master. Pei Xiu asking about practice shows that he still believed there was something he needed to practice.

I am not saying that, since the Way cannot be cultivated, we can behave recklessly, ignoring the law of causality. The Way is like water that flows ever onward, naturally finding its way even in the dark of night. In the same manner, the Way has nothing to do with intentionally trying or not trying to cultivate it.

Pei Xiu inquired, "If these are words intended to entice people with dull spiritual faculties, then I'm not yet clear about what dharma is taught to people with superior faculties."

The master responded, "If they are people of superior spiritual faculties, then where would they be looking for someone to follow? Even one's own self cannot be found; how much less likely would there be some distinct dharma they could cognize? Haven't you noticed that in the scriptural teachings it says, 'What form would each of these dharmas take?'"[47]

云此即是引接鈍根人語 未審接上根人復說何法 師云 若是上根人 何處更就人覓他 自己尚不可得 何況更別有法當情不見教中云 法法何狀.

The saying that you "awaken on your own without a teacher" (*wushi ziwu / musa ja-o* 無師自悟) means that if you open your eyes, you may go your own way. Even if you achieve only the fruition of arhatship, you will already have reached a state high enough to become a teacher in your own right and thus will no longer need guidance.

Pei Xiu, because he had not fully matured, kept asking questions. You cannot attain the Way by cultivating it. The moment you attain enlightenment and see what you have turned your back on, you just have to let go. That's all there is to it. But the words "let go" are also a forced expression that we use because there is no other way to express the matter.

I am not denying that the Way should be cultivated. Even the Buddha cultivated ascetic practices in order to attain great enlightenment (*mahābodhi*) at Bodhgayā. Sometimes, certain causes and conditions make it seem as if something is to be attained through cultivation; at other times, there are causes and conditions that make cultivation irrelevant. If you have firm understanding and can digest different expressions, nothing will shake you.

Pei Xiu said, "Were this the case, there would be utterly no need to seek anything at all."

The master responded, "Since that's the way it is, you should conserve your mental energy."

Pei Xiu said, "In that case, everything would be eliminated. There can't just be nothing."

The master asked, "Who taught anyone that it is nothing? What is that 'it'? What is it you are seeking?"

云若如此 則都不要求覓也 師云 若與麼則省心力 云如是則渾成斷絕不可是無也 師云 阿誰教他無 他是阿誰 爾擬覓他.

There can be nothing else except the matter that is simply such. When you seek it, it is immediately concealed. But when you stop seeking it, it is completely obvious.

Pei Xiu feared he would fall into emptiness if he eliminated thoughts. However, this matter cannot be understood through reasoning.

Pei Xiu asked, "Since you don't allow me to look for it, why then don't you just tell me to eradicate it?"

The master answered, "If you don't look for it, it will be at rest. Who said it needs to be eradicated? Look at the empty space right in front of you. How could you ever produce or eradicate it?"

云既不許覓 何故又言 莫斷他 師云 若不覓便休 即誰教爾斷 爾見目前虛空 作麼生斷他.

To think that there is a separate thing that needs to be eradicated is a mistake. The point is whether you thoroughly know it or not. It is also a mistake to seek it when you don't know it. The Way is already fully revealed. Nothing needs to be eliminated or sought.

After having an experience through your meditation practice, there is nothing you need to do but pass the time by going along with the flow of causes and conditions.

Pei Xiu asked, "Can this dharma in fact be identical to empty space, or not?"

The master answered, "Morning and evening, has empty space ever said to you that there is identity and difference? I offered such an explanation provisionally, but you immediately interpreted it conceptually."

云 此法可得便同虛空否 師云 虛空早晚向你道有同有異 我暫如此說 你便向者裏生解.

Do not cling to words and produce conceptual interpretations.

If you spend time with a master advanced in his practice, it is as if you listen to the dharma without listening and the master preaches the dharma without preaching.

It is wrong to say that the Buddha preached the *Lotus Sūtra* on Vulture Peak with his mouth. He did not say a word. Nonetheless, the countless bodhisattvas and śrāvaka disciples gathered around the Buddha enjoyed his sermon.

Pei Xiu asked, "Shouldn't we generate conceptual interpretations to help people understand?"

The master answered, "I have never stopped you from doing that. But you must know that conceptual interpretations involve cogitation. Once cogitation arises, wisdom is shunted aside."

云應是不與人生解耶 師云 我不曾障你 要且解屬於情 情生則智隔.

Whether or not you produce conceptual interpretations, there is nothing to discriminate between, for originally nothing is conceptualized. Since you do not yet understand that defilements and deluded thoughts are not different from bodhi and nirvāṇa, you say ignorant things, arousing discriminative thought.

You need not intentionally remove what is transiently appearing in accord with causes and conditions. When the time is right, things will appear, change, and disappear.

Pei Xiu asked, "Correct me if I am wrong, but it sounds like you are saying I shouldn't cogitate on it."

The master answered, "If there's no cogitation, who is it who asks whether that's correct?"

云向者裏莫生情是否 師云 若不生情 阿誰道是.

It is said that you should use your mind like a bird flying all day long without leaving any trace behind. This does not mean you don't think. When you think, you think dynamically, like waves swelling in the ocean, and once you release those thoughts, you leave no trace behind. It is pointless to commit foolish acts, thinking about it and arguing about whether your thoughts are discriminative.

If you turn one thought around, all will originally be just as it is and unmoving.

Pei Xiu asked, "Why is it, no matter what I ask, master, you refute my words?"

The master answered, "You're one who doesn't understand what he's told. So what refutations are you talking about?"

問 纔向和尚處發言 為甚麼便言話墮 師云 汝自是不解語人 有甚麼墮負.

Master Huangbo here means, "If you don't understand, it's your mistake; it's not that the words are mistaken." Whether or not Pei Xiu became attached to the words, his questions showed that he was still generating discrimination. Whatever Master Huangbo said, had Pei Xiu simply not been so affected by the master's words, that would have sufficed. Pei Xiu, however, just proved that his training was still not sufficiently mature.

9. The Mind of the Great Vehicle

Pei Xiu asked, "So far, all the many words you have spoken are just refutations. But you still haven't pointed out any real dharma to us."

The master answered, "Real dharma is free from distortions (*viparyāsa*). Even the way you framed this question is itself a distortion. What real dharma are you seeking?"

問 向來如許多言說 皆是抵敵語 都未曾有實法 指示於人
師云 實法無顛倒 汝今問處 自生顛倒 覓甚麼實法

The true characteristic of things has never functioned separately from the dharma even once. You simply do not see it, and as a consequence you produce distortions and deluded thoughts.

Pei Xiu asked, "If the way I framed my question is itself a distortion, how would the master frame his response?"

The master answered, "You should get something to see your own reflection. Pay no attention to others." He continued, "You are like a stupid dog that sees something move and starts barking, unaware that it's the wind blowing the plants and trees." He added, "This Seon school of ours, since the transmission began until now, has never taught people to seek knowledge or conceptual understanding. It only says, 'Study the Way.' And even these were just words to cajole [people to practice]. The Way also cannot be studied. If your thoughts are inclined toward learning and understanding, you will to the contrary become confused about the Way.

云 既是問處 自生顛倒 和尚答處如何 師云 爾且將物照面看 莫管他人 又云 秪如箇癡狗相似 見物動處便吠 風吹草木也不別 又云 我此禪宗 從上相承已來 不曾教人求知求解 只云 學道 早是接引之詞 然道亦不可學 情存學解 却成迷道.

There is no Way to be cultivated, so what is there for you to cultivate? When you seek the Way through conceptual understanding, you assume that satisfying your intellectual curiosity is Buddhist training, not knowing you are making a mistake. This is not Buddhist training.

Whether you are enjoying the day or not, the master Huangbo focuses only on whether you are in conformity with the original share (*benfen/bonbon* 本分) of the enlightened nature.

"The Way that has no fixed locus is called the mind of the Great Vehicle. This mind does not exist inside, outside, or in between. In reality, it has no fixed locus.

道無方所 名大乘心 此心不在內外中間 實無方所.

In this way, the mind transcends any fixed locus. It is not influenced by time or space.

You live your life immersed in discriminative thought, missing what is truly important. Once you turn one thought around, discriminating wisely means that you are no longer discriminating among things. You may discriminate all day long, but nothing is being discriminated.

"First of all, do not generate intellectual understanding. I just tell you now that the place where ratiocination comes to an end is the Way. If ratiocination comes to an end, the mind will have no fixed locus. This Way is immaculate and originally nameless. It is only for the sake of the people of this world who do not know this and who are confounded by their thinking that all the buddhas appear to refute this state of affairs.

第一不得作知解 只是說汝 如今情量盡處爲道 情量若盡 心無方所 此道天真 本無名字 只為世人不識迷在情中 所以諸佛出來 說破此事.

People keep seeking, generating discriminative understanding. Although that may be how they have learned and gained understanding in the past, it will not reveal the Way. They cannot escape falsity because they themselves are creating mirages and deceiving themselves with those mirages. They must seek to solve the fundamental issue as soon as possible by meeting a master whose eyes are open.

"Fearing that no one would understand, [the buddhas] provisionally gave it the name the 'Way.' Do not generate conceptual understanding while holding on to this name.

恐汝諸人不了 權立道名 不可守名而生解.

When people hear the term *Way*, they cling to that name and create mirages from it. They delude themselves into believing that they have attained enlightenment. In fact, they only know what they have learned. These are just thoughts about the Way, not enlightenment. With this kind of understanding, without the experience of sudden enlightenment, you can never digest anything.

"Therefore, it is said, 'Once you've caught the fish, you can forget about the weir.'[48]

故云 得魚忘筌.

Having achieved your goal, you need no longer cling to expedients. There is nothing more foolish than to continue carrying the raft once you've crossed the raging river of birth and death.

"Once body and mind are spontaneous, you will reach the

Way and know the mind. Having reached the original fount, they are called *śramaṇas*.

身心自然 達道識心 達本源故 號為沙門.

Even if you do not shave your head, if you realize the Way, you are a *śramaṇa* (renunciant).

Turning one thought around to see the original form and proceeding to that point where the buddha and you are not different is what is meant by the gate of liberation or the gate of nonduality. If you enter this gate, you are a śramaṇa. But if you keep coming and going through this gate of nonduality, you are not a śramaṇa.

"The 'fruits of renunciation' (*śrāmaṇyaphala*) are accomplished not by learning but by bringing a halt to deliberation. If you now set out to seek the mind with the mind, you are only borrowing another's house, learning through mere imitation. When will you ever have any attainment? The ancients had such keen minds that, even hearing just one word, they ceased their learning. They were called practitioners who ceased learning, acted spontaneously, and relaxed in the Way. Practitioners today only wish to gain much knowledge and much understanding, to extensively explore the meaning of texts. They call this 'practice,' but they don't understand that much knowledge and much understanding, to the contrary, become a barrier.

沙門果者 息慮而成 不從學得 汝如今將心求心 傍他家舍秖擬學取 有甚麼得時 古人心利纔聞一言便乃絕學 所以喚作絕學無為閒道人 今時人只欲得多知多解 廣求文義 喚作修行 不知多知多解翻成壅塞.

When those who have great academic potential learn a lot and spread their knowledge to satisfy others' curiosity, people admire them. But if you want to carry on the tradition of the buddhas and patriarchs, do not cling to secular learning.

> **"Just knowing a lot is like a baby who gulps down curdled milk with no sense at all of being able to digest it. Practitioners of the Way in the three vehicles are all like this. They can be called 'those who consume without digesting.' This so-called conceptual knowledge is not digested, and it all becomes toxic—it all belongs to the cycle of birth and death. In true suchness, none of this is relevant. Therefore, it is said, 'There is no such sword in our royal armory.'"[49]**

> 唯知多與兒酥乳喫 消與不消 都總不知 三乘學道人 皆是此樣 盡名食不消者 所謂知解不消 皆為毒藥 盡向生滅中取 真如之中 都無此事 故云 我王庫內無如是刀.

Only when you attain sudden enlightenment and see the nature do you remove discriminative thought. You may have learned that all the phenomena appearing before you are originally illusions, but if you never actually realize this for yourself, your knowledge will remain nothing but delusion. You live your whole life making discriminations. But once you attain enlightenment, you will no longer discriminate. From that moment forward, you can draw on the power of *unconstrained conduct* (*wu'ai xing / muae haeng* 無礙行) by which you act without doing anything. This is something totally different from *veiled conduct* and *veiled consumption* (*muxing mushi / makhaeng maksik* 幕行幕食).

If you ground your life in discriminative thought without drawing on the power of enlightenment, you will live as if tumbling from thought to thought.

There is originally not a single thing in the royal armory. Since there is not a single thing in it, the myriad dharmas derive from it.

> **"All the intellectual understanding you have previously accumulated should be removed and emptied so there is no further discrimination; this is the empty tathāgatagarbha (womb or embryo of the buddhas). The tathāgatagarbha contains not even the slightest mote of dust. It is in fact the appearance in the world of the Dharma King [the Buddha], who destroys [all notions of] existence. [The Buddha] also said, 'I did not obtain**

> **even the slightest dharma at Dīpaṃkara Buddha's residence.'[50] This statement means that you just empty out ratiocination and intellectual understanding. If you dissolve both extrinsic and instrinic, your thinking will come to an end, and you will have nothing to rely on or cling to. This is what it means to be a 'person without concerns.'[51]**
>
> 從前所有一切解處 盡須併却令空 更無分別 即是空如來藏 如來藏者 更無纖塵可有 即是破有法王出現世間 亦云 我於然燈佛所 無少法可得 此語只為空爾情量知解 但銷鎔表裏情盡都無依執 是無事人.

The opening lines of Yongjia Zhenjue's "Song of Realizing the Way" describe this state:

> The leisurely person of the Way who has ceased all learning and
> has nothing more to do (*wuwei/muwi* 無爲),
> neither removes deluded thoughts nor seeks truth.[52]

The master Linji Yixuan also strongly advocated being a "person without concerns."[53] The Seon school as as whole values being such a person without concerns.

> **"The three vehicles' nets of teachings are remedies administered in response to spiritual capacity. They are spoken in accordance with particular circumstances and are established only temporarily. Each and every one of [those teachings] is different. If you understand this, you will not be deluded. It is most crucial that you do not generate intellectual understanding by holding fast to the words of a single teaching given on a single occasion. Why? There is no fixed dharma the Tathāgata could have preached. This school of ours would never comment on such a thing. Know only that resting the mind is what what we mean by relaxing. No conceptions before nor thoughts afterward are necessary."**

> 三乘教網 秖是應機之藥 隨宜所說 臨時施設 各各不同 但能了知 即不被惑 第一不得於一機一教邊守文作解 何以如此 實無有定法 如來可說 我此宗門 不論此事 但知息心即休 更不用思前慮後.

According to the *Diamond Sūtra*, "There are no fixed dharmas."[54] Only when the mind is revealed will you be able to rest. You cannot rest your thoughts even if you intend to. Without an awakening, you will never be able to digest this.

10. Mind Is the Buddha

Pei Xiu asked, "Since long ago, people have been saying, 'Mind is the buddha.' Yet I am not sure which mind is the buddha."

問 從上來皆云 即心是佛 未審即那箇心是佛.

This question shows that Pei Xiu had a lingering stereotypical conception of what is meant by *buddha*. He did not know that defilements were nothing other than bodhi. Pei Xiu knew only that the original mind was different from the discriminative mind, and so he asked this kind of question.

The master responded, "How many minds do you have?"

Pei Xiu said, "Is the worldly mind the buddha or is the noble mind the buddha?"

師云 爾有幾箇心 云 為復即凡心是佛 即聖心是佛.

Pei Xiu asked this question because he thought that the noble mind of a sage was somehow different from the worldly mind of an ordinary person. Although people may have seen the nature, unless they can control the habituations generated by subtle delusions, they continue to have ceaseless tension in their minds. Here, since Pei Xiu was in that very situation, he kept asking this sort of question.

Given how forthright he is here, Pei Xiu may have known that his question derived from discriminative thought. It is hard to say for sure, but he may have asked this question intentionally to help future practitioners resolve their doubts.

Whether or not he understood the implication of his question, he accumulated great merit by posing it to Master Huangbo and handing down the record of it to future generations.

The master asked, "So where are these worldly and noble minds?"

Pei Xiu answered, "Nowadays, in the teachings of the three vehicles, it is said that there are both worldlings (*pṛthagjana*) and noble ones (*ārya*). Why would the master suggest that there are neither?"

師云 爾何處有凡聖心耶 云 即今三乘中 說有凡聖 和尚何得言無.

Pei Xiu here expresses confusion because Master Huangbo seems to assert that, in the three vehicles, no distinctions are made between worldlings and saints. Pei Xiu suggests that the master's assertion runs contrary to Buddhist scriptures.

When people see the nature, they should realize that such terms as *worldling* and *saint* are mere relative concepts and ultimately are illusions. However, when the power of enlightenment is weak, dualistic thought prevails.

The master replied, "In the three vehicles, it says clearly that the minds of worldlings and saints are delusions. You seem now not to understand this and instead cling to their existence, mistaking something empty for something real. How is this not a delusion? Being a delusion, it confuses your mind. You need only eliminate [such dualistic notions as] the state of worldlings and the realm of the saints; then, there will there be no separate buddha outside the mind.

師云 三乘中 分明向爾道 凡聖心是妄 爾今不解 返執為有 將空作實 豈不是妄 妄故迷心 汝但除却凡情聖境 心外更無別佛.

Although Pei Xiu had experienced a spiritual breakthrough, he was unable to realize that ordinary people's minds were not different from the minds of the saints. He still had not had a penetrating awakening. He had seen the nature, but he could not escape his deeply engrained habituations.

If you have a sudden awakening and see the real characteristic of things thoroughly, you will realize that everything is merely an illusory mirage, and you will not make a distinction between saints and worldlings.

> **"The Patriarch [Bodhidharma] came from the West and directly pointed out that all people, in their entirety, are buddhas. You now do not understand this and are instead clinging to worldling or noble and galloping after everything outside. You are deluding yourselves to your own mind. I say to you that that very mind is the buddha. To arouse a single thought or sensibility is to fall into a discrepant destiny.**
>
> 祖師西來直指一切人全體是佛 汝今不識 執凡執聖向外馳騁 還自迷心 所以向汝道 即心是佛 一念情生 即墮異趣.

If even one thought is confused, you will create another mirage and will not be able to escape the six destinies in the cycle of birth and death. While all the various mirages are ceaselessly created and destroyed, the original foundation of the nature never changes.

You must realize this fact. If you study Buddhist teachings without realizing this, you could easily end up falling deeper in the pit of intellectual understanding.

Therefore, you must feel "this mind is the buddha" with your whole body and see through everything that is internal and external.

> **"Since time immemorial, it has never been different from what it is today; there is no discrepant dharma. This is what is called 'achieving complete, perfect enlightenment.'"**
>
> 無始已來不異今日 無有異法故名成等正覺.

There is no separate complete, perfect enlightenment to achieve.

The moment you realize "This is it!" you will never again be tricked by mirages. This is because, although the mind conjures up all sorts of mirages, those mirages have never actually happened.

Pei Xiu asked, "What is the rationale behind the 'is'[55] to which the master just referred?"

The master answered, "What rationale are you looking for? The moment there is the slightest rationale, that very mind will be discrepant."

云 和尚所言即者 是何道理 師云 覓什麼道理 纔有道理 便即心異.

If it is that very mind, it is in fact the buddha; do not think that there is any different buddha. There can be no distinction between saint and worldling. The mind of the buddha and the mind of sentient beings are originally nondual. If you realize this, you are not shaken by any other mirages. The noble are those who develop faith so that they are able to live their lives with confidence in the path they are following.

Whether one is a saint or a worldling is decided by karma. One becomes a saint or a worldling through his or her own efforts. However, there is no sage or worldling from the perspective of the original mind, which is pristine.

Pei Xiu asked, "You just said, 'Since time immemorial, it has never been different from what it is today.' What does this mean?"

The master answered, "You diverge from it only because of your searching. If you stop searching, where would there be any difference?"

云 前言無始已來 不異今日 此理如何 師云 秖為覓故 汝自異他 汝若不覓 何處有異.

If you seek it, you will be far off the mark. If you let it go, it will flow naturally, following its own course. Why do you commit a foolish act to get even more?

Master Huangbo could give this teaching because he had the experience of sudden awakening. When those who have not attained enlightenment hear these words, they will either fall into blankness or interpret them erratically. Since Pei Xiu had already seen the original true characteristic of things, the master told him not to seek anything else.

Pei Xiu asked, "Since they are not different, why even say '[mind] is [the buddha]'?"

The master answered, "If you do not acknowledge that there are worldlings and saints, who would tell you that '[mind] is [the buddha]'? If that 'is' is not 'is,' then 'mind' is also not really 'mind.' If 'mind' and 'is' are both forgotten, where else would you expect to search for the dharma?"

云既是不異 何更用說即 師云 汝若不認凡聖 阿誰向汝道即
即若不即 心亦不心 可中心即俱忘 阿爾便擬向何處覓去.

If from the very beginning there is nothing to seek, there is no need to say "is." In order to help Pei Xiu seek and understand what distinguishes "saint" and "worldling," the master employed this term "is" provisionally.

11. The Mind-to-Mind Transmission

Pei Xiu asked, "Since delusions can hinder our minds, I'm still unclear on how we are to expel delusions right now."

問 妄能障自心 未審而今以何遣妄.

Everyone in the world has such thoughts. But if they just open their eyes, they will see that there are originally no delusions. Here, Pei Xiu asks what he should do about the mirages that keep arising in his mind.

The master said, "To generate delusions in order to expel delusions is also a delusion. Delusions originally have no root; they exist only because of discrimination. If you simply cease thinking in terms of worldling and saint, you naturally will be free from delusions. If you then try to expel more of them, you would find not even a hair's breadth of anything to rely on or cling to. This is what is meant by the line, 'I have sacrificed both my arms, so it is certain that I will achieve buddhahood.'"[56]

師云 起妄遣妄亦成妄 妄本無根 秖因分別而有 爾但於凡聖兩處情盡 自然無妄 更擬 若為遣他 都不得有纖毫依執 名為我捨兩臂 必當得佛.

One thought creates all the diversity of phenomena. If you discard relative differences and abandon both extremes, delusions will no longer exist.

Master Huangbo could have stopped Pei Xiu's discriminations through shouts or beatings here. However, since there was something deficient in his understanding, the master kindly explained to Pei Xiu the reason for his delusions.

The story of a bodhisattva making a vow to cut off both his arms as an act of self-immolation so that he may achieve buddhahood comes from the *Lotus Sūtra* chapter on "The Previous Acts of the Bodhisattva Medicine King."

Pei Xiu asked, "Since there is nothing left to rely on or cling to, how does the serial transmission [from master to disciple] occur?"

The master replied, "They transmit the mind with the mind."

Pei Xiu asked, "If they transmit the mind to each other, then why do you say that the mind is nonexistent?"

The master answered, "Not attaining a single dharma is what is called 'transmitting the mind.' If you understand this mind, then there is no mind and no dharma."

云 既無依執 當何相承 師云 以心傳心 云 若心相傳 云何言心亦無 師云 不得一法 名為傳心 若了此心 即是無心無法.

This very thing transcends both existence and nonexistence. This being so, that thing appears or disappears without leaving a trace.

There is neither mind nor dharma in the true characteristic of things. Realizing this is transmitting the dharma from mind to mind.

Pei Xiu asked, "If there is no mind and no dharma, then why do you call it 'transmission'?"

The master replied, "The moment you hear me say, 'transmit the mind,' you presume there is something to be attained. This is why a patriarch said,

The moment you recognize the nature of the mind,
you can say only that it is inconceivable.
Perfectly clear, there is nothing to be attained.

Once you get it, you won't say you have any such understanding.[57]

If I tried to teach you this, how would you ever be able to handle it?"

云 若無心無法 云何名傳 師云 汝聞道傳心 將謂有可得也 所以祖師云 認得心性時 可說不思議 了了無所得 得時不說知 此事若教汝會 何堪也.

Once you see the nature, the rest will follow without much effort. Therefore, do not pay foolish attention to the matter of transmission. If you let it go, it will take its own course naturally. When you try to do something about it, you will be far off the mark.

If your karma is heavy, things will be not go easily for you, even if you have opened your eyes. You cannot avoid the fruits of your previous acts. Karmic fruitions include not only what you experience physically; they also include delusions.

Don't forget to thank the buddhas and bodhisattvas for helping you realize the inconceivable reality faster and more easily.

12. Mind and Realms

Once you have understood, both the mind and realms are nonexistent. "Existence" and "nonexistence" are concepts we create. From the vantage point of truth, it cannot be said that they exist or do not exist.

Unless you experience and digest this matter for yourself, you will be unable to grasp it. It is therefore said that you must open your own eyes.

> **Pei Xiu asked, "How could the empty space right before my eyes not be a realm? How do you see the mind without pointing to its realms?"**
>
> **The master answered, "What mind is it that is instructing you to look toward its realms? Even if you were able to see something there, it is actually the mind that is illuminating its realms.**
>
> 問 秖如目前虛空 可不是境 豈無指境見心乎 師云 甚麼心教汝向境上見 設汝見得 只是個照境底心.

The fundamental quality of what we call "empty space" is that it is a realm that involves sensory experience. Although we already are able to see our own minds, eyes, or empty space, we delude ourselves into thinking that we are unable to see.

Just turn one thought around. It would be foolish to say that you are seeing or not seeing. As soon as you open your mouth, you will be off the mark. If you know why we describe it this way, you can definitively see what is unchanging amid change, and you will not be swayed by the changes happening right before your eyes.

Just like reflections in the mirror, when the barbarians arrive, the barbarians appear in the mind; when the Chinese arrive, it is the Chinese who appear.

"It is like your face reflected in a mirror: even though your eyes and eyebrows appear clearly, those are intrinsically just a reflection. How can this have anything to do with you?"

如人以鏡照面 縱然得見眉目分明 元來秖是影像 何關汝事.

Both seer and seen are illusions. My reflection in a mirror is not I, but what sees my reflection in a mirror is not I either. There's no question, however, that an "I" is there.

You must perceive this for yourself. Everything besides this is unnecessary, nothing but discursive thought. You quibble over right and wrong, but you're simply adding to this discrimination. It has nothing to do with your original face or the true nature.

Pei Xiu asked, "But if it is not due to the reflections, when else would we ever be able to see [our faces]?"

The master answered, "If you are still wading through causation, you are inevitably relying on conventional things. When will you ever have a moment of understanding? Has no one ever said to you, 'I open my hand to show it to you, but there's nothing there'? It is a waste of effort to futilely explain it several thousand various ways."

云若不因照 何時得見 師云 若也涉因 常須假物 有什麼了時 汝不見他向汝道 撒手似君 無一物 徒勞謾說數千般.

True insight does not involve either seeing or not seeing, but Pei Xiu here asked because of his discriminatory thoughts. Even though you have trained in Buddhism, conceptual understanding, like a splinter in your finger, cannot easily be removed.

When you attain enlightenment, you see that even though people say various things about those mirages, all mirages belong to this matter of the mind.

> **Pei Xiu asked, "For those who have understood clearly, is it that the reflection is of something that isn't there?"**
>
> **The master answered, "Were nothing there, what would be reflected? Stop talking in your sleep with open eyes!"**
>
> 云 他若識了 照亦無物耶 師云 若是無物 更何用照 爾莫開眼寱語去.

Because something is there, it can be reflected. The difference is whether you realize this, whether you see this. If you see this but are still confused, there is nothing more to say except "give it time." Do not try to hasten the process. Just let things go their own way, and inevitably a day will come when you will naturally understand everything. Since Pei Xiu tried to rush this understanding, Master Huangbo told him that the best course was to just kill time like a fool.

This may seem to be turning one's back on the buddha, but it is not. Master Huangbo, who had the power to open practitioners' eyes, offered his teachings to Pei Xiu, who had just opened his eyes, like a mother caring for her child. Pei Xiu also demonstrated well what he had to do to fulfill his filial duty as a son.

13. A Person without Concerns

The master entered the hall and said, "To have hundreds of types of knowledge is not as good as to be without seeking; that is best of all. A person of the Way is a person without concerns. In reality, there are not countless types of minds, and there are no principles to be explained. Be without concerns. You're dismissed!"

上堂云 百種多知 不如無求 最第一也 道人是無事人 實無許多般心 亦無道理可說 無事 散去.

According to *Vimalakīrti's Instructions*, "'To seek the dharma' means that there should be no dharmas whatsoever that you seek."[58] In the *Two Accesses and Four Practices Treatise* (*Erru sixing lun* 二入四行論), Bodhidharma also talked about, "Seeking nothing is truly the gateway to practice. This is the practice that seeks nothing, which leaves behind all attachments."[59] The master Linji also referred to a "person without concerns."

Time cures everything. This matter being clearly revealed—nothing else is worth seeking.

If you have lived your life perpetually seeking something and finally come upon the opportunity to change yourself all at once, be thankful. Even so, it is not easy to digest this change all at once. Your eyes may brighten, but until you attain a penetrating awakening for yourself, you will continue seeking something, just as you have always done.

If you spend enough time with a master who can help you digest such a change, you will get better—and not just yourself: everyone around you will get better as well.

14. Acting Effortlessly

Pei Xiu asked, "What is conventional truth?"

The master answered, "What's the point of discussing such entanglements? All is originally pristine; why pursue such a dialogue using provisional language? Merely being free from all states of mind—that is 'uncontaminated knowledge' (*anāsravajñāna*).

問如何是世諦 師云 說葛藤作什麼 本來清淨 何假言說問答 但無一切心即名無漏智.

When people hear the words "free from all states of mind" they take this to mean, "You should be free from thoughts and conceptions." However, these words still include the injunction "should." Sudden awakening means you know effortlessly that you originally are free from thought. If you think you need to learn something and act according to what you have learned, you are still anchored to the Great Vehicle.

There is nothing better than to take the conveyance of the Supreme Vehicle and offer teachings in accordance with people's capacities.

Conventional truth (*saṃvṛtisatya*) refers to mundane principles. Pei Xiu asked about mundane principles, but Master Huangbo answered from the ultimate standpoint of absolute truth (*paramārthasatya*).

Pei Xiu's practice was still not that mature; but no matter how stifling his questions, Huangbo showed him the kindness that only a great Seon master can offer.

"Every day, whether you are walking, standing, sitting, or reclining, and whatever it is you say, if you merely stop clinging

to conditioned dharmas, then every utterance and blink of your eyes will be identical to the uncontaminated (*anāsrava*).

汝每日行住坐臥一切言語 但莫著有為法 出言瞬目 盡同無漏.

If you awaken to your original face, you will know that, regardless of your efforts, the contaminants (*āsrava*) are originally nonexistent. But if this is not the case, you will inevitably discriminate between contaminated and uncontaminated. "I'm practicing, so why don't these discriminations and delusions disappear from my mind?" "My mind is often obstructed by trivial matters and is far from being unobstructed. What should I do?" These types of questions all involve clinging to conditioned phenomena. The true characteristic of things is that they are originally unconditioned (*asaṃskṛta*) and uncontaminated (*anāsrava*). You must realize that this is how it has always been. If you make an effort to escape, it will be impossible even after three incalculable eons.

"Nowadays, as the final age of the dharma approaches, many of those who train in the way of Seon cling to sounds and sights; why don't they associate with their minds? Their minds are instead like empty space, like a withered tree or a stone, or like the cold ashes of an extinguished fire.

如今末法向去 多是學禪道者皆著一切聲色 何不與我心 心同虛空去 如枯木石頭去 如寒灰死火去.

After you attain enlightenment, your discriminations will, over time, gradually diminish. Do not practice with the intent of trying to accomplish something. See for yourself the conditions in which you can do everything without actually doing anything.

Once you have clearly seen the fundamental source, let it all go and allow time to pass. If you have not yet seen it, quickly seek out a spiritual mentor to help you.

"Then and only then will you have a slight correspondence [with the Way]. But if this is not the case, then one of these days you will be interrogated by old man Yama.

方有少分相應 若不如是 他日盡被閻老子拷爾在.

Since you leave traces behind, you can be tracked by Yama, the king of the hells. If you are an arhat or a pratyekabuddha, you will have a mind-made body (*manomayakāya*), which means you can choose to be reborn where you want and Yama will not be able to catch you.

At that spot where all mirages vanish and there are no longer any distinctions between the buddhas and you, there will be nothing you need to say. But if you are not even aware of the mirages that are now appearing before you, you will just end up wandering the rebirth destinies of sentient beings and being startled by ghosts.

"If you leave behind all dharmas that are subject to existence and nonexistence, your mind will become like the orb of the sun that is always present in the sky, its radiance shining naturally without [making any effort to] shine. Isn't that a situation where you should conserve your strength?

爾但離却有無諸法 心如日輪常在虛空 光明自然不照而照 不是省力底事.

If you simply let go, everything will naturally disappear; but if you attempt to remove things intentionally, they will turn into things that deceive you. Therefore, it is said, "Where you conserve strength is where you gain strength."[60]

"When you reach this point, you will have nowhere to roost; then your actions will be the actions of the buddhas. This is what is meant by 'You should give rise to a mind that does not abide anywhere.'[61] This is your pristine dharma body; this is called *anuttara[samyaksaṃ]bodhi*.

到此之時 無棲泊處 即是行諸佛行 便是應無所住而生其心 此是爾清淨法身 名為阿耨菩提.

Anuttarasamyaksaṃbodhi means "supreme, perfect enlightenment." This is not something you develop through learning; you reach it through a penetrative awakening. It gives you the strength to never be deceived. Everywhere you go is a place of truth. Everything you do is a buddha's actions. Although you use your mind, no trace is left behind.

"Without understanding what this means, though you may gain much knowledge through your studies and cultivate such ascetic practices as wearing grass garments and eating tree bark, you will not recognize your own mind. These are all deviant practices, certain to make you one of Māra's minions. If you practice in this manner, how would you benefit?

若不會此意 縱爾學得多知 勤苦修行 草衣木食 不識自心 盡名邪行 定作天魔眷屬 如此修行 當復何益.

Though you reach a position where everyone admires you for your extensive ascetic practices, those are all useless if you do not attain awakening.

You must open your eyes to supreme, perfect enlightenment; then you will gain the strength that makes the impossible possible. Otherwise, you will end up deceiving yourself and others.

"Zhigong said, 'The buddha is originally created by your own mind; how could he be found in words and letters?'[62] Even though you fill your mind by training in the three levels of sagacity, the four fruitions, and the ten stages, you will still be sitting amid the worldlings and the saints.[63]

志公云 佛本是自心作 那得向文字中求 饒爾學得三賢四果 十地滿心 也秖是在凡聖內坐.

A worldling may attain the level of a saint and continue along the path toward becoming an even greater sage, but everything he or she has done is still useless. When you simultaneously hear "you should become a saint" and "becoming a saint is useless," you will be confused if your Buddhist practice is not sufficiently clarified. However, those who begin to have some power in their practice can distinguish which words are right and which are wrong, which are deep and which are shallow.

> **"Have you not heard? 'All compounded things are impermanent. They are dharmas that are subject to production and cessation.'[64]**
>
> **Its velocity spent, an arrow falls back to earth,**
> **the future lives you have earned will not be as you hope.**
> **How could this compare to the unconditioned real characteristic of things,**
> **where in one leap you directly access the stage of the tathāgatas?[65]**
>
> **Since you are not this sort of person, you need to extensively study the knowledge and understanding of the gate established by the ancients that brings transformation.**
>
> 不見道 諸行無常 是生滅法 勢力盡箭還墜 招得來生不如意 爭似無為實相門 一超直入如來地 為爾不是與麼人 須要向古人建化門廣學知解.

Since Pei Xiu had already opened his eyes, the master recommended that he mature his knowledge regarding expedients. If you expand your knowledge without having this experience of opening your eyes, then the more you practice, the more deluded you will become. But the more you train after having opened your eyes, the deeper will become your knowledge of expedients.

The lines "All compounded things (*saṃskāra*) are impermanent;/ they are dharmas that are subject to production and cessation" are a part of a quatrain from the *Mahāparinirvāṇa Sūtra*. This phrase is very popular and often called the "Snowy Mountains Gāthā" or the "Gāthā on the Impermanence of All Compounded Things."[66] The second half of the quatrain is: "Once production and cessation cease,/ their tranquil extinction is bliss."[67] After that verse, the master quotes from Yongjia's "Song of Realizing the Way."

The gate of the "real characteristic of things" (*shixiang/silsang* 實相; *tattvaṣya lakṣaṇaṃ / dharmatā*) represents the perspective that all dharmas manifest the true principle.

> **"Zhigong said, 'If you have not yet met a supramundane bright teacher, you are ingesting in vain the dharma medicine of the Great Vehicle.'[68]**
>
> 志公云 不逢出世明師 枉服大乘法藥.

You may believe you have had a breakthrough in your practice, but you should nonetheless seek out a reliable Seon teacher whose eyes are bright and ask for his or her guidance. If you arrogantly say, "I have opened my eyes and have become a spiritual mentor myself. I don't need any more teachers," you will fall into the so-called "malady of a spiritual mentor." If that happens, you will inevitably become confused and lost, losing any chance of being guided toward a right path.

> **"From now on, simply practice no-mind at all times, whether walking, standing, sitting, or reclining. If you continue in this way for a long time, you will definitely experience some real attainment. Because you lack strength, you cannot make a sudden leap forward. But if you simply continue for three years, five years, or ten years, by all means you will be able to make a start[69] and you will naturally comprehend. But if you can't do this and instead try to force yourself to train in Seon and train on the Way, what would this have to do with the Buddhadharma?**
>
> 爾如今一切時中行住坐臥 但學無心 久久須實得 為爾力量

小 不能頓超 但得三年五年或十年 須得箇入頭處 自然會去為爾不能如是 須要將心學禪學道 佛法有甚麼交涉.

If you just have faith and are patient, your practice will naturally mature; there's no need to hurry. Let time pass, and five or ten years hence, you will find yourself transformed. If you do not have faith and commit foolish acts, maladies will occur despite your practice. You may think you are following the Buddha's teachings, but these conditioned dharmas, which you think you need to do something about, are in fact far from the Buddhadharma.

"Therefore, it is said, 'Everything the Tathāgata preached was intended to edify people. It is like distracting a child from crying by pretending that a yellow leaf is made of gold, even though that is obviously not the case.'[70]

故云 如來所說 皆為化人 如將黃葉 為金止小兒啼 決定不實.

The Buddha's teachings are intended as expedient explanations to help sentient beings fully realize the truth. The Buddha kindly offers explanations so that sentient beings will not give up in the middle of the journey, losing their faith. If people know this fact, they will not cling to expedients by mistaking them for true practices. This is not denying the need to learn expedients. But Master Huangbo is here guarding against wasting time by clinging to provisional means.

Those who know nothing can sometimes be better practitioners. They meet a good teacher, experience a breakthrough, and allow time to pass, not paying too much attention to practices that are provisional.

The story of pretending a yellow leaf is gold comes from the *Mahāparinirvāṇa Sūtra.*

"If you presume there is actually something to attain, you are not a member of our school; what will this have to do with your original essence? Therefore, a sūtra says, 'That there is in reality not the slightest dharma that can be attained is called

> ***anuttara[samyak]saṃbodhi.*'[71] If you can comprehend this meaning, you then will understand that 'the Buddha's Way and Māra's way are both in error.'[72]**
>
> 若有實得 非我宗門下客 且與爾本體有甚交涉 故經云 實無少法可得 名為阿耨菩提 若也 會得此意 方知佛道魔道俱錯.

From the standpoint of the original place, the dharma is also a conjured mirage that can therefore not be considered real. To all who have turned their backs on truth, Seon directly reveals the essential and profound meaning of the truth by demonstrating that there is originally no wisdom or ignorance whatsoever. To those who do not see this fact right away, Seon opens the door of enlightenment through meditative training.

The line "the Buddha's Way and Māra's way are both in error" comes from Baozhi's "Verses in Praise of the Mahāyāna." It is wrong to discriminate between the Buddha's Way and Māra's way. If you get caught in these two great evils, you will dislike suffering and seek only pleasure. If you awaken to the original root of birth and death, you will see that your original essence is empty; so where could there be buddhas and māras? They are just discriminations created by deluded thought.

> **"[That state] is originally pure, clear, and lucid. It has no such characteristics as square and round, big and small, or long and short. It is uncontaminanted and unconditioned, free from delusion and awakening.**
>
> **Once you clearly see that there is not a single thing,**
> **There will also be no human beings and no buddhas,**
> **Chiliocosms as numerous as sand will be like foam on**
> **the sea,**
> **All the saints and sages will be like flashes of lightning.[73]**
>
> 本來清淨皎皎地 無方圓無大小無長短等相 無漏無為無迷

無悟 了了見無一物 亦無人亦無佛 大千沙界海中漚 一切聖賢如電拂.

From the beginning of the world up to the present, all compounded things are impermanent. However, if you have a penetrative awakening to the true characteristic that is the foundation of the production and cessation of these impermanent mirages, then even though you cannot explain it to others, you will know it for yourself and will always be free and comfortable.

"Nothing is like the mind. The true dharma body is the same in the buddhas and patriarchs from the past to the present. Where could there be a flaw as minute as a single strand of hair? If you already comprehend what this means, you must exert yourself until the end of your current life, for you can never be certain when you exhale that you aren't taking your last breath."

一切不如心 真實法身 從古至今與佛祖一般 何處欠少一毫毛 既會如是意 大須努力 盡今生去 出息不保入息.

People may know what it means to perform some action diligently. But what they may not know is whether this diligence is leading to ruin. If they do know, they will be able to do something without doing anything. The difference between whether people know and don't know is as huge as that between heaven and earth.

There are, however, differences in the degree of knowing. You can see these differences when you examine how people have tried to help others. This is because you can see whether in their lives they strenuously cultivated Buddhist practices or wasted their time.

15. Huineng Becomes the Sixth Patriarch

Pei Xiu asked, "The Sixth Patriarch could not read scriptures, so how could he inherit the robe and become a patriarch? Chief Monk Shenxiu was the 'head seat' [*shouzuo*/*sujwa* 首座, i.e., leader] of five hundred, an instructor (*ācārya*) who taught thirty-two scriptures and treatises. Why didn't he inherit the robe?"

The master replied, "[Shenxiu] still had thoughts and presumed there were conditioned dharmas to be practiced and realized. For this reason, the Fifth Patriarch chose the Sixth Patriarch [Huineng]. At that time, the Sixth Patriarch just conformed in silence and attained the Tathāgata's extremely profound meaning that was privately entrusted. This is why the dharma was conferred on him.

問 六祖不會經書 何得傳衣為祖 秀上座是五百人首座 為教授師 講得三十二本經論 云何不傳衣 師云 為他有心 是有為法 所修所證將為是也 所以五祖付六祖 六祖當時秖是默契 得密授如來甚深意 所以付法與他.

The verse Shenxiu 神秀 (606–706) posted basically says, "If dust alights,/ diligently wipe it clean."[74] This is a conditioned teaching in which the mind retains characteristics.

The verse the Sixth Patriarch offered in response basically says, "The mind has no place where dust can alight,/ so there is no need to wipe it clean." This reveals the unconditioned dharma.

Afterward, the Sixth Patriarch spent eight months pounding rice and thereby had time to reflect on his experience. Then he said, "I have finished pounding rice. Now, I have only to sift it." The Fifth Patriarch, who realized that the time to transmit the dharma had come, called the Sixth Patriarch to his room in the middle of the night and preached to him the *Diamond Sūtra*. Right then and there, the Sixth Patriarch achieved a penetrative awakening and said, "How could I have known that my self-nature is originally pristine?"

"Have you not heard it said?:

Dharma is originally a dharma that is no dharma.
The dharma that is no dharma is also a dharma.
Now when I confer this no dharma,
how would you understand the dharma to be this dharma or that dharma?[75]

If you comprehend what this means, you will then be called a person who has left the household life; you will then be someone who enjoys practice.

汝不見道 法本法無法 無法法亦法 今付無法時 法法何曾法
若會此意 方名出家兒 方好修行.

The scriptures teach that those who have left the household life receive precepts and become members of the saṅgha in order to pay homage to the three jewels of the buddha, the dharma, and the saṅgha.

On the other hand, in Seon, only those who have opened their eyes are called those who have left the household life. Even though you do not shave your head and still live in a town, if you open your eyes, you will be called one who has left the household life.

At the fundamental place, you are not bound by whether the dharma is existent or nonexistent. Why then would it matter whether you have received the precepts? However, if you become attached to enlightenment and do not stop valorizing causes and conditions, as long as you have a physical body, you will not be able to escape one whit of causality.

"If you cannot believe this, then tell me why Chief Monk Daoming rushed to the summit of Mount Dayu to find the Sixth

Patriarch? The Sixth Patriarch asked him, 'What did you come in search of, the robe or the dharma?'

"Daoming replied, 'I haven't come for the robe; I've only come for the dharma.'

"The Sixth Patriarch said, 'Gather your thoughts for a moment and don't think of either good or evil.' Daoming did as he was told. The Sixth Patriarch said, 'When you're not thinking of good and not thinking of evil—at that very moment, bring me Chief Monk Daoming's original face before your parents conceived you.'[76] At these words, Daoming suddenly silently conformed [with the Way].

"He then bowed respectfully and said, 'I am like a person who has drunk water and knows for himself whether it is cold or warm. While I was living in the Fifth Patriarch's congregation, I wasted thirty years of practice. Today, I have finally realized my previous mistakes.'

"The Sixth Patriarch said, 'So it is. Having arrived here, you finally know that the Patriarch [Bodhidharma's] coming from the West, pointing directly to people's minds, and seeing the nature and achieving buddhahood does not involve speech.'[77]

若不信 云何明上座 走來大庾嶺頭 尋六祖 六祖便問 汝來求何事 為求衣 為求法 明上座云 不為衣來 但為法來 六祖云 汝且暫時斂念 善惡都莫思量 明乃稟語 六祖云 不思善不思惡 正當與麼時 還我明上座 父母未生時面目來 明於言下 忽然默契 便禮拜云 如人飲水冷煖自知 某甲在五祖會中枉用三十年工夫 今日方省前非 六祖云 如是 到此之時 方知祖師西來 直指人心 見性成佛 不在言說.

Chief Monk Daoming's original name was Huiming 慧明. After he awakened, out of deference for the Sixth Patriarch Huineng, he stopped using the Sinograph "Hui," which also appeared in his teacher's name, and changed his name to Daoming.

Daoming had been a fifth-rank general in the Chinese army before he ordained as a monk and was a disciple of Huineng's rival, Shenxiu. When Shenxiu's inner circle thought that Huineng had stolen the robe and bowl symbolizing the patriarchy from their rightful recipient, they tried to track Huineng down in order to retrieve the symbols of the patriarchy for Shenxiu. Because of Daoming's military background, he was able to catch up more quickly with the Sixth Patriarch than others. Seeing Daoming approach, the Sixth Patriarch hid, placing the robe and bowl on a rock. Daoming at first tried to return to Shenxiu with the robe and bowl, but he "turned one thought around" and instead sought Huineng's teachings. Although Daoming did not initially chase after the Sixth Patriarch to seek the dharma, he didn't miss this opportunity to ask about the dharma. Right then and there, he conformed with the Way and illuminated the nature.

"Have you not heard how Ānanda asked Mahākāśyapa, 'Did the World-Honored One separately transmit anything besides his golden garment?'

"Mahākāśyapa called Ānanda over and Ānanda complied. Mahākāśyapa ordered, 'Knock over the flagpole in front of the gate!'[78] This was the patriarch's symbolic flag.

"How was it that Ānanda served as [the Buddha's] attendant for thirty years, only to be admonished by the Buddha for acquiring knowledge that comes from extensive learning: 'For you to study knowledge for a thousand days is not as good as studying the Way for just one day. If you do not study the Way, it will be difficult to digest even a drop of water.'"[79]

豈不見 阿難問迦葉云 世尊傳金襴外 別傳何物 迦葉召阿難 阿難應諾 迦葉云 倒却門前刹竿著 此便是祖師之標榜也 甚生阿難三十年為侍者 秖為多聞智慧 被佛訶云 汝千日學慧 不如一日學道 若不學道 滴水難消.

When Ānanda asked, "What dharma did the World-Honored One transmit?" Mahākāśyapa just told him, "Knock over the flagpole in front of the gate," without giving any further explanation. As the Buddha's longtime attendant, Ānanda had heard numerous teachings but failed to attain enlightenment. Only after the Buddha passed away was he finally enlightened, thanks to his senior dharma brother Mahākāśyapa, and became a patriarch himself.

The householder Pei Xiu attained enlightenment through the intercession of Master Huangbo and was able to digest these words thanks to the power of sudden enlightenment. In this way, know that the experience of sudden enlightenment is truly useful and precious.

Part II

The Wanling Record

(*Wanling lu* 宛陵錄)

1. The Way Means Awakening to the Mind

Grand Councilor Pei Xiu asked the master:

裴相公問師曰.

Both *Essentials of Transmitting the Mind-Dharma* and the *Wanling Record* are records of Master Huangbo's exchanges with Pei Xiu. The former text was written in 842 during the Tang dynasty when Pei Xiu served as governor of Zhongling 鍾陵. The latter was compiled six years later, in 848, in Wanling. Wanling was the capital of Anhui province, located in the hill areas south of the Yangtze River, and served as a major transportation hub.

Essentials refers to the questioner "Pei Xiu" without any honorific title, while the *Wanling Record* uses his title "grand councilor."[80] Considering this variation, it seems that *Essentials* was written by Pei Xiu himself while the *Wanling Record* was compiled by disciples of the master who were present during Pei Xiu's visits with Huangbo.

"Of the four or five hundred people in this mountain [assembly], how many have gained the master's dharma?"

The master replied, "It is impossible to count the number of those who have gained it. Why? The Way involves awakening to the mind. How could it involve speech? Language is only used to help immature children understand."

山中四五百人 幾人得和尚法 師云 得者莫測其數 何故 道在心悟 豈在言說 言說只是化童蒙耳.

Language is merely a means to help people realize the Way, like pretending a yellow leaf is real gold to make a child stop crying. Therefore you should not think that there is real meaning in language.

This statement is made from the standpoint of the Way. It is not that there is something wrong with language itself. What the master said here is that language is only a means, not the goal.

I can feel the immeasurable weight of the master's words, "It is impossible to count the number of those who have gained it."

2. No-Mind Is the Way

Pei Xiu asked, "What is buddha?"

The master replied, "The mind is buddha. No-mind is the Way.

問 如何是佛 師云 即心是佛 無心是道.

Here, something that cannot be named is called the "mind." This mind is nothing but the buddha and no-mind. "No-mind" refers to everyday mind. Although everyday mind is revealed in front of your eyes, you cannot describe its limit. There is no spot where you can pinpoint its location, saying, "Here it is!" The mind that you cannot say either exists or does not exist is called "no-mind." It has never revealed any form that can be called "the mind"; but it is not that it does not reveal itself, either.

Seon masters say, "It is revealed anywhere and at any time, but you do not realize this fact because you have not attained enlightenment."

"If you neither arouse your mind nor allow yourself to think in terms of such mental conceptions as existence and nonexistence, long and short, self and others, and subject and object, then the mind is originally buddha and buddha is originally the mind.

但無生心動念 有無長短 彼我能所等心 心本是佛 佛本是心.

If the dualistic thoughts that discriminate and distinguish among things are eradicated, the mind will then indeed be the buddha.

"The mind is like empty space. Therefore it is said, 'The true dharma body of the buddha is like empty space.'[81]

心如虛空 所以云 佛真法身 猶若虛空.

Since the mind is like empty space, it is not known when and how it was created. It transcends the level of cognition. Empty space does not change even the slightest, whether in the past, present, or future. The mind is just like this. Since people try to describe or even name the mind that is like empty space, they think there must be this kind of mind or that kind of mind. But how can there be discriminations such as wide and narrow, large and small, or close and distant in either empty space or the mind itself?

Empty space may be like the mind, but unlike the mind, empty space has no numinous awareness (*lingzhi*/*yeongji* 靈知). Empty space and the mind are alike in their emptiness and tranquility. However, empty space cannot tell the difference between warm and cold when water is sprayed into the air; only the mind can know warmth and cold.

Although empty space cannot become a buddha, comparing the mind to empty space is valid because they share some similarities.

"Do not seek [the buddha] separately. Seeking anything will inevitably lead to suffering.

不用別求 有求皆苦.

If the mind is indeed buddha, and because the myriad things are also the mind, there is no need to seek the buddha elsewhere.

You're always seeking something, thinking, "I should find the buddha. I should realize buddhahood." However, you should first turn this one thought around. If you think you need to find something and you pursue it, you will only stain yourself with more dirt.

Master Huangbo asserted, "There is originally nothing to be attained."

"Even if you cultivate the six perfections and the myriad [bodhisattva] practices for as many kalpas as there are grains

of sand in the Ganges and gain the bodhi of the buddhas, this still will not be the ultimate. Why is this? This is because they are associated with conditioned creation.

設使恒沙劫 行六度萬行 得佛菩提 亦非究竟 何以故 為屬因緣造作故.

Even though you cultivate the myriad practices of the bodhisattvas, you are still not ready to attain supreme enlightenment. The six perfections and the myriad bodhisattva practices are nothing but mirages that constantly change, being dragged along by karmic conditioning. The moment you realize that there is something that is immutable, everything that is subject to change will be seen as false.

What is created by causes and conditions are conditioned dharmas (*saṃskṛtadharma*). For this reason, the *Diamond Sūtra* says, "All conditioned dharmas are like a dream, a mirage, a bubble, and a shadow; they are like the morning dew or a flash of lightning."[82]

"And once such causes and conditions come to an end, they revert to impermanence.

因緣若盡 還歸無常.

The dharma body remains the same, whether it is in the hells or the heavens, for it has never been created or altered. However, anything that is produced through causes and conditions inevitably changes, and such ephemeral things are all vain and false.

"Therefore, it is said,

> **The reward body and the transformation body are not the true buddha.**
> **They also are not the one who preaches the dharma.**[83]

所以云 報化非真佛 亦非說法者.

The dharma body, reward body, and transformation body can be compared to the moon, moonlight, and the shadows cast by the moon, respectively. If the moon has risen, there will be moonlight, which casts shadows. Therefore the reward body and transformation body are created in accordance with karmic causes and conditions. They are not the one who preaches the dharma.

"You need only recognize that your own mind involves neither self nor person but is originally a buddha."

但識自心 無我無人 本來是佛.

Since originally there are no real conceptions of self and person, it would be foolish to try to eradicate such conceptions. How can you eradicate something that does not exist? If you realize that there are originally no such conceptions, you will realize that all conceptions of a self (*ātman*), a person (*pudgala*), a living being (*sattva*), or a soul (*jīva*) are nothing but shadows. Seeing that such things appear in accordance with the proper conditions, do not think that these are things you need to eradicate.

Do not foolishly try to remove conceptions. Try instead to thoroughly realize that originally no such conception exists.

3. Put Your Mind to Rest

Pei Xiu asked, "For the saints, no-mind is the buddha. For worldlings, wouldn't no-mind mean that they end up being submerged in emptiness and quiescence?"

問 聖人 無心即是佛 凡夫 無心莫沈空寂否.

The minds of saints and worldlings are not different because both are originally no-mind. Sentient beings who do not know this fact tend to discriminate between saints and worldlings. Therefore masters with bright eyes develop expedients to help break down sentient beings' delusions and provide an opportunity for those who have aroused faith to practice Buddhism.

The master replied, "In the dharma, there are no saints or worldlings and no submersion in quiescence, either. The dharma may originally be nonexistent, but do not then generate a view that it is nonexistent. The dharma may originally not be nonexistent, but do not then generate a view that it is existent.

師云 法無凡聖亦無沈寂 法本不有 莫作無見 法本不無 莫作有見.

Since those who have had a breakthrough in their training know that there are originally no dharmas to be established, they never create such a view. They employ such views without actually employing anything. They know that, in the mind, there is no distinction between saints and worldlings.

Although it may seem that the minds of saints and worldlings exist separately, what is really happening is that their different karma makes them appear to be different.

In the mind, how would there be either saints or worldlings?

"Whether [the dharma] is existent or nonexistent is entirely a discriminative view that is like a phantasm.[84]

有之與無 盡是情見 猶如幻翳.

Since all discriminations in the phenomenal realm are created by the sense consciousnesses, be fooled by phantasms no longer.

Opening the true eye of the Way, you will transcend all discriminations and dualistic views involving the mundane world and embrace these relative values within the nondual middle way. Therefore enlightened people have overcome all dualistic tensions and live freely in their everyday mind.

Practice diligently with a distinguished master, never neglecting self-examination. Such is the good fortune that comes to practitioners.

"This is why it is said, 'Seeing and hearing are like phantasms.'[85] **Sensing and perceiving are indeed what it means to be a sentient being. In the gate of the patriarchs and teachers, we only discuss resting the [mind's] operations and remaining oblivious to views.**

所以云 見聞如幻翳 知覺乃眾生 祖師門中 只論息機忘見.

Although there is originally no distinction between buddhas and sentient beings, people discriminate between the two, creating false impressions because of their ignorance. When sentient beings realize that they themselves are buddhas, all discriminations will disappear.

Although you generate various thoughts all day long, nothing is generated. If you perfectly realize this fact, discrimination will cease.

"Therefore, 'If you remain oblivious to mental impulses, the Buddha Way will thrive; but if you discriminate, Māra's minions will swarm.'"[86]

所以 忘機則佛道隆 分別則魔軍熾.

Since there is no mind to rest, there is no need even to say, "Remain oblivious to mental impulses." But Master Huangbo said such words out of his concern for his disciples.

4. No Mind and No Dharma

Pei Xiu asked, "Since the mind is originally a buddha, should I cultivate the six perfections and the myriad bodhisattva practices or not?"

問 心既本來是佛 還修六度萬行否.

Grand Councilor Pei Xiu here is asking, "If I have already seen the mind, is it still necessary for me to cultivate the six perfections and the myriad bodhisattva practices?" Even though though he knew that he could not solve the issues of birth, aging, sickness, and death through conceptual understanding, he asked this question because of his habituations.

The master replied, "Awakening resides in the mind; it has nothing to do with the six perfections and the myriad bodhisattva practices. The six perfections and the myriad practices all involve the gate of propagation; they are ancillary matters associated with assisting others and saving living creatures.

師云 悟在於心 非關六度萬行 六度萬行 盡是化門 接物度生邊事.

Strictly speaking, the six perfections and the myriad practices of the bodhisattva path are just expedients designed to help people realize the mind. Though you may cultivate the six perfections and the myriad bodhisattva practices for eons on end, it still means you are creating karma.

Awakening resides only in the mind. All practices that do not involve awakening are insignificant and trivial in comparison. However, ignorant people who hear these words do not understand them and cannot even enter the path leading to the Way. Therefore expedients are established to help these people cross over to the other shore.

If people have an awakening, they should be able to let go of their knowledge. Even though Pei Xiu attained sudden awakening, he could not let go of the knowledge that he had previously acquired.

Such conceptual knowledge always ends up becoming a hindrance. People gain some knowledge, and then they become curious and want to gain some more. Once people learn a lot, they want to use their knowledge. Therefore knowledge that people have not realized through their own practice becomes a poison and an impediment to their Buddhist training.

If people attain a great awakening, all intellectual hindrances vanish. Pei Xiu asked these questions because he was not yet mature in his practice. Master Huangbo removed the veils of obscurity for him, leading him directly to the point.

> **"Even though [you may attain] bodhi, suchness, the characteristic of reality, liberation, or the dharma body and directly reach the sanctified ranks of the ten stages or the four fruitions, all these involve the [expedient] gate of salvation. They have nothing to do with the buddha mind.**
>
> 設使菩提 真如實際解脫法身 直至十地四果聖位 盡是度門非關佛心.

All gradual stages are far removed from the Way. Turn one thought around and realize completely the fact that a buddha's nature and your nature are not different. Those who are not mature enough in their training keep asking these kinds of questions. If you find this is how you are as well, try to develop the power that comes from having firmly established the unwavering mind, so you are no longer dragged around by such foolish thoughts.

Truly, if you just let go of those things rather than trying to remove them, they will all vanish, just as clouds naturally vanish, revealing the empty sky.

Bodhidharma speaks of the buddha mind in his *Two Accesses and Four Practices Treatise*: "That the mind is free from discriminative characteristics is called true suchness; that the mind cannot be altered is called dharma-nature; that the mind is attached to nothing is called liberation; that the mind-nature is free from impediments is called bodhi; that the mind-nature is tranquil and extinct is called nirvāṇa."[87]

"The mind is indeed the buddha. Therefore, among all the gates leading to salvation, the buddha mind is foremost.

心即是佛 所以一切諸度門中 佛心第一.

Pei Xiu awakened the moment he met Master Huangbo, but because his initial awakening was not yet complete, he often asked this kind of question. Master Huangbo, therefore, spoke directly of the fundamental matter so that he would be able to see reality. The master pointed out that Pei Xiu was ignorant and confused.

This dialogue form is, in fact, similar to that which we see in the *Diamond Sūtra* between the Buddha and Subhūti. Some say that Subhūti had already realized everything but asked such questions as if he did not already know the answers. Others argue that Subhūti asked questions because had yet to attain perfect enlightenment. If the latter is the case, Subhūti is like Pei Xiu.

In the *Diamond Sūtra*, although Subhūti opens his wisdom eye, he still has discriminative thoughts and thus generates defilements. He then asks how to open the dharma eye that is like that of a bodhisattva who transcends all thoughts and conceptions. The Buddha tells him how to open the dharma eye, which is beyond even the wisdom eye.[88]

"Only if there are no states of mind involving birth and death, defilements, and so forth is there then no need for such dharmas as bodhi.

但無生死煩惱等心 即不用菩提等法.

There is nothing that can be named "mind." It is not that the mind does not exist; rather, it reveals itself as causes and conditions are produced. Whether good or evil, there is no exception to this rule.

There is neither birth and death nor defilements; they are all shadows created through corresponding causes and conditions. Not knowing this fact, people try to remove all these shadows. If they suddenly turn one thought around and realize that all shadows are originally empty, their minds will be at rest. If this happens, not only birth and death and defilements but also nirvāṇa and bodhi will be at rest. Whether it is this or that is all relative. Therefore, if one is extinguished, the other will naturally be extinguished as well.

"Therefore, it is said,

The Buddha taught all dharmas
to eliminate all states of mind.
Since I retain no states of mind,
what need is there for all dharmas?[89]

所以道 佛說一切法 度我一切心 我無一切心 何用一切法.

The Sixth Patriarch Huineng made the above statement. It is like saying, "Since I am not sick, I need no medication." The Seon teachings stand firmly at this level of confidence. Inheriting this spirit, the master Linji declared, "Wherever you go, you are master; wherever you stand, all is authentic."[90]

Seon points out the shortcut to becoming a truly free person.

"From the Buddha to the patriarchs, they speak only of the one mind and the one-vehicle.

從佛至祖 並不論別事 唯論一心 亦云一乘.

The buddhas and patriarchs revealed only the original state of reality. The "Skillful Means" chapter of the *Lotus Sūtra* calls the "one vehicle" the "one Buddha Vehicle."[91] From the standpoint that all sentient beings are able to attain buddhahood, "one vehicle" means the following: "The teaching that saves people is not two. It alone is ultimately true."

"Therefore,

> **Though you look scrupulously in all ten directions,**
> **there is no other vehicle. . . .**
> **There are no branches or leaves left in this congregation;**
> **there are only well-ripened fruits.**[92]

所以 十方諦求 更無餘乘 此衆無枝葉 唯有諸貞實.

The *Lotus Sūtra* tells the story that, after those of lesser spiritual capacity had all departed from the assembly, the Buddha then explained the one Buddha Vehicle only to his disciples who had opened their eyes. You must read the scripture with the dharma eye to understand its real meaning; do not simply say from the standpoint of worldlings that "the *Lotus Sūtra* is the greatest of all scriptures!" You have to understand why it is the greatest.

However perfectly you may understand the principle conceptually, it is just like Linji's three statements (*sanju/samgu* 三句). Those who realize the third statement cannot save even themselves. If people realize the second statement, they can become masters of humans and heavenly beings. If people realize the first statement, they will have the power to surpass the buddhas and patriarchs.[93] Only when you have this kind of power can you understand the true meaning of the one Buddha Vehicle.

"Consequently, this meaning is hard to believe. Bodhidharma came to this land and arrived at the two kingdoms of Liang and Wei. Only one person, the great master [Hui] Ke, confidentially believed in his own mind, and through [Bodhidharma's] words, he then understood that the mind is the buddha.

所以此意難信 達摩來此土 至梁魏二國 秖有可大師一人 密信自心 言下便會 即心是佛.

There is inevitably a limit in training through learning and understanding. Only when you have the majestic power that enables you to have faith in the real characteristic of things can you believe it, whether you say you believe or you don't.

The master Bodhidharma came to China from South India and became the first patriarch of the Seon school. When Huike 慧可 (487–593) questioned him, Bodhidharma opened Huike's mind-eye by teaching him how to pacify his mind (*anxin/ansim* 安心). Bodhidharma said to Huike, "You have acquired my marrow." Thus Huike became the Second Patriarch of the Seon school.[94]

"That both body and mind do not exist—that is called the great Way. Since the great Way is originally equanimous, you will develop deep faith that all living creatures have the same identical true nature.

身心俱無 是名大道 大道本來平等 所以深信含生 同一真性

The Way has neither characteristics nor name; the designation "Way" is forced on it. Original equanimousness means absolute, not relative, equanimousness. It refers to something that remains the same throughout past, present, and future.

All sentient beings result from that true nature. There are no creations that are separate from that nature. Mirages change in various ways. However, the place of the true form—that is, the nature—cannot be two. You should generate faith in this nondual nature. Faith indicates the unwavering state of mind, in which there is the full realization of the nature.

Bodhidharma says in the *Two Accesses and Four Practices Treatise*, "The access via principle means deeply believing that all beings, whether worldlings or saints, have the same true nature, and it is merely because of being mistakenly obscured by adventitious defilements that this true nature is not able to be revealed."[95]

"The mind is not different from the nature; the nature is indeed the mind. One whose mind is not different from the nature—we call that person a patriarch.

心性不異 即性即心 心不異性 名之為祖.

The phrase, "The nature is indeed the mind," is an abbreviation of the longer phrase that offers the Seon guideline for awakening: "Directly pointing to the human mind/ so that one may see the nature and attain buddhahood." The basic stance of the Seon school is to prompt people to see the nature by pointing directly to the mind. A person whose mind accords with the nature becomes a patriarch.

Such a patriarch is a "living patriarch" (*huozu*/*hwalcho* 活祖). He or she is a noble and free person, who at this very spot lives with vivacity. Linji says, "That your states of mind are not different—we call that 'the living patriarch.'"[96]

"Therefore, it is said,

The moment you recognize the nature of the mind,
you can only say it is inconceivable."[97]

所以云 認得心性時 可說不思議.

This comes from the transmission verse of Haklena, the twenty-third patriarch of India. The entire gāthā is as follows:

The moment you recognize the nature of the mind,
you can only say it is inconceivable.
Since you thoroughly understand that there is nothing to be attained,
the moment there is attainment, you cannot say that you know.[98]

Haklena's master, the twenty-second Indian patriarch Manorhita, also has a well-known transmission verse:

Although the mind is made manifest through the myriad sense realms,
it truly leaves no trace wherever it appears.
If you go with the flow and recognize the nature,
you will have neither joys nor worries.[99]

5. Nothing to Learn

Pei Xiu asked, "Does the Buddha save sentient beings or does he not?"

The master replied, "'There are in reality no sentient beings whom the Buddha saves.'[100]

問 佛度衆生否 師云 實無衆生如來度者.

Śākyamuni Buddha, the transformation body, appeared in order to save people with whom he shared affinities. However, from an ultimate perspective, where all appearances are transcended, he saves people without actually saving anyone. At the level where existence and nonexistence are utterly transcended, even the word "salvation" is misleading.

"'If even self is unascertainable, how could nonself ever be ascertained?'[101] Neither the Buddha nor sentient beings can be ascertained."

我尙不可得 非我何可得 佛與衆生 皆不可得.

These words are quoted from the "Dharma Gate of Nonduality" chapter of *Vimalakīrti's Instructions*. And just as the *Heart Sūtra* also says, "because there is nothing to be attained," so too all things ultimately are unascertainable. This matter is incomprehensible, whether things have form or are formless.

The Buddha opened a way for those having difficulty realizing this fact, so they could see this matter with the eye of wisdom. He bestowed his compassion on sentient beings who were living in ignorance by accepting false appearances as real; he kindled the light in their minds by illuminating them with the brightness of his wisdom.

[Pei Xiu asked,] "It is said, '[The Buddha] manifested the thirty-two major marks and saved sentient beings.'[102] How dare you say that this did not happen?"

云 現有三十二相及度眾生 何得言無.

The Buddha exercised compassion on behalf of sentient beings, and all the things he preached were expedients that derived from his concern for ignorant sentient beings.

Pei Xiu's question here really means, "Since the Buddha possesses the thirty-two major marks and eighty minor marks of a sage, shouldn't sentient beings also possess these marks if they are in fact buddhas? And shouldn't they try to become buddhas so they too can save other sentient beings? How could you, Master, say that all these things are false? I don't understand what you mean."

The master replied, "'Whatever characteristics there may be, all of those are spurious. But if you see that all characteristics are free from characteristics, you will see the Tathāgata.'[103]

師云 凡所有相皆是虛妄 若見諸相非相 即見如來.

These famous lines come from the *Diamond Sūtra*. Although the master could just have ignored Pei Xiu's misguided questions, Huangbo kindly answered them all.

"Both buddhas and sentient beings are utterly false views that you have created. Because you do not recognize the original mind, in vain you create such views and understandings.

佛與眾生盡是汝作妄見 只為不識本心 謾作見解.

Since time immemorial, there have been no grounds for explaining in words the fact that all sentient beings are endowed with the original mind. When people try to understand this intellectually, they commit the mistake of regarding what is a mere concept as something that exists in reality.

If people see the nature, they will see reality and naturally understand everything, unmediated by words. But because they cling to their intellectual understanding, they generate wrong views.

> **"The very moment you create the notion that there is a 'buddha,' you are obstructed by that 'buddha.' The moment you create the notion that there are 'sentient beings,' you are obstructed by those 'sentient beings.' If you create such notions as 'ordinary' and 'saint,' 'pure' and 'impure,' those will all become obstructions.**
>
> 纔作佛見便被佛障 作衆生見 被衆生障 作凡作聖作淨作穢等見 盡成其障.

The very moment you allow one thought to arise, you are far removed from the buddha. There is a big difference between thinking with understanding and thinking without understanding. If you generate a view with an eye that is able to perceive all causes and conditions, you will not be hindered by that view. But if you have a mistaken thought, you will inevitably get off track.

> **By obstructing your mind, all these [views] lead to the cycle of rebirth, like an ape that throws one thing away and picks up another without ever taking a break. The highest training of all is invariably no-training.**
>
> 障汝心故總成輪轉 猶如獼猴放一捉一無有歇期 一等是學直須無學

If you arouse one thought, you will be born again and assume another form. Since sentient beings arouse delusions without rest, they are not expected to escape this sea of suffering. No-training (*aśaikṣa*) refers to the state in which one attains arhatship and thus has nothing more to study or to practice. However, Seon goes beyond the levels of training or no-training and teaches that, in our natures, there is originally nothing we need to learn.

> **There is neither worldling nor saint; neither pure nor impure; neither large nor small. It is uncontaminated and unconditioned.**[104]
>
> 無凡無聖 無淨無垢 無大無小 無漏無為.

The nature of sentient beings is originally thus. However, listening to these words, people think they need to get rid of everything in order to become thus. Regardless of the actions they take, things are originally thus. Even though people should fully believe these facts, they misguidedly think: "Do we have to resolve and eradicate our karma in order to become thus?" If you let go of all such thoughts, the idea of "nothing" will also fade away.

> **"In this way, the one mind is assiduously adorned with skillful means.**[105]
>
> 如是一心中 方便勤莊嚴.

All characteristics are created; they are not there from the start. You should be your own master, staying always in accord with conditions and seeing the reality of the middle way that is nondual. These words that appear above are part of this verse from the *Brahmā's Net Sūtra*:

> You should investigate silently
> the true characteristic of all dharmas,
> which is neither produced nor extinguished,
> neither permanent nor annihilated,
> neither one nor two,
> neither coming nor going.
> In this way, the one mind
> is assiduously adorned with skillful means.[106]

"I hear that you have studied all the twelve categories of the teachings of the three vehicles. You should relinquish completely all views and understanding.

聽汝學得三乘十二分教 一切見解總須捨却.

When people hear the word "relinquish," they intentionally try to renounce those things. This shows that they are deluded.

From the perspective of "nothing," there is originally nothing to abandon or take. Then, what can you relinquish or retain? Only from this perspective can you understand the word "relinquish." Only then will you not try to relinquish or retain anything—that is, you will let go of both retention and relinquishment.

The "twelve categories of the teachings of the three vehicles" refers to the three vehicles of the śrāvakas, pratyekabuddhas, and bodhisattvas and the twelve different genres of the scriptural teachings of the Buddha.[107] Thus the "twelve categories of the teachings of the three vehicles" is a categorization of the Buddha's teachings in terms of style and content.

"Therefore 'I have abandoned everything I have and am just lying here on my sickbed' refers precisely to not generating any sort of view.

所以除去所有 唯置一床寢疾而臥 秖是不起諸見.

The words above were spoken by the layman Vimalakīrti and appear in the "Mañjuśrī's Questions" chapter of *Vimalakīrti's Instructions*.[108] The layman was not bound or hindered by what he possessed. He uttered this remark after investigating the causal relationships of things. His words reveal that everything is empty and false.

"If there is not a single dharma that is ascertainable, you will not be obstructed by dharmas. You transcend the three realms of existence and the spheres of both worldlings and saints.

Then and only then will you will deserve to be called a 'supramundane buddha.'

無一法可得 不被法障 透脫三界凡聖境域 始得名為出世佛.

Those who are ignorant think that they have to reach the realm of the buddhas in order to attain buddhahood. Although trying to become buddhas, they shoot themselves in the foot by creating discriminative views.

Those who realize the nature do not discriminate between buddhas and sentient beings; they go their own ways, not caring about taking up or abandoning anything.

"Therefore, it is said, 'I bow my head before that which, like empty space, has no support.'[109] I have left behind non-Buddhist paths.

所以云 稽首如空無所依. 出過外道.

Non-Buddhist paths lead people to commit misguided deeds. Even some people in the Great Vehicle do things as if they were followers of the vehicles of the śrāvakas or pratyekabuddhas. Since even adherents of the Great Vehicle at times make mistakes, ancient masters speak only of the one Buddha Vehicle. If you arouse a discriminative thought, you will be mistaken.

"That which, like empty space, has no support" refers to that realm where all dichotomies and discriminations are eradicated. The above words are part of a song in praise of the buddha that appears in the "Buddha Realm" chapter of *Vimalakīrti's Instructions*.

"Since the mind is already undifferentiated, dharmas are also undifferentiated; since the mind is already unconditioned, dharmas are also unconditioned. The myriad dharmas all derive from transmutations of the mind.

心既不異 法亦不異 心既無為 法亦無為 萬法盡由心變

The mind and dharmas are nondual. The mind is like empty space. In empty space, there is no past, present, or future. This is just how the mind is. For these reasons, it is unconditioned.

It is said, "You should realize that all things originate from the mind. There is no right or wrong in all those things that are subject to change." You should not be deceived by these words, which were never intended to deceive others.

> **"Therefore, [it is said,] 'Since my mind is empty, all dharmas are empty; so too are the thousands of types and the myriad species.'**[110]
>
> 所以 我心空故諸法空 千品萬類悉皆同.

At the very moment you see the nature, you should know, "All dharmas are originally empty. They are all false." If you have had such an experience, you must completely believe in it. However, discriminative thoughts may arise and confuse you, causing you to go back to being who you were before. Since all sentient beings are endowed with the nature, once you see that nature, that's it! Do not think that there is something more you need to see or that you need to engage in various foolish deeds.

> **"The realm of space that spreads out in all the ten directions is identical to the essence of the one mind. Since the mind is originally undifferentiated, dharmas also are undifferentiated. It is only because your views and understanding are not the same that distinctions appear.**
>
> 盡十方空界同一心體 心本不異法亦不異 秖為汝見解不同 所以差別.

People create all kinds of false distinctions by discriminating large and small, right and wrong. Through his enlightenment, the Buddha demonstrated that all these characteristics were not different from each other. Thanks to him, people can realize this fact and arouse faith in the Buddhist teachings, saying "So it is!" This faith will bring an end to endless wandering in saṃsāra.

"'It is just like all heavenly beings, who eat together from the same bejeweled bowl but, depending on their merit and virtue, the color of their meals is different.'[111]

譬如諸天共寶器食 隨其福德飯色有異.

When eating from same bowl, some people will say, "Delicious!" while others will say, "How tasteless!" They have different perspectives because their karma differs. The analogy Huangbo uses here is also an unattributed quotation from the preface to the "Buddha Realm" chapter of *Vimalakīrti's Instructions*.

The Sixth Patriarch Huineng also said that worldly blessings derive from chasing characteristics, while genuine spiritual merit derives from staying far removed from characteristics.[112]

"All the buddhas in the ten directions have in fact never attained even a modicum of dharma—this is called *anuttara[samyaksaṃ]bodhi.*[113]

十方諸佛 實無少法可得 名為阿耨菩提.

The Buddhadharma is not something that has been newly attained and revealed. It is already there to be recognized, so it doesn't need to be created. You simply must realize for yourself what has always been there: "Ah! This is what it is! Since I was deceived by false things, I have spent my life doing foolish things. Now I realize that I have been deceived by mirages. The nature of the buddha is not different from the nature of sentient beings. This nondual nature is what all people should awaken to."

Anuttarasamyaksaṃbodhi—supreme, unexcelled enlightenment—is in fact always right in front of our eyes, but we need to see the nature in order to to realize this fact.

Since this realm cannot be expressed, it is called "inconceivable."

> **"There is only this one mind; there are no differentiated characteristics. It is also has no luminosity or colorations, nothing superior or inferior.**
>
> 秖是一心實無異相 亦無光彩 亦無勝負.

The sky has no brightness of its own: when dawn comes, it becomes light; when sunset comes, it gets dark.

Śākyamuni Buddha saw the morning star and attained enlightenment, after which he saved ignorant sentient beings who were wandering around in darkness. He ensured they would not lose their original mind by helping them to realize their natures for themselves, and he established the spiritual faculties that would help them avoid being dragged around by illusory things.

> **"Since there is no superior, there are no characteristics of a buddha; since there is no inferior, there are no characteristics of a sentient being."**
>
> 無勝故無佛相。無負故無眾生相

At that point, the myriad dharmas are all equal in the one mind. Therefore there are no characteristics of a sentient being who admires and worships the buddha and no characteristics of a buddha who saves sentient beings. Therefore it is called the *nondual dharma*.

> **Pei Xiu asked, "Since the mind is formless, how could it be that a buddha does not possess all the thirty-two major marks and eighty minor marks and does not edify and save all sentient beings?"**
>
> 云心既無相 豈得全無三十二相八十種好化度眾生耶.

Since Pei Xiu had not transcended the realm of characteristics, he could not avoid discriminating between buddhas and sentient beings.

But Master Huangbo said from the start, "All buddhas and sentient beings share the same one mind. There is no other dharma. This one mind itself is the buddha. The buddha and sentient beings are not different."

It is hard to say why Pei Xiu asked the above question. Clinging to characteristics and persisting in looking outside for truth, he likely did not understand the meaning of the master's words and continued to ask foolish questions.

The master said, "The thirty-two major marks involve characteristics. [Therefore, it is said,] 'Whatever characteristics there may be, all of those are spurious.' The eighty minor marks involve materiality. [Therefore, it is said,]

Those who look for me in my physical form, . . .
those people practice a deviant path.
They will never be able to see the Tathāgata."[114]

師云 三十二相屬相 凡所有相 皆是虛妄 八十種好屬色 若以色見我 是人行邪道 不能見如來.

Pei Xiu discriminated in terms of characteristics and materiality, so Master Huangbo kindly guided him with these lines from the *Diamond Sūtra*. The difference between Pei Xiu and Master Huangbo was that the grand councilor may have had some slight experience of the root, but he could not remove discriminative thought because he was still influenced by subtle delusions; the master thoroughly saw the true characteristic of the middle way, which transcends all characteristics.

In other words, Pei Xiu's question was slanted toward extreme views, while Master Huangbo followed the middle way and provided an opportunity for Pei Xiu to break through his discriminative delusions. The difference between the two is as great as that between heaven and earth. Therefore the ancient teachers advised that one should first awaken to the mind.

6. There Is Only the One Mind

Pei Xiu asked, "Is the nature of the buddha and the nature of sentient beings the same or different?"

問 佛性與衆生性 為同為別.

If you say that their natures are same, I will strike you with my staff; if you say that they are different, I will strike you with my staff. However meticulously Master Huangbo showed him the dharma, Pei Xiu could not digest the master's words. Master Huangbo was careful to ensure that Pei Xiu would not misunderstand and cling to the master's words.

The master replied, "Their natures are neither the same nor different. If, from the standpoint of the three-vehicle teachings, it is explained that there is a buddha nature and a nature of sentient beings, then there will accordingly be causes and effects associated with the three vehicles, which will involve identities and differences.

師云 性無同異 若約三乘教 即說有佛性有衆生性 遂有三乘因果 即有同異.

"Whether it is the buddha nature or the nature of sentient beings, the essence of that nature involves neither sameness nor difference." However, from the standpoint of the teachings of the three vehicles sentient beings are sentient beings and buddhas are buddhas. The law of causality clearly does exist, so differences inevitably appear.

"But from the standpoint of the Buddha Vehicle and the transmission of the patriarchs, we do not discuss such things. There is only the one mind, which involves neither identity nor difference, neither cause nor effect.

若約佛乘及祖師相傳 即不說如是事 唯有一心 非同非異 非因非果.

Pei Xiu's questions derive from the intellectual knowledge he had gained through learning, but Master Huangbo kindly and yet clearly revealed to him the truth about the basic tenets of the house of Seon.

If your master points directly to the mind of human beings, and you are able to see the nature and attain buddhahood, then you will realize that all sorts of causes and effects and various types of discriminative thoughts are simply false: there is nothing other than this one mind. Since there is just this one mind, the reality of things is clearly and easily revealed.

The revelation of the one mind is recorded in the 1,700 *gongan* cases of the Seon school and are transmitted in the many discourse records of the Seon masters.

Master Huangbo's disciple Linji Yixuan said after his enlightenment, "Fundamentally, there is nothing special in Huangbo's Buddhadharma."[115] Seon is just this simple and clear!

"Therefore, it is said,

There is only this path of the One Vehicle.
There are not two or three,
except what the Buddha teaches expediently."[116]

所以云 唯此一乘道 無二亦無三 除佛方便說.

If your eye for the one mind becomes penetrating, you will see that only the one mind is the real characteristic of things while the two or three vehicles are just mirages. Seon just points directly to this true characteristic of nonduality.

However, the Buddha offered expedient teachings in accord with sentient beings' mental capacities in order to guide them to enlightenment. Therefore those teachings are included in the discussion of the path.

Later, bright-eyed Seon masters created such meditation techniques as examination of meditative topics (*kanhua/ganhwa* 看話) and silent illumination (*mozhao/mukjo* 默照) out of concern for practitioners who failed to realize the truth the moment the master spoke.

7. The Bodhisattva Boundless Body

Pei Xiu asked, "Why can't Boundless Body Bodhisattva see the top of the Tathāgata's head?"

The master replied, "In fact, he shouldn't be able to see it. Why? He shouldn't be able to see it because Boundless Body Bodhisattva is himself the Tathāgata.

問 無邊身菩薩 為什麼不見 如來頂相 師云 實無可見 何以故 無邊身菩薩 便是如來 不應更見.

Before Grant Councilor Pei Xiu met Master Huangbo, he had befriended Guifeng Zongmi. Since Zongmi was the fifth patriarch of both the Huayan doctrinal school and the Heze school of Chan, he was versed in both Chan and scholastic teachings. Therefore, Pei Xiu asked the above question.

Boundless Body (*Anantakāya 無邊身) Bodhisattva appears in the first chapter of the *Mahāparinirvāṇa Sūtra*.[117] The gist of what Pei Xiu asks here is why Boundless Body Bodhisattva, who has no boundaries, can't see the top of the Tathāgata's head even through the power of his awesome virtue?

Since Boundless Body Bodhisattva is the Tathāgata himself, it is absurd to suggest that the Tathāgata would look at the top of his own head.

"We only teach you this:

Don't create the notion of a buddha so that you don't succumb to the limits of a buddha;
don't create the notion of sentient beings so that you don't succumb to the limits of sentient beings.

Don't create the notion of existence so that you don't succumb to the limits of existence;
don't create the notion of nonexistence so that you don't succumb to the limits of non-existence.
Don't create the notion of ordinariness so that you don't succumb to the limits of ordinariness;
don't create the notion of sanctity so that you don't succumb to the limits of sanctity.

秖教爾 不作佛見 不落佛邊 不作衆生見 不落衆生邊 不作有見 不落有邊 不作無見 不落無邊 不作凡見 不落凡邊 不作聖見 不落聖邊.

The Buddhadharma involves no-thought, signlessness, and nonabiding; but these words are just expedient means to help practitioners not to abide in or cling to anything, anywhere.

Buddha and sentient beings are two limits, or extreme views. Therefore, if you seek a buddha, you will fall into the extreme view that a buddha exists separately from you.

Those who are deluded try to gain something good, but good and evil are also two extremes. If you seek either of the two, you succumb to that limit.

"Only by being free from all views will one have a boundless body. But if one has even the semblance of a view, one will be called a non-Buddhist.

但無諸見 即是無邊身 若有見處 即名外道.

Since the Buddhadharma is originally pristine, it is free from all impediments and is luminous and bright. Therefore, if you say that you have seen something or gained something, you are entrapped in extreme views.

If you meet the buddha, you kill him; if you meet the patriarch, you kill him; only then can you claim that you share something, however tiny, with Boundless Body Bodhisattva.

"Non-Buddhists delight in all views; bodhisattvas remain unmoved by all views. A 'thus come one' (*tathāgata*) means the quality of being thus with all dharmas.

外道者樂於諸見 菩薩於諸見而不動 如來者即諸法如義.

A "non-Buddhist" refers to one who clings to views and moves one's mind toward the outside. On the contrary, bodhisattvas are originally just calm and unmoving; they stay silently in accord with the original nature. Bodhisattvas move all day long without ever really moving. A "tathāgata" means that whatever he encounters, he remains always thus; whether rainy or windy, he remains originally thus and unmoving.

"Therefore, it is said, 'Maitreya is also thus; all the sages and saints are also thus.'[118] Thusness is neither produced nor extinguished; thusness neither sees nor hears. The top of the Tathāgata's head can be seen completely but also not seen completely. Therefore he does not fall into the limit of 'completeness.'

所以云 彌勒亦如也 眾聖賢亦如也 如即無生 如即無滅 如即無見 如即無聞 如來頂即是圓見 亦無圓見故不落圓邊.

"That which is thus and unmoving" is neither created, changed, nor extinguished; so what causality can it involve? It has nothing to do with either causality or dependent origination. Can people believe that it is constantly in motion and yet has never moved? This is why it is said to be inconceivable. Only when you know its final resting place can you understand it without being disturbed by appearances.

"Therefore, 'a buddha's body is unconditioned and does not capitulate to any numerical category.'[119]

所以 佛身無為不墮諸數.

Like Boundless Body Bodhisattva, a buddha's body is also limitless: where it begins or ends cannot be determined. Because it has no form, it is the biggest of the big and the smallest of the small. It appears big or small in accordance with the process of dependent origination, but its real characteristic is that it is immeasurable. Therefore you should be able to carefully watch this place right now without succumbing to the two extremes of big and small.

> **"Provisionally, it [i.e., a buddha's body] is compared to empty space.**
>
> > **It is perfect like the great void,**
> > **without deficiency or redundancy.**[120]
>
> 權以虛空為喻 圓同太虛 無欠無餘.

"Empty space" refers to the original form before all forms were created. Since its limits cannot be determined, it is compared to empty space.

The above line is an unattributed quotation from the Third Patriarch Sengcan's *Verses on Faith in Mind.*

> **"Be at leisure and without concerns. Do not try forcibly to contend that it involves some other realm, for attachment to such rhetoric is what leads to discursive thought.**
>
> 等閑無事 莫強辯他境 辯著便成識.

The three vehicles try to explain it, but the one vehicle directly penetrates into it. This is because this principle cannot be gained through the discriminative mind.

When a bright-eyed master is asked about the Way, he or she directly reveals the true characteristic of reality that is right before your eyes. In that moment, if you are ready, you will understand it; but if not, the doubt that you have had from the beginning will deepen, making matters worse. Seon meditation stays far removed from discursive thought by emphasizing the importance of doubt.

"Therefore, it is said,

> **Perfection is immersion in the sea of consciousness.**
> **Cycling through rebirths is like a tumbleweed blown by the wind.**[121]

所以云 圓成沈識海 流轉若飄蓬.

Perfection (*pariniṣpanna*) refers to the original place. When a thought arises in accord with causes and conditions, sentient beings immediately follow it. Then they end up being blown around like tumbleweeds, believing that they have lost the original place.

This is why the three realms of existence are called the "sea of suffering," while the original place is the "sea of consciousness."

When the principle of nonduality is revealed, the original place is seen to be always as it is, whether delusions have arisen or not.

The quotation above is taken from Fu Dashi's verse commentary to the *Diamond Sūtra*. The line that follows it says: "If you wish to comprehend the acquiescence to the nonproduction [of dharmas] (*anutpattikadharmakṣānti*),/ eradicate all traces of compounded things that are external to the mind."

"You just say, 'This is what I know, this is what I have learned, this is awakening, this is liberation, this is logical.' Where you are strong, things go as you wish; where you are weak, things do not go as you wish. What is the use of such persumptions? I say to you: be at leisure and without concerns; do not use your mind aimlessly.

秖道 我知也 學得也 契悟也 解脫也 有道理也 強處即如意 弱處即不如意 似者箇見解 有什麼用處 我向汝道 等閑無事 莫謾用心.

You may be calm where you are strong, but if you become shaken by an unexpected occurrence, your practice of Buddhism still has a long ways to go.

Master Huangbo advised Pei Xiu to let go of all conceptual understanding and focus on nonaction, so that he would not disturb his mind to no avail. Since Pei Xiu experienced a kind of breakthrough in his first encounter with Huangbo, the master asked him to abandon all views and intellectual understanding and return to the originally tranquil and pure mind that is unconditioned.

"You need not seek truth.
Just bring views to an end.[122]

不用求真 唯須息見.

The above line is a quotation from Master Sengcan's *Verses on Faith in Mind*. If you illuminate the mind just once, let go of everything and check your faith. Discriminative thoughts may arise and mental conflict may develop, but you should let go of conceptual understanding and rely on your faith. The biggest obstacle in your practice is conceptual understanding.

Therefore, when students practice illuminating the mind, a master tells them to let go of what they have learned—"relinquish doctrine and enter Seon" (*sagyo ipseon* 捨教入禪).

"Therefore,
Inside views and outside views are both wrong.
The Buddha's Way and Māra's way are both evil.[123]

所以 內見外見俱錯 佛道魔道俱惡.

This line is a quote from Master Baozhi's "Verses in Praise of the Mahāyāna." Since the Buddhadharma involves both the middle way and the nondual dharma, it is neither inside nor outside. Since we are originally endowed with everything and have nothing new we need to gain, we should neither seek the Buddha nor try to eliminate the demon Māra.

Afflictions are identical to bodhi; buddha and sentient beings cannot be differentiated. The instant you try to eradicate evil in order to accomplish good, you fall into duality. Therefore the authentic good is the middle way, where the distinctions between good and evil or right and wrong are eradicated.

> **"Therefore, Mañjuśrī aroused dualistic views for just a moment and was condemned to the concentric Iron-Ring Mountains.**
>
> 所以文殊暫起二見 貶向二鐵圍山.

This story of Mañjuśrī comes from the *Recitations of the Buddhas Sūtra.*[124] The Iron-Ring Mountains (Cakravāḍa) are places like the hells that demarcate the perimeter of a world system. They are concentric ranges that therefore exist at the edges of the world. The moment the bodhisattva Mañjuśrī generated relative views, he became far removed from the scenery of the original place.

> **"Mañjuśrī embodies the wisdom of reality, while Samantabhadra embodies the wisdom of expedients. Expedients and reality counteract each other, but ultimately there is neither expedient nor real; there is only the one mind.**
>
> 文殊即實智 普賢即權智 權實相對治 究竟亦無權實 唯是一心.

Since the buddhas' appearances produce countless Mañjuśrīs and Samantabhadras, it is natural that Mañjuśrī and Samantabhadra would eventually return to the buddhas. In the ultimate realm, real and expedient both vanish; but the tathāgatas require both real and expedient in order to save sentient beings.

The ultimate realm is the place of the original characteristic of reality. Even though it is said that one should reach the ultimate realm through applying expedients, from the standpoint of what is fundamental, the ultimate realm is nothing special: right where you are standing is the ultimate realm.

"The mind, moreover, involves neither buddhas nor sentient beings; it is free from discriminative views. The very moment you create the view that there are buddhas, you also create the view that there are sentient beings.

心且不佛不眾生 無有異見 纔有佛見 便作眾生見.

The mind is not a buddha and it is not a sentient being. The moment one thought arises, you become a sentient being. Buddhas and sentient beings are both extreme views, which betray the nondual dharma.

If you let go of both buddhas and sentient beings, the middle way will appear right in front of you.

"The view of existence and nonexistence, and the view of eternalism and annihilationism, form concentric Iron-Ring Mountains that sequester you within the obstruction of views. The patriarchs point directly to the fact that the essence of the original mind of all sentient beings is originally a buddha, so it cannot be perfected through provisional practices and is not associated with gradual attainment; it involves neither brightness nor darkness.

有見無見 常見斷見 便成二鐵圍山 被見障故 祖師直指 一切眾生本心本體本來是佛 不假修成 不屬漸次 不是明暗.

The *Flower Garland Sūtra* says, "Mind, buddha, and sentient beings:/ there is no distinction among these three."[125] This is why sentient beings are buddhas.

The patriarchs only point directly to this fact. They do not try to explain it indirectly, because if they did, they would end up implanting intellectual views in their students. When patriarchs point directly, students either experience realization right then and there, or they at least deepen their sense of doubt, which serves as a catalyst for their sudden awakening.

The mind is not realized through successive practices or a series of stages. If you cannot digest these words, you will be prone to complaint, saying you're not even sure whether you are supposed to practice. However, the essential point of Seon practice is right there. As soon as true practitioners hear these words, they understand the reality of the mind, and their practice moves in the right direction.

> **"Since it is not bright, there is no-brightness [viz., ignorance]; since it is not dark, there is no-darkness. Therefore, 'there is no ignorance and also no extinction of ignorance.'[126] Whoever enters the gate of our school must have this sort of aspiration. The act of seeing is what is called *dharma*. Seeing the dharma is what is called *buddha*. Where both buddha and dharma are nonexistent is what is called *saṅgha*.**
>
> 不是明故無明 不是暗故無暗 所以 無無明 亦無無明盡 入我此宗門 切須在意如此 見得名之為法 見法故名之為佛 佛法俱無名之為僧.

There is neither brightness nor darkness in empty space. If light shines through it, space is bright; if there is no light, it is dark. But whatever light or darkness there might be, empty space is always just empty. Therefore, in the mind there is originally neither the darkness that is ignorance nor the light that is the extinction of ignorance.

The mind is brightened or darkened in accordance with causes and conditions. Since it cannot be named, it involves neither the buddha nor the dharma. The situation in which both the buddha and the dharma have disappeared is called the saṅgha. To put this bluntly, those who have not realized truth do not really belong to the saṅgha.

Being a disciple of the Buddha is a huge responsibility. Seon offers straight talk about this, holding nothing back.

> **"This is called the unconditioned saṅgha;[127] this is also called the three jewels in their single essence.**
>
> 喚作無為僧 亦名一體三寶.

In the experience of awakening, buddha, dharma, and saṅgha become a single essence that is free from all differentiation. In this moment, there is nothing that can be called buddha, dharma, or saṅgha. If you are in conformity with that nondifferentiation, then you have already taken refuge in the three jewels, whether you are an ordained member of the saṅgha or not.

> **"Now, those who seek the dharma should seek it without attachment to buddha, dharma, or congregation; there should be nothing that they seek.**[128]
>
> 夫求法者 不著佛求 不著法求 不著衆求 應無所求

You awaken to the dharma that has already been revealed; you do not awaken to a dharma that you create anew. If you look correctly and realize the dharma that is right before you, you naturally eradicate the intention to seek anything, without being told, "Do not cling to anything!"

Therefore Master Yongjia sings in his "Song of Realizing the Way":

> The leisurely person of the Way who has ceased all learning and
> has nothing more to do,
> neither removes deluded thoughts nor seeks truth.[129]

> **"Since you seek without attachment to the buddha, there is no buddha; since you seek without attachment to the dharma, there is no dharma; since you seek without attachment to the congregation, there is no saṅgha."**
>
> 不著佛求故無佛 不著法求故無法 不著衆求故無僧.

The twelve categories of three-vehicle teachings say that you should take refuge in buddha, dharma, and saṅgha. The supreme principle of the one Buddha Vehicle foments no disputes even though it abandons all words and letters, because it is free from literary forms. There is no fixed rule in the Buddha Vehicle; therefore it does not posit even buddha, dharma, or saṅgha.

Once you accord with the Buddha Vehicle, there is nothing to take up or abandon because all things are buddha, dharma, and saṅgha. Before awakening, buddha, dharma, and saṅgha are fantasies; but once you have opened your mind, all things are buddha, dharma, and saṅgha.

8. The Enlightenment Site of Truth

Pei Xiu asked, "Master, we see you preaching the dharma right now. How can you say that there is no saṅgha and no dharma?"

問 和尚見今說法 何得言無僧亦無法.

Here, Pei Xiu is still enmeshed in language and does not understand the import of Master Huangbo's words. Therefore Pei Xiu does not understand why the master said there is no dharma and no saṅgha, since, in his eyes, the master obviously was a member of the saṅgha and preached the dharma. This is why he asks this question. Although Pei Xiu comes off as hopelessly incorrigible, it is extremely fortunate that people after him can hear the master's answers to his questions.

The master replied, "If you presume that there is a dharma that can be preached, you are 'seeking me through the sound of my voice.'[130]

師云 汝若見有法可說 即是以音聲求我.

If you delude yourself into thinking that there is a dharma that can be preached, this is what the four-line verse of the *Diamond Sūtra* implies in calling it the "deviant path," which means seeking the buddha through his voice.

One who is a Seon master can put buddhas and demons into the same basket and discard it without leaving a trace.

> **"If you presume there is an 'I,' then that becomes a locus of clinging. The dharma is also not the dharma; the dharma is the mind.**
>
> 若見有我 即是處所 法亦無法 法即是心.

If you posit that there is an "I" or a "dharma," you will cling to what is called "I" or "dharma" and get stuck there.

The Buddhadharma does not abide in anything. The Sixth Patriarch also emphasized *nonabiding* as being his fundamental principle. Since everything is just mind, there cannot be anything else.

> **"Therefore a patriarch said:**
>
> **When this mind-dharma has been entrusted,**
> **how there can be this or that dharma that is called the *dharma*?**
> **When there is neither dharma nor original mind,**
> **only then will you understand the dharma [transmitted from] mind to mind.**[131]
>
> 所以祖師云 付此心法時 法法何曾法 無法無本心 始解心心法.

When Seon patriarchs transmitted from mind to mind the sublime mind of nirvāṇa, they did not in fact transmit even a single dharma. The patriarchs simply guided their disciples to realize what all sentient beings originally possess; these patriarchs added or subtracted nothing.

All sentient beings possess and use that mind perfectly. It is not that the buddhas have more of this mind or that sentient beings have less.

Even though you perceive there really does seem to be a transmission between master and disciple, realize that there is in fact no dharma or original mind that is transmitted. Only then will you understand the principle that the dharma or the mind is transmitted without anything actually being transmitted.

However, ordinary beings should not simply parrot these words. They should practice strenuously in order to silently accord with them and be joyful.

The first two lines in the above verse are part of Śākyamuni Buddha's dharma-transmission verse to the second Indian patriarch, Mahākāśyapa. The latter two lines are taken from the verses of the fourth and sixth patriarchs of India.

"The realization that there is not a single dharma to be attained is called 'sitting at the enlightenment site.' An *enlightenment site* (*bodhimaṇḍa*) just means not giving rise to any views.

實無一法可得名坐道場 道場者秖是不起諸見.

The site where buddhas are selected (*xuanfochang*/*seonbuljang* 選佛場) is a place where not a single dharma is attained. This is an enlightenment site, where all right and wrong views, speculations, and discriminations are eradicated. The buddhas always sit at this site. Even were delusions to appear at this site, they would be purified by the buddhas' majestic power. It is like empty space, where not a single thing can be established.

A true practitioner should sit at this site and see the buddha directly, use the dharma carefully, respect the entire saṅgha, and live comfortably, in perfect harmony.

If you realize that a true enlightenment site is that place where not a single dharma is attained, wherever you are will be a pure land, where lotus flowers blossom.

"Awakening to the fact that dharmas are originally empty is called the empty tathāgatagarbha.

Originally there is not a single thing,
so where can dust alight?[132]

If you understand the meaning here, what need is there to speak of wandering leisurely?"

悟法本空 喚作空如來藏 本來無一物 何處有塵埃 若得此中意 逍遙何所論.

If a pristine enlightenment site is created, there will be no sentient beings who need to be saved. Since the dharma is originally empty, it is not something that is either good or bad. Be grateful to the Buddhadharma for helping you to understanding this meaning as you course with the flow of causes and conditions with a simple and clear spirit. In this way, your practice will deepen and widen.

After studying under Master Huangbo, the lay practitioner Pei Xiu probably lived a leisurely life without worldly cares. Pei Xiu's tomb is located in Weishan. After Huangbo passed away, Pei Xiu spent the rest of his life relying on the guidance of Weishan/Guishan Lingyou 潙山靈祐 (771–853), a renowned Seon master of his time and cofounder of the Weiyang/Guiyang school of Chan.

9. Originally There Is Not a Single Thing

Pei Xiu asked, "'Originally there is not a single thing.' But is it then correct or not to say there is 'no-thing'?"

問 本來無一物 無物便是否

The Sixth Patriarch's famous verse, "Originally there is not a single thing,/ so where can dust alight?," was delivered in response to his rival Shenxiu's verse, "At all times, strive to polish it./ Do not let dust collect." Shenxiu had not yet seen the mind but tried to express enlightenment from the standpoint of the conditioned (*saṃskṛta*, *youwei/yuwi* 有爲) realm, while the patriarch revealed the unconditioned (*asaṃskṛta*, *wuwei/muwi* 無爲) enlightenment site, where not a single dharma can be ascertained. Huineng was simply responding to Master Shenxiu's view. His use of the phrase "not a single thing" revealed he still had a trace of attachment to the notion of "nonexistence." After his exchange of verses, Huineng attained sudden awakening thanks to the intercession of the Fifth Patriarch Hongren 弘忍 (601–74), who privately instructed him on the *Diamond Sūtra*. Huineng overcame his attachment to the dichotomy between "existence" and "nonexistence" and declared this lion's roar: "Who would have thought that the self-nature is itself originally pristine!"[133]

The master answered, "'Nonexistence' is also not correct. Bodhi has no fixed locus, but it is also not free from knowledge and understanding."

師云 無亦不是 菩提無是處 亦無無知解.

Master Nanyue Huairang received the Sixth Patriarch's dharma. When he visited the Sixth Patriarch, Huineng asked him, "What thing has come in this manner?" After eight years of study, Huairang answered this question by saying, "It is not right even to call it a thing," and received certification of his enlightenment.[134]

The Buddhadharma is not a relative concept that can be described in terms of existence or nonexistence. It involves neither delusion nor bodhi, neither ignorance nor the extinction of ignorance.

10. Why Did Bodhidharma Come from the West?

Pei Xiu asked, "What is buddha?"

問 何者是佛.

Depending on who asks "What is buddha?" the result can vary. If the questioner painstakingly grapples with this question day and night, he or she can attain awakening just by a Seon master's striking and shouting. Seon masters who have an eye for the truth have answered the question in different ways. Some for example, say one word directly, others sit with their backs to the questioner, or give a thumb's up, or strike the questioner. These acts served as a trigger prompting their disciples to awakening.

It is just like a chick pecking at its shell from the inside while the mother hen pecks from the outside: the chick hatches from its shell more quickly.

The master replied, "Your mind is buddha. Buddha is the mind. The mind and the buddha are not different. Therefore, it is said, 'The mind is buddha.' Apart from the mind, there is no other buddha.'"

師云 汝心是佛 佛即是心 心佛不異 故云 即心是佛 若離於心別更無佛.

Since even a person like Pei Xiu, who had already awakened to his mind, wanted his understanding to be checked by the master. Huangbo answered him directly, by saying, "Your mind is buddha."

Mazu Daoyi often asked his students, "It is not mind, it is not buddha, it is not a thing. So what is it?"[135]

Pei Xiu asked, "If our own minds are buddha, why did the Patriarch [Bodhidharma] come from the West to transmit it?"

云若自心是佛 祖師西來如何傳授.

Unless you firmly believe that your mind is buddha, it is easy for you to misunderstand that there is something that is transmitted.

"The Patriarch's intention in coming from the West" (*zushi xilai yi / chosa seorae ui* 祖師西來意) is just the one mind. There is no separate dharma.

The master replied, "The Patriarch came from the West only to transmit the mind that is buddha. He directly pointed to the fact that your minds are originally buddhas. Each and every mind is no different. This is why he is called a patriarch."

師云 祖師西來 唯傳心佛 直指汝等心本來是佛 心心不異 故名為祖.

The Seon school refers to the "mind-to-mind transmission," but there is actually no one who transmits or receives anything; this expression simply means that the mind is connected to the mind. Do not be content with just understanding this expression intellectually. Check it for yourself. Pei Xiu knew what this meant, but he had not fully digested it, so he felt anxious. That is why he keeps asking the same question. In truth, if you attain thorough penetration, you must see a Seon master. You cannot check yourself with a mind that understands intellectually. Only if you awaken to your mind will you be able to find 'peace of mind and the correct course in life' (*anxin liming / ansim immyeong* 安心立命).

"If right here and now you perceive this intention, you will suddenly transcend all the ranks in the three vehicles. This is the original buddha. It is not something achieved by provisional practices."

若直下見此意 即頓超三乘一切諸位 本來是佛 不假修成.

Whether mind or buddha, they are just revealed, like stamping a seal in the air. If you understand this, you will not commit a foolish act like mastering a series of stages in practice because you know that there is nothing to rely on.

When people realize what it is that they are inherently endowed with, they do not rely on practice.

Pei Xiu asked, "If this is the case, when all the buddhas in the ten directions appeared in the world, what dharma did they teach?"

云 若如此 十方諸佛出世說於何法.

We say that the buddhas "appeared," but they never truly appeared even once. In terms of conditioned dharmas, Śākyamuni Buddha may have appeared in the world 2,500 years ago, but in terms of the unconditioned dharma, all the buddhas in ten directions have never come or gone.

After Śākyamuni Buddha was born under the Sorrowless (Aśoka) Tree (Wuyou shu / Muu su 無憂樹), he took seven steps, pointed up to the sky with one hand and down to the ground with the other, and declared, "In the heavens above and the earth below, I alone am honored." The master Yunmen Wenyan 雲門文偃 (864–949) commented boldly on this event: "If I had seen him do this, I would have struck him dead with a single blow and fed him to the dogs."[136]

You need to be able to intuit the point of these words.

The master said, "All the buddhas in the ten directions appeared in the world only to preach the dharma of the one mind.

師云 十方諸佛出世 秖共說一心法.

The Buddhadharma only reveals the dharma of the one mind. You have to penetrate it. If you think one thought in order to understand it, you will be far off the mark!

If you do not penetrate, then raise a doubt at that spot where you cannot penetrate. But if you deploy your intellect, you will be far removed from the Buddhadharma.

"Therefore the Buddha secretly entrusted it to Mahākāśyapa. The essence of this one-mind dharma extends throughout empty space and pervades the dharma realm; we call this 'all the buddhas.'

Although we may discuss this dharma, how can you understand what it is through words? You cannot perceive what it is through the sense faculties or sense objects; you can only silently accord with it.

所以佛密付與摩訶大迦葉 此一心法體 盡虛空遍法界 名為諸佛 理論這個法 豈是汝於言句上 解得他 亦不是於一機一境上見得他 此意 唯是默契得.

Although the mind is always with you—past, present, and future—if you do not accord with the Buddhadharma and attain it for yourself, you will cling to things, and life will exhaust you.

Fortunately, Śākyamuni Buddha attained great awakening and revealed the way for sentient beings to live a new life with wisdom: by liberating themselves from ignorance. His teachings have been passed down through successive generations of masters to the present.

However, even if this were not so, the mind would still flow along in accordance with causes and conditions. It is not a function of whether Buddhism exists. This was so before the realms of the cosmos were created, and it has been so ever since they were created. It will be so wherever, whenever, or even whether heaven and earth are created or destroyed.

You must awaken to this fact!

"This one gate is called the 'unconditioned dharma gate.'

這一門 名為無為法門.

All the buddhas transmitted only the dharma of the one mind. Since it cannot be revealed through either form or color, it was transmitted silently from mind to mind. The dharma gate that is conveyed through this mind-to-mind transmission is called the "unconditioned dharma gate."

In the realm of conditioned dharmas, a subject carries out intentional actions in order to control and manipulate objects. However, the Buddhadharma is the unconditioned dharma. This means it is possible to let go of all intentional actions and naturally accord with the mind that is originally the buddha.

"If you wish to comprehend it, you need only know it is no-mind. Then, unexpectedly, you will have an awakening. If you use your mind to try and learn something about it, you will end up further from it.

若欲會得 但知無心 忽悟即得 若用心擬學取 即轉遠去.

If you wish to enter the realm of the unconditioned dharma, which is non-action, you need only realize that your mind is originally no-mind and let go of all intentionality. In the realm of the unconditioned dharma, you do nothing, but there is nothing that is not done. The more you try to understand it intellectually, the further you will be from that original state of no-mind.

Master Huangbo here advises you to suddenly realize no-mind. If you try to understand it by studying, you will end up going astray.

"If the mind is free from forks in the road (*qilu/kiro* 岐路) and from both clinging and rejection, then the mind will be like stone or wood. Only then will you have a share in the path of training."

若無岐路心一切取捨心 心如木石 始有學道分.

If you cling to or reject things with a mind that discriminates among things, you will end up falling into extreme views and lose the middle way. Only when your mind becomes no-mind do you begin to partake of the path of training (*sikṣāmārga*).

> **[Pei Xiu] asked, "Various deluded thoughts are appearing this very moment. How can you say these don't exist?"**
>
> 云 如今現有種種妄念 何以言無.

Since Pei Xiu here is entrapped in the mirages created by causes and conditions, he falls into the bifurcation of existence and nonexistence. Deluded thoughts that appear in accordance with causes and conditions are false. You should know that they are not real.

If you do not know the true source, you will fall into the realm of characteristics and be entrapped by illusory mirages. Your mind will be also disturbed by those characteristics and mirages. Whether a cloud floats by or the wind blows, empty space is void, as it has always been.

If you do not know how to see the nature that has no foundation, you will cling to characteristics and will never be able to stop disputing over right and wrong.

> **The master replied, "Delusions originally have no essence; they are what arise from your mind. If you recognize that the mind is buddha and that the mind is originally free from delusions, then how would you give rise to thoughts that could be acknowledged as deluded?"**
>
> 師云 妄本無體 即是汝心所起 汝若識心是佛 心本無妄 那得起心更認於妄.

The instant you awaken to the fact that your mind is originally buddha, you recognize that there are originally no false forms. You will then be able personally to confirm that there are no other forms distinct from this truth.

When you do not understand something during your encounter with a Seon master, raise a doubt and investigate it. As your study matures over a long period, the master's intention is eventually revealed. This training technique has been standardized by later generations of teachers as *ganhwa Seon*—questioning meditation on topics of contemplation.

You must understand that the mind of doubt (*yixin/uisim* 疑心) is the lifeblood of ganhwa Seon. As the mind of doubt deepens into the sensation of doubt (*yiqing/uijeong* 疑情) and eventually the mass of doubt (*yituan/uidan* 疑團), the true import of the *hwadu*, or meditative topic, will be fully illuminated when the moment is right.

"If you neither produce mental states nor think thoughts, then naturally you will be free from delusion. Therefore, it is said, 'If the mind arises, various dharmas arise; if the mind ceases, various dharmas cease.'"[137]

汝若不生心動念 自然無妄 所以云 心生則種種法生 心滅則種種法滅.

You may give rise to thoughts while encountering objects all day long, but if you know that your mind is always such and just as it is, it does not matter that thoughts arise and disappear. You are no longer inveigled by mirages. If you give rise to thoughts while being moved by objects and do not know this fact, you will engage in ceaseless discriminating actions. If you are awakened, even delusions will be sublime, but if you are not awakened, even the sublime will become a delusion.

Therefore the *Awakening of Faith* says, "If thoughts arise, various dharmas arise; if thoughts cease, various dharmas cease."

Pei Xiu asked, "Now, at the very moment deluded thoughts arise, where is the buddha?"

云 今正妄念起時 佛在何處.

Pei Xiu asks this question, one that is difficult to broach with a Seon master, on behalf of all of us. Every Seon practitioner has probably asked the following questions at least once during training: We're told we're originally buddhas, so why do deluded thoughts keep arising in our minds? Where is the buddha when these deluded thoughts arise?

> **The master replied, "Now, the moment you are aware that delusions are arising—that awareness is precisely buddha. Were there no deluded thoughts, there would be no buddhas.**
>
> 師云 汝今覺妄起時 覺正是佛 可中若無妄念 佛亦無.

The Buddhist doctrinal teachings contrast sentient beings with buddhas and defilements with wisdom. Seon does not give such explanations. Rather, it directly points to the fact that defilements are nothing other than wisdom and sentient beings are nothing other than buddhas.

Where there are deluded thoughts, there is buddha. Were there no deluded thoughts, there would be no buddha. In the original mind, "there is no ignorance but also no extinction of ignorance."[138] Reject both extreme views and reveal nonduality.

> **"Why is this so? By generating thoughts and creating a view that there are buddhas, you are presuming that buddhas need to be produced. By creating a view that there are sentient beings, you are presuming that sentient beings need to be saved. Generating mental states and thinking thoughts all derive from having a point of view.**
>
> 何故如此 為汝起心作佛見 便謂有佛可成 作衆生見 便謂有衆生可度 起心動念總是汝見處.

When practitioners are new to Buddhism and not mature in their practice, Seon masters will employ provisional descriptions to teach them, saying for example that the buddhas save all sentient beings. As these neophytes delve deeper into their practice based on initial confidence in the master's words, they will open the correct eye of the Buddhadharma.

To the mature in practice with a discerning eye, Seon masters directly reveal the true characteristics of things, just as Master Huangpo does here for Pei Xiu. Relative concepts such as sentient beings and buddhas never apply to the mind. At this place right before your eyes, there are neither buddhas to be achieved nor sentient beings to be saved. If you discriminate between buddhas and sentient beings, you are just creating views.

"If you are free from all views, then where would the buddhas be? It is like Mañjuśrī, who as soon as he generated the view that there was a buddha, was condemned to the concentric Iron-Ring Mountains."

若無一切見 佛有何處所 如文殊纔起佛見便貶向二鐵圍山.

That spot where you generate a thought is your buddha nature. You cannot generate even a single thought without the buddha nature. The thoughts that arise are like mirages, but if you do not chase after these mirages, a lotus flower will blossom at every step you take.

Even Mañjuśrī would fall into the hells if he aroused a view.

Though you may speak all day long, not even a single word is spoken.

Pei Xiu asked, "Now, at the very moment of awakening, where is buddha?"

云 今正悟時 佛在何處.

In a situation like this, it would be better to strike down with a mighty blow even a highly placed official like Pei Xiu. Even though the master keeps telling him that if he keeps opening his mouth, he will be far off the mark, Pei Xiu, with his lingering intellectual tendencies, cannot keep his mind clear. He therefore asks a question concerning what he is most curious about.

The master replied, "What does your question come from? What does your perception arise from? Speaking and keeping silent, action and stillness, and all sounds and sights are all the

buddha's events. Where else would you seek the buddha? You cannot put a head on top of your head or add lips to your lips.

師云 問從何來 覺從何起 語默動靜一切聲色 盡是佛事 何處覓佛 不可更頭上安頭 嘴上加嘴.

Every movement, every question, every thought, every sound, and every sight arises just at this place. Whether walking, standing, sitting, or reclining, whether speaking or keeping silent, whether active or still, none are not the buddha's events. If you do not realize this, you will inevitably and futilely wander all around the world.

That guy who is wandering around is the buddha! Not knowing this, you pointlessly smear excrement on the buddha's head.

"Simply stop generating discrepant views; then, mountains are mountains, water is water, monastics are monastics, and laypeople are laypeople. Mountains, streams, and the great earth, the sun, the moon, and the stars—none exist outside your mind. The entire trichiliocosm all derives from your own self. Where else would all these many things be?

但莫生異見 山是山 水是水 僧是僧 俗是俗 山河大地 日月星辰 總不出汝心 三千世界 都來是汝箇自己 何處有許多般.

If you stop generating views, the things before your eyes reveal themselves exactly as they are. They are unchanging and have never left this place, from time immemorial to the present. Since past, present, and future have all vanished, it is just this, now and forever. However, unless you have awakened, you will be unable to escape the fetters of karma. You will pass your entire life painfully oppressed by those fetters.

"There are no dharmas outside the mind, so the green mountains that fill your eyes and the realm of empty space are utterly

transparent. You cannot generate even a hair's breadth of views and understanding.

心外無法 滿目青山 虛空世界 皎皎地 無絲髮許與汝作見解.

There is no mind outside the dharmas and no dharmas outside the mind. Yellow is yellow; green is green. Without thinking, you raise your head and look right in front of you: your eyes are filled with green mountains; the mountains are tall; the water is flowing.

It is not green mountains or empty space that create views. You create mirages yourself and laugh and cry while wrestling with them. How beautiful is a person laughing aloud after waking from a spring dream!

Therefore all sounds and sights are the buddha's eye of wisdom. Dharmas do not arise on their own; they are produced in dependence on the perceptual environment. Because those things exhibit variations, there are all sorts of things to know.

所以一切聲色 是佛之慧目 法不孤起 仗境方生 為物之故有其多智.

All sounds and sights are the buddha's appearance. If you are enveloped in ignorance, you will not be able to understand these words. People try to put what they learn into practice. However, it is all too easy to become unwittingly attached to that and become stubborn, rigidly confined within yourself.

Whenever you *try* to become a buddha, you end up becoming a devil. This is why you must be humble during your mental cultivation, always guarding your original intention.

To have nothing to attain is the right way forward.

Since all things are differentiated in accord with the perceptual environment, you must have wisdom that is able to deal with countless situations. However different may be the forms they assume, if you know the fundamental source, they will all return to a single form.

"You may speak all day long, but what have you said? You may listen all day long, but what have you heard? For this reason, Śākyamuni Buddha may have taught for forty-nine years, but he never actually said even a single word."

終日說何曾說 終日聞何曾聞 所以釋迦四十九年說 未嘗說著一字.

Although you may speak all day, you have never really spoken even one word. Although you may listen all day, you have never really heard even one word.

Just as many reflections appear and disappear in a bright mirror, the myriad things pass by this immutable place.

If you know and use your mind, the thirty-six thousand days of the hundred years of your lifespan are just repetitions of this one place and nothing more. Every day's events pass by evanescently, while this place remains completely unmoving.

It is like saying that, although Śākyamuni Buddha preached his whole life, he never actually preached anything.

If you brighten your wisdom, your life will be full, and everything will go smoothly.

Pei Xiu asked, "If this is so, then where is bodhi?"

The master replied, "Bodhi is not anywhere.

云 若如此 何處是菩提 師云 菩提無是處.

Master Huangbo does not test Pei Xiu. Rather, through this encounter dialogue, the master gives elaborate responses to Pei Xiu's questions.

Ordinarily, if a person asks a question like the above, a Seon master would compel the questioner to raise a doubt by rendering him speechless or he would use various means to help him suddenly awaken.

If you are awakened, you are not confined by the three periods of past, present, and future or by the six directions of east, west, north, south, up, and down.

Time and space are also nothing but mirages produced in accord with the law of causality.

> **"The buddhas do not attain bodhi, but sentient beings also do not lose bodhi. It can neither be attained with the body nor sought with the mind. All sentient beings are marked by bodhi."**
>
> 佛亦不得菩提 眾生亦不失菩提 不可以身得 不可以心求 一切眾生即菩提相.

Since the whole world is replete in the one mind, there can be no awakening outside this mind.

The buddhas do not attain any special awakening, and sentient beings are never apart from awakening. It's just that the buddhas have awakened to this fact while sentient beings have not. Therefore there is not the slightest distinction between the mind, the buddhas, and sentient beings. If you do not understand this, you will have only "distorted views and dream-like conceptions."[139]

> **Pei Xiu asked, "How do we arouse the bodhi mind?"**
>
> 云 如何發菩提心.

Pei Xiu's question is this: even though sentient beings live amid awakening, they have not yet been able to *arouse the bodhi mind* (*bodhicittotpāda*). What can they do to arouse that mind?

His underlying question may well be: since sentient beings are already perfect and complete, is it really necessary to arouse the bodhi mind? Intellectuals can easily fall into this kind of trap.

> **The master replied, "Bodhi is not something to be attained. Right now you need only arouse this mind that**

is unascertainable, which is certain that there is not a single dharma that can be attained. That is the bodhi mind.

師云 菩提無所得 爾今但發無所得心 決定不得一法 即菩提心.

Bodhi means awakening, but awakening is not something that can be attained. This is because bodhi is inherent to us. Hence, the Buddha compared people seeking awakening to "a head seeking its head."

However, since sentient beings are deceived by the mirages of their karma and have not realized this fact, they should abandon "distorted views and dream-like conceptions " through the help of a spiritual mentor.

"Bodhi has no abiding place; this is why it is not something that is attained.

菩提無住處 是故無有得者.

The mind is not originally something that is abiding. Therefore it is not an object to be gained or lost. Since the bodhi mind does not abide anywhere, where would it be?

"Therefore, [Śākyamuni Buddha] said, 'When I was at Dīpaṃkara Buddha's abode, there was not the slightest dharma for me to attain. The Buddha then made the prophecy (*vyākaraṇa*) of my future awakening.'[140]

故云 我於然燈佛所 無有少法可得 佛即與我授記.

If there is not even a single dharma for you to attain, that means you have achieved perfect awakening.

In the same manner, the nonduality of the one mind, as something that cannot be described with words and letters and that is transmitted outside the scriptural teachings, is transmitted through the mind-to-mind transmission.

However, since there is nothing that is attained, there is also nothing that is transmitted. That is why the Sixth Patriarch said, "The self-nature is originally pure in and of itself; it is neither produced nor extinguished; we are originally endowed with it; it is originally unmoving. Therefore the self-nature is able to produce the myriad dharmas."[141]

Since it is originally perfect in and of itself, nothing can be added to it.

"Know clearly that all sentient beings are originally bodhi. There is no further bodhi you need to attain.

明知一切眾生本是菩提 不應更得菩提.

If you believe that all sentient beings are intrinsically endowed with bodhi, you can rest the mind that chases things outside. Seeking something outside is not Buddhist. Only when you believe that the seeking mind is identical to the original mind with which you are inherently endowed and you move toward the unconditioned path will you partake of Seon practice.

"Now, you may have heard that you must generate the bodhi mind, which suggests that you use this mind to train yourself to achieve the Buddhadharma. But merely by being intent on becoming a buddha, though you may practice for three asaṃkhyeya kalpas, you will end up attaining only a buddha's reward or transformation body. What connection would this have with the fundamental buddha of the true nature? Therefore, it is said,

You may seek outside for the buddha that has characteristics, but it has nothing to do with you."[142]

爾今聞發菩提心 將謂一箇心 學取佛去 唯擬作佛 任爾三秖劫修 亦秖得箇報化佛 與爾本源真性佛 有何交涉 故云 外求有相佛 與汝不相似.

The dharma body is perfect just as it is; it has nothing that needs to be augmented or diminished.

If you are told to generate the bodhi mind and thus try to seek the buddha by arousing your mind, it is like placing a head on top of your head.

True practitioners know how to both increase and decrease. This is because, while others may see them sitting still, they are in fact fiercely striving against their most deep-rooted and subtle desires.

11. The Simile of Mercury

Pei Xiu asked, "As we are originally buddhas, how can there be four modes of birth and six rebirth destinies, each with various physical forms and appearances and each different?"

問 本既是佛 那得更有四生六道 種種形貌不同.

The four modes of birth (*yoni*) are egg-born, womb-born, moisture-born, and metamorphic-born. Human beings are womb-born while heavenly beings are metamorphic-born. Birds are egg-born and most insects are traditionally said to be moisture-born. The six rebirth destinies (*gati*) refer to the six kinds of rebirth that sentient beings undergo: birth as the denizens of the hells, hungry ghosts, animals, demigods, humans, and heavenly beings. The question here is: Why are there these different kinds of rebirths if all sentient beings are endowed with the buddha nature?

The master replied, "The essence of all the buddhas is perfect, with nothing to be added or subtracted. Although it flows into the six rebirth destinies, in each and every place it remains perfect. It is present in myriad species, for each and every one of them is a buddha.

師云 諸佛體圓 更無增減 流入六道 處處皆圓 萬類之中 個個是佛.

Although these outward appearances may change in various ways, the buddha nature has never changed. It is unmoving just as it is and is always clear.

It is just that sentient beings cycle through rebirths, assuming various physical forms.

Regardless of the physical forms in which they appear, if they look for an opportunity to encounter the Buddhadharma and they open their eyes to the fundamental source, they will be able at any time to recover their original mind. Even though the forms they take may be infinitely different, the nature of each and every one of those forms is neither produced nor extinguished, neither augmented nor diminished.

"It is like a drop of mercury: when divided over many places, each and every individual droplet is still round; but when no longer divided, they will combine back into a single drop. This is [what is meant by] 'one is all; all is one.'[143]

譬如一團水銀 分散諸處 顆顆皆圓 若不分時 秖是一塊 此一即一切 一切即一.

Mercury always stays round regardless of whether it is condensed or dispersed, or comingled with something different. The original nature of the myriad dharmas is just like mercury: even were it combined with something else, it would remain a round drop; even were it to be divided, each droplet would remain round.

Therefore, the Buddha says that we do not need to taste every spot in the entire ocean to make sure they all have the taste of seawater.[144] Similarly, all the buddhas and sentient beings in all the universes share just this one mind.

Therefore, if you come into accord with your own mind, you will reveal at once the secret of the universe.

'One is all; all is one' refers to the principle of the unimpeded interpenetration between phenomenon and phenomena (*shishi wu'ai / sasa muae* 事事無礙) in Flower Garland thought.

"The various physical shapes and appearances may be compared to dwellings. You may leave a donkey stable and enter a

human dwelling; [likewise,] you may leave a human body and take a heavenly body.

種種形貌 喻如屋舍 捨驢屋入人屋 捨人身至天身.

Time in the heavens passes quickly, and heavenly beings may fall to a lesser rebirth when their merit runs out. Time in the hells passes slowly, but denizens of the hells may escape and rise to a better rebirth after they have exhausted all of their karmic debts. In this way, sentient beings are reborn throughout the six rebirth destinies, descending or ascending.

Because the bodhisattva Kṣitigarbha could not ignore the suffering of the hell denizens, he took a vow to "dim his light and comingle with the dust" (*heguang tongchen* / *hwagwang dongjin* 和光同塵)—that is, to continually take rebirth in the world of suffering in order to save all sentient beings.

"You may eventually even enter the dwellings of śrāvakas, pratyekabuddhas, bodhisattvas, or buddhas, but these are all places you choose to either take up or abandon, which is what accounts for their differences. But how could there be any differences in the nature of their original source?"

乃至聲聞緣覺菩薩佛屋 皆是汝取捨處 所以有別 本源之性 何得有別.

The myriad changes in these physical appearances all occur in accord with causes and conditions. But no matter what appearances things may take, they are not worth clinging to any longer.

12. The Buddha's Loving-Kindness and Compassion

Pei Xiu asked, "Why do all the buddhas cultivate loving-kindness and compassion and preach the dharma to sentient beings?"

The master replied, "The buddhas' loving-kindness and compassion are unconditional; therefore they are called great loving-kindness and compassion."

問 諸佛如何行大慈悲 為衆生說法 師云 佛慈悲者無緣 故名大慈悲.

The buddhas' loving-kindness and compassion do not distinguish whether you have karmic affinities with them or not. Their compassion is unconditional. There is neither a subject who bestows compassion nor an object who receives it. This great loving-kindness and compassion treats everyone equally.

***Loving-kindness* means not presuming that buddhas need to be produced. *Compassion* means not presuming that sentient beings need to be saved.**

慈者不見有佛可成 悲者不見有衆生可度.

At its most basic level, the mind of compassion aims to remove suffering and give pleasure. Since sentient beings suffer from immeasurable amounts of pain and agony in this sea of suffering, they should draw close to the Buddha's teachings so they can transform their pain and agony into pleasure. At this level, sentient beings are told to trust and rely on the Buddha because the Buddha will compassionately cure their suffering.

Seon masters take a different approach. They teach the fastest path to those who want to realize the truth and transcend the sea of suffering itself. Seon masters, therefore, employ such special techniques as striking and shouting in order to directly reveal the truth to their students here and now.

True compassion means to know the fact that there are neither buddhas nor sentient beings and to put this into practice by realizing the nonduality of the middle way.

"The dharma he preaches is neither preached nor revealed, and those who hear that dharma neither hear nor attain anything. It is as if a magician preaches the dharma to people he has conjured. How can I say that I comprehended or awakened to this dharma upon hearing the words of a spiritual mentor (*kalyāṇamitra*)?

其所說法 無說無示 其聽法者 無聞無得 譬如幻士為幻人說法 這個法 若為道 我從善知識言下領得會也悟也.

Regardless of the dharma preached, nothing has actually been preached.

When the bodhisattva Avalokiteśvara preaches the dharma to the youth Sudhana [in the *Flower Garland Sūtra*], the youth listens to the bodhisattva without listening to anything. This is preaching without preaching anything and listening without listening to anything.

To give a slightly different story from the Song dynasty, when the Seon adept Xuedou Zhongxian 雪竇重顯 (980–1052) was planning to go to the monastery of Lingyinsi 靈隱寺 in Hangzhou to train, the scholar Zeng Hui 曾會 (952–1033) wrote him a recommendation letter to take to the abbot there, who was his old friend. With this recommendation letter, Xuedou would have received special treatment at the monastery. However, he did not show the letter to the abbot and instead strenuously practiced as a rank-and-file monk in the monastery's meditation hall. One day, after Xuedou had been practicing there for three years, his recommender Zeng Hui visited the monastery. He saw Xuedou sitting at the lowest seat and asked Xuedou why. Xuedou answered, "I was grateful to receive your letter, but because the monastery provides such a great setting for practice, I concluded I could focus more on my practice by not showing the letter."

You practitioners should be able to maintain everyday mind, enduring whatever you face, no matter how exhausted you are, without complaint. However, you should cultivate Buddhist practice without thinking that you need to cultivate anything.

"Regarding loving-kindness and compassion, say that I prompt you to arouse states of mind, think thoughts, and study others' views and interpretations. If you have not had a personal awakening to the original mind, all this ultimately will bring no benefit."

這個慈悲 若為汝起心動念學得他見解 不是自悟本心 究竟無益.

The unconditional compassion that suddenly arises from that place where there is originally not a single dharma is bestowed everywhere and at every time, with neither redundancy nor deficiency.

The compassion bestowed when you have karmic affinities with someone is of course compassion, but you should nonetheless deeply immerse yourself in the ineffable ocean of the unconditional compassion that is bestowed regardless of karmic affinities. Then you will be able to say, "How deeply grateful I am that I was born in this world and am able to study and practice Buddhism." Even so, however, can you recognize that this also involves characteristics?

13. The Most Strenuous Practice

Pei Xiu asked, "What is vigor (*vīrya*)?"

The master replied, "That body and mind do not arise is called the most strenuous form of vigor.

問 何者是精進 師云 身心不起 是名第一牢強精進.

Since sentient beings have varying spiritual capacities, there are different degrees of *vigor*—that is, energy for practice—and various expedients that are applied. For those of lesser spiritual capacity, sitting long hours could be seen as vigor; for those a little more advanced, then the concurrent practice of both concentration (*samādhi*) and wisdom (*prajñā*) could be regarded as vigor.

However, the vigor of those of superior spiritual capacity cannot be perceived, even by spirits. Such people have an unfailingly discerning eye, which countenances all sorts of changes and yet never changes itself, even amid hundreds of thousands of samādhis. They think all day long without thinking a single thought. They cultivate without cultivating anything. Were this not the case, then whatever they did or did not practice would all fall under the law of causality. Do you understand the principle that real vigor is not vigorous?

"Just arousing the mind and seeking outside is what is called 'King Kaliṅga loved hunting.' That the mind does not wander outside is the 'asectic Kṣāntivādin.' That body and mind are both nonexistent is the 'path to buddhahood.'"

纔起心向外求者 名為歌利王愛游獵去 心不外遊 即是忍辱仙人 身心俱無 即是佛道.

The analogy here refers to a story about King Kaliṅga in the fourteenth section of the *Diamond Sūtra*:

> Subhuti, the Tathāgata has explained that the perfection of forbearance (*kṣāntipāramitā*) is not the perfection of forbearance; this is called the perfection of forbearance. Why is this? Subhūti, long ago when King Kaliṅga was dismembering my body, at that time, I retained no conception of a self, no conception of a person, no conception of a sentient being, no conception of a living being. Why is this? Long ago, at the time I was being torn limb from limb, had I retained any conception of a self, a person, a living being, or a soul, I would have felt anger and animosity.[145]

In one of his previous lifetimes, the Buddha was an asectic named Kṣāntivādin. He was practicing in the forest where the arrogant and violent King Kaliṅga hunted. While the king was asleep, his courtesans went out for a walk and came across the acsetic sitting under a tree. Impressed by his pure and undefiled demeanor, they asked him to preach the dharma to them. When the king awoke and found the ascetic preaching to his court ladies, the king got jealous and cut off the ascetic's nose and ears, and finally his arms and legs. The ascetic, however, did not lose his peace of mind and stopped an angry dragon king from avenging him and hurting King Kaliṅga. By demonstrating such inconceivable compassion, the ascetic sought to remove the king's three poisons of greed, hatred, and delusion. The king deeply regretted what he had done and returned, chastened, to his palace.

If someone's mind arises in accordance with external objects and clings to them, he or she will become like the hunter King Kaliṅga. On the contrary, if one rests his or her mind and stays in accord with the original place, he or she will become like the ascetic Kṣāntivādin. Those whose minds go outside will follow the way of non-Buddhists and become violent. But if their minds exercise forbearance, they will practice with vigorous effort and become generous ascetics.

In other words, if a thought arises and chases external phenomena, it is like someone who goes outside and causes all sorts of trouble. If a thought turns inward and becomes one with the original mind, it is like someone who rests comfortably at home. True practice refers to the "thought that is no-thought," which stays far removed from all characteristics. The Sixth Patriarch said, "No-thought is the fundamental tenet."[146] "No-thought" does not mean that you literally have no thoughts. It rather means that, even though you may think thoughts all day long, there are no thoughts that have actually been aroused.

Therefore the Sixth Patriarch placed primary importance on seeing the nature (*jianxing*/*gyeongseong* 見性). You should make strenuous efforts to see the nature, but without actually making such an effort. This is called "cultivating without cultivating anything."

Even this form of cultivation still retains a trace of practice, but the Buddha completely removed even these subtlest of traces. Only when you see your self-nature and attain great understanding of it can you exercise true vigor. Before that point, you cannot practice vigorously, even though you wish to do so. If you practice vigorously in the wrong way, you will be mistaken or foolish.

Even though you may have opened your own eyes, the true way of practice is to help and encourage your fellow religious in their training.

14. The Practice of No-Mind

Pei Xiu asked, "If I practice no-mind, will I succeed in attaining this Way or not?"

The master replied, "No-mind is the practice of this Way. Why do you ask whether there is something to attain or not attain?

問 若無心行 此道得否 師云 無心便是行此道 更說什麼得與不得.

When it is said that no-mind is the practice of the Way, *no-mind* does not mean that you are supposed to get rid of your mind. The mind cannot be defined in terms of the concepts of existence or nonexistence. As the original no-mind, no-mind does not involve doing something or doing nothing. Therefore the original state of no-mind is to be unascertainable.

"Moreover, it is as if, in the blink of an eye, you aroused a thought and the sense spheres appeared. But if you do not have even a single thought, then the sense spheres will be forgotten and the mind will be naturally extinguished. There will be nothing further that needs to be sought."

且如瞥起一念 便是境 若無一念 便是境忘 心自滅 無復可追尋.

If you arouse a single thought, this is not no-mind. No-mind occurs not because you try to be without mind. Rather, you demonstrate no-mind in both pleasant and unpleasant circumstances because you are originally in a state of no-mind.

Once you see the nature, even then though you may think all day long, you always remain in a state of no-mind.

15. Transcending the Three Realms of Existence

Pei Xiu asked, "What does it mean to escape the three realms of existence?"

The master replied, "'Do not think at all about good and evil';[147] right then and there you will escape the three realms of existence.

問 如何是出三界 師云 善惡都莫思量 當處便出三界.

As an expedient, sentient beings are told to escape from the sensuous realm, the realm of subtle materiality, and the immaterial realm; these three realms of existence are said to be like a burning house. However, there are actually no three realms from which one needs to escape.

If you do not think about good and evil, you will not be dragged around by the mirages of good and evil. It is then that you can realize your self-nature. This is in fact the place that transcends the three realms. You should be able to illuminate your original face right at the very spot where all notions of good and evil are eradicated.

"The tathāgatas appear in the world to pulverize these three types of existence. If you have no states of mind, the three realms will also not exist.

如來出世 為破三有 若無一切心 三界亦非有.

Since the tathāgatas are always just as they are, they neither come nor go. They appear in the world without actually appearing.

If we truly understand the three realms, we know that they are originally nonexistent. Establishing as existent something that is nonexistent is an expedient description.

The mind is not something that exists or does not exist. If there is no mind, there are no three realms. If you try to remove the mind, the very mind that tries to remove the mind instead becomes another dust mote. Therefore, until the end of time, it is impossible ever to remove the mind.

> **"If you pulverize the smallest mote of dust[148] into a hundred pieces and get rid of ninty-nine of them but one piece still remains, then the Mahāyāna can never prevail. Only when all hundred pieces are removed can the Mahāyāna prevail."**
>
> 如一微塵破為百分 九十九分是無 一分是有 摩訶衍不能勝出 百分俱無 摩訶衍始能勝出.

Foolish efforts to destroy delusions are meaningless. Accept the reality that there is nothing to be destroyed and digest this fact by experiencing it for yourself.

When you raise a hwadu, you are not trying to destroy anything. You are instead generating the mind of doubt, building it into the sensation of doubt, and ultimately turning it into a mass of doubt.

In Mahāyāna practice, you do not attain bodhi by removing defilements. Rather, you realize the fact that defilements are in fact identical to bodhi. Bodhi simply means recognizing that you are originally awakened. It is not that you attain something totally new. Therefore, it is often said, "You awaken to the fact that there is nothing to attain."[149]

"Removing all hundred pieces" does not literally mean removing all defilements. Rather, it means that there is originally nothing to be removed. The truth, there from the very beginning, is completely revealed right before your eyes; it is only because your eyes are blinded by your own delusions that you cannot see it. Therefore, escaping the three realms of existence means that you realize the fact that the three realms are nothing but mirages.

The Buddha said that the three realms are mind alone, which means that the three realms are created by the mind. This implies that all causes and conditions originate in the mind and thereby generate all sorts of phenomena.

You are probably curious what this mind that creates all phenomena is.

Only when you see the nature through a sudden awakening can you digest such a teaching. Otherwise, you will be like a dog chasing a dirt clod someone threw.

Master Huangbo, from beginning to end, taught the unconditioned dharma; he did not teach his students to study conditioned dharmas. But he also taught that practitioners should not abide in the unconditioned dharma. Those of you who gain some insight should be able to look at yourselves for the briefest of moments, which will make you tremble. Then your spine immediately straightens, and you have an experience that accords with what you have practiced thus far. Staying far removed from all views, whether they involve signs or signlessness, you digest the unconditioned dharma that is separate from signs and attain the sudden awakening that transcends signlessness.

You should open your eyes to the value of the precious Buddhadharma through making strenuous efforts in practice. If you seek out and cultivate only practices that are comfortable and easy, the wisdom of the buddhas and patriarchs will be discontinued, and the Buddhadharma of this world will become a nuisance.

Arouse faith in the Mahāyāna and do not be dragged around by expedient teachings. Pass the time calmly, and apply yourself freely yet vigorously.

16. Ascending the Hall (Shangtang) Sermon

[Master Huangbo] ascended the hall [to deliver a sermon] and said, "The mind is buddha. All the buddhas above and the wriggling beings that possess numinosity below have the buddha nature and the same essence of the one mind.

上堂云 即心是佛 上至諸佛 下至蠢動含靈 皆有佛性 同一心體.

The phrase "the mind is buddha" sometimes carries a sting and sometimes does not. When practitioners know its meaning, that's fine. But when they don't, the phrase will be extremely difficult to digest. The scriptural teachings adhere strictly to the phrase "the mind is buddha." But in Seon, if you say that "the mind is buddha," you will be beaten with a staff.

All sentient beings without exception possess the buddha nature and the very same mind. Therefore the Buddhadharma is the dharma that is nondual, equanimous, and unconditioned.

"Therefore Bodhidharma came from the West just to transmit the one-mind dharma. He directly pointed to the fact that all sentient beings are originally buddhas.

所以達摩從西天來 唯傳一心法 直指一切衆生 本來是佛.

All sentient beings may originally be buddhas, but if they are ignorant, they will be deceived by mirages and cycle through rebirth in the six destinies. When they awaken to the mind, they realize that everything is empty regardless of outward appearances.

However, according to Seon, such an explanation can easily create delusions, so you should let go of it without hesitation. The moment you cling to an explanation, you turn your back on awakening. That is why a master sometimes gives an explanation and at other times dismisses it. The master's intention is to avoid falling into either of the two views.

> **"You do not need to engage in provisional practices. Instead, you need only right now recognize your own mind and see your own original nature. There is nothing else you need to seek.**
>
> 不假修行 但如今識取自心見自本性 更莫別求.

Once you see the nature, it does not matter whether you practice any further or not. However, most of you want to keep practicing because you still think you lack something. The mind is, in fact, so close that it is quite easy to see it. Sentient beings want at least a taste of that experience. It is like wanting to check how hot spicy bean paste actually is by dipping a fingertip into it and licking it.

> **"How can you recognize your own mind? That which right now is speaking is precisely your mind.**
>
> 云何識自心 即如今言語者正是汝心.

Apart from this mind, there is nothing else that enables you to speak. Master Huangbo here explains that "that which right now is speaking" is what is called "mind." This mind that is functioning right now is the nature. There can be nothing else.

You should accord with the truth right here and right now. If you try to understand this intellectually, you will be far off the mark.

> **"If you were to neither speak nor act, the mind's essence would**

be like empty space, without form or shape, without direction or location.

若不言語 又不作用 心體如虛空相似 無有相貌 亦無方所.

Before even a single dharma is created, the original mind has neither form nor direction. Nonetheless, this mind functions in various ways in accordance with causes and conditions. Those who cling to characteristics would not understand it if you said, "That which has neither form nor location is what is now speaking." But you should still believe that the original mind evolves in different ways in accordance with causes and conditions. As your belief matures, you will come into accord with the truth; and once you accord with the truth, everything will be revealed right before you. When that happens, you will be able to digest all the words of the buddhas and patriarchs.

If you do not understand the discourse records of the patriarchs, then, recognizing the fact that you are a blind fool, make a vow to attain awakening. If you earnestly practice as if you were a thirsty person seeking water, then what hinders your understanding will be removed, and everything will be clearly revealed. Your experience will correspond to the patriarchs' words, just like an arrow hitting the bull's eye.

"But it also is not entirely nonexistent. It exists but is imperceptible. Therefore, a patriarch [Puṇyamitra] said,

The true nature is secreted away in the mind ground;
it has neither head nor tail.
It transforms into things depending on conditions;
out of convenience, we say that it 'knows.'[150]

亦不一向是無 有而不可見 故祖師云 眞性心地藏 無頭亦無尾 應緣而化物 方便呼為智.

This is the dharma-transmission verse of Puṇyamitra, the twenty-sixth Indian patriarch. There is originally neither wisdom nor ignorance in the mind. We force the name "mind" on it. Where can you find the true mind?

You may have affinities than enable you to encounter the Buddha's teachings and attain awakening, but guard against the risk that you just learn and grasp those teachings intellectually and end up extremely arrogant.

If you come to have a little bit of understanding of the Buddhadharma, you might say: "It is said that whether walking, standing, sitting, or reclining, whether speaking or keeping silence, whether active or still, nothing is not the mind. It is also said that I should awaken to the mind. What do these statements mean? You use the mind, and I also use the mind. Whether awakened or unawakened, whether aged or a newly born, everyone possesses and uses the same mind. Is there any other mind? Since this mind is that mind and that mind is this mind, what more minds should we realize? Aren't these all mistaken words? If this is the mind, we should just believe it. That's all!"

But even though you arouse intellectual understanding and discriminate between what is right or wrong, you may still have some discomfort in mind that makes you worry, "Have I still not realized the mind?" Although you think you know it all in your head, if you are not content, you will definitely find yourself blocked. Your knowledge instead becomes an illness that leads you to deceive yourself. You need to come face to face with a spiritual mentor, receive his or her guidance, and delve deeply into true doubt.

> **"But even when [the mind] is not responding to conditions, we cannot say that it either exists or does not exist. Even in the very moment when it is responding to conditions, it is leaving behind no trace.**
>
> 若不應緣之時 不可言其有無 正應之時 亦無蹤跡.

Whether the mind is functioning or not, since it has no form, we cannot say that the mind exists or does not exist. However hard you look, you'll find no proof that the mind exists. But since it has great capacity and great functioning, we also cannot say that the mind does not exist.

It surely functions, but since it leaves no traces, it is hard to discover what the mind actually is. Until you wake up from "distorted views and dreamlike conceptions," you may listen to this explanation countless times, but you will not understand what the mind is. Once your mass of doubt has exploded, however, you will just nod your head naturally.

"Since you have understood in this manner and these days are simply roosting in nothingness, you are definitely following the road of all the buddhas.

既知如此 如今但向無中棲泊 即是行諸佛路.

"Nonabiding" (*muju* 無住) refers to roosting in the nothingness that transcends the extremes of both existence and nonexistence. Once you have finally made the decision to wake up from this persistent nightmare, your Buddhist practice will mature.

"A scripture advises, 'Give rise to a mind that does not abide anywhere.'[151]

經云 應無所住而生其心.

In the *Diamond Sūtra*, when Subhūti asks to the Buddha how a bodhisattva maintains the mind after he or she has generated the thought of enlightenment, the Buddha says, "Give rise to a mind that does not abide anywhere." The Sixth Patriarch Huineng suddenly awakened after hearing this phrase.

When awakened, we will know that our mind originally is nonabiding. Therefore a bodhisattva can arouse a mind that does not abide anywhere.

That 'all sentient beings cycle through birth and death'[152] means that they wander on conditioned by their intentions, incessantly creating minds in the six rebirth destinies so that they experience all sorts of suffering. Vimalakīrti said, 'The minds of people who are difficult to teach are like gibbons and macaques. This is why they need various teachings and restrictions to regulate their minds, so that they will subsequently be tamed.'[153]

一切眾生輪迴生死者 意緣走作心於六道不停 致使受種種苦 淨名云 難化之人 心如猿猴 故以若干種法制禦其心 然後調伏.

Because their minds do not stay quietly at home but wander outside, sentient beings take rebirth among the six destinies in the endless cycle of birth and death. When you arouse one thought in response to external phenomena, thoughts follow one after another so that you squander your entire life. Life is but a dream. Before long, your hair will be gray and the burial grounds of the Beimang Hills 北邙山 north of the ancient Chinese capital of Luoyang will be close at hand.

The minds of those who have been wandering for years are like monkeys that cannot stay still even for a moment and are constantly snooping around. When your mind is like this monkey, constantly trying to go outside, it must first be calmed by applying some expedient means and then regulated. Only then will you be able to attain 'peace of mind and the correct course in life' (*anxin liming / mimmyeong*) in accord with the truth by revealing your original mind.

Even those who have a small measure of experience in their mind can at times regress in their practice due to past karmic propensities. Although Pei Xiu tasted something the moment he met Master Huangbo, he still had a suspicious and curious mind, like that of a monkey. Pei Xiu spent years staying close to the master, asking questions to tame his mind.

"Therefore, 'If the mind arises, various dharmas arise; if the mind ceases, various dharmas cease.'[154]

所以心生種種法生 心滅種種法滅.

When a thought arises, all sorts of external phenomena arise accordingly. Likewise, when a thought disappears, all sorts of external phenomena disappear accordingly. However, if you try to remain in no-thought and signlessness, you will fall instead into a non-Buddhist path. Any thought of trying tries to remain in no-thought and signlessness is searching outside for the mind and creates all sorts of troubles.

Just trust that the self-nature of bodhi is originally pure and let go of all your useless efforts. Then the original source will be naturally revealed. You cannot just stay still and let your mind wander all over the place, learning all sorts of so-called good teachings. In doing so, you will not digest those teachings and will end up simply adding to your intellectual obstructions. Thus you will stray far from your native land.

"Therefore, know that 'all dharmas are created by the mind'[155] and even the six rebirth destinies, including humans, heavenly beings, hell denizens, and demigods, are all created by the mind. If you would nowadays master no-mind, immediately put to rest all conditioning and arouse no delusory thoughts and discrimination. There then will be no self or others, no craving or aversion, no love or hate, no winning or losing.

故知一切諸法皆由心造 乃至人天地獄六道修羅 盡由心造 如今但學無心 頓息諸緣 莫生妄想分別 無人無我 無貪瞋 無憎愛無勝負.

"All dharmas are created by the mind" means the same as the passage we saw just before, "If the mind arises, various dharmas arise; if the mind ceases, various dharmas cease." Therefore the mind is called the fundamental cause. Since the mind brings about the process of rebirth through the six destinies, if you turn your mind around, all relative phenomena will disappear.

If you master no-mind by putting to rest all the conditions that create external phenomena, then all sorts of speculations and discriminations will vanish as quickly as "a snowflake falling onto a red-hot brazier."[156] But do not make an effort to maintain no-mind, because such efforts are also based on discriminations; rather, allow no-mind to occur naturally without effort.

"Merely eliminate various sorts of delusory thinking, and the nature will of itself be originally pristine. This is cultivating the dharma of bodhi, which is equal to that of the buddhas.

但除却如許多種妄想 性自本來清淨 即是修行菩提法佛等.

Whether or not you eliminate delusory thinking, the mind will be originally pristine of itself. Thus you do not need to grapple with delusory thoughts. It is not that your mind becomes pristine after removing defilements. If you maintain no-mind, you realize that your mind is originally pristine and has no connection to delusory thoughts. If, however, you make an effort to remove delusions, your efforts will continue until the end of time.

> **"If you do not comprehend the meaning [of these words], then even though you train extensively and practice arduously, eating tree bark and wearing grass garments, you will not recognize your own mind. All these are called deviant practices.**
>
> 若不會此意 縱爾廣學勤苦修行 木食草衣 不識自心 皆名邪行.

We practice in order to know our own minds, not to perform asceticism or self-mortification.

The Sixth Patriarch only mentioned "seeing the nature"; he did not discuss meditative absorption (*dhyāna*) or liberation (*vimokṣa*). You should be trying to see the nature so that you can wake up from your "distorted views and dream-like conceptions," as the *Heart Sūtra* explains; you should not be trying to cultivate meditative absorption or to attain liberation from within this dream.

As the clouds disperse, the green mountains will naturally appear. Do not intentionally create the clouds of meditative absorption or liberation. If you create something intentionally, no matter how good it might be, you will be far removed from the dharma of nonduality. Without understanding the import of this, then no matter what practices you cultivate, they will never bear fruit.

> **"All [such practices] will lead to rebirth as the divinity Māra, as a non-Buddhist, or as a land or water spirit. What benefit will there be in practicing in this fashion? Master Zhi said, "This very body is created by your own mind. How can you search for it in words and letters?"[157] If you now just know your**

own mind and put to rest conceptual thought and delusory thinking, then the dusty tribulations [defilements] will naturally not arise.

Vimalakīrti said, 'I am just lying here on my sickbed'[158]—that is, his mind was not arising. Nowadays, you are lying on your sickbed and must put an end to all your clinging to karmic conditions; then delusory thoughts will cease. That is bodhi.

盡作天魔外道水陸諸神 如此修行 當復何益 志公云 本體是自心作 那得文字中求 如今但識自心 息却思惟妄想 塵勞自然不生 淨名云 唯置一床寢疾而臥 心不起也 如今臥疾 攀緣都息 妄想歇滅 即是菩提.

If you prize intellectual understanding and supernatural powers but do not know your mind, you will become a vassal of the demon king Pāpīyāṃs and hinder practitioners from cultivating right practices, or you will fall into baleful destinies and become a lowly spirit of the land or water.

Focus your practice on revealing your own mind. If you foolishly search outside, you will become a prodigal son and wander for years as a beggar. Since the mind is originally complete and perfect in and of itself, there is nothing that you need to cultivate. Just accept that your mind is originally pure and let go of the mind that seeks something outside. You may look foolish sometimes, but the sprout of bodhi will grow rapidly. Bodhidharma also advised, "Externally, put to rest all conditioning; internally, make the mind free from panting."[159]

All ancient masters clearly presented the road of practice. If, like Vimalakīrti lying on his sickbed, you put to rest all your clinging to karmic conditions and discriminative thinking, then that very spot will be the pure land where lotus flowers bloom. Although you may be busy all day long, you should be able to remain free and unobstructed thanks to the everyday mind that is not busy.

"Nowadays, if your mind is disordered and unsettled, then even though you may master all the levels of the three vehicles' four fruitions and ten stages, in the end, you are still sitting

with saints and worldlings. All compounded things eventually return to impermanence, and there will be a time when all your strength will be exhausted. Just like an arrow shot into the sky falls back to earth when its velocity is spent, so too you will return to the cycle of birth and death. If you practice in this manner, you will never understand the Buddha's intent and will receive bitter suffering in vain. How could this not but be a great mistake?

如今若心裏紛紛不定 任爾學到三乘四果十地諸位 合殺秖向凡聖中坐 諸行盡歸無常 勢力皆有盡期 猶如箭射於空 力盡還墮 却歸生死輪迴 如斯修行不解佛意 虛受辛苦 豈非大錯.

According to the teachings of the three vehicles of śrāvakas, pratyekabuddhas, and bodhisattvas, you practice and attain the four fruitions of stream enterer, once-returner, nonreturner, and arhat, or else you progress further and reach the ten stages of the bodhisattva path. But though you master all of these levels, you would still not be able to escape the dichotomous states of saints and worldlings. Even if you enjoy pleasure and happiness in the heavens—the highest realm in saṃsāra—through the merit you accumulated in previous lifetimes, once that merit is exhausted, you will end up falling to lower realms of existence.

The Buddha preached that we should escape the six rebirth destinies, not try to ascend through them. Do not slumber away dreaming great dreams; awaken from your sleep. You may be dreaming a good dream at the moment, but if you keep sleeping, eventually nightmares will come.

The same is true for trying to develop no-mind through practice. Since this sort of no-mind eventually turns back into discrimination and delusory thought, you must attain the original no-mind that transcends the mind's existence or nonexistence. Once you wake up, there will be nothing but what has been originally revealed.

Although practitioners discover no-mind, if they try to approach it intellectually, they will be immediately engulfed in the clouds of birth and death and sink back into utter darkness.

"Master Zhi said, 'If you have not yet met a supramundane bright teacher, you are ingesting in vain the dharma medicine of the Great Vehicle.'[160] If you will now just practice no-mind at all times, whether walking, standing, sitting, or reclining, there will then be nothing to discriminate, nothing to rely on, and nothing to abide in. You will cavort playfully (*renyun tengteng / imun deungdeung* 任運騰騰) all day long, like a simpleton.

志公云 未逢出世明師 枉服大乘法藥 如今但一切時中 行住坐臥 但學無心 亦無分別亦無依倚 亦無住著 終日任運騰騰 如癡人相似.

Mundane affairs always derive from dichotomies, but supramundane matters always transcend subject and object. A bright-eyed enlightened master helps practitioners break their bad habit of approaching the Buddhadharma from a dualistic perspective. Hence, if you do not meet such a master, no matter how long you practice, you will still remain in discriminating delusion, painting a false picture. The more you practice alone and as you like, the greater your intellectual understanding becomes. The good medicine of the Great Vehicle then changes into something that reeks like the dregs of alcohol.

A true practitioner should live a life of nonaction, eating when hungry and sleeping when tired. Then, in accordance with conditions, he or she will be able to respond naturally and reflexively, like a flash of lightning.

"Although no one in this world may recognize you, you still need not teach others to either recognize or not recognize you. Your mind is like coarse stone with no fissures or cracks, so no dharmas are able to penetrate your mind. Transfixed, you are free from clinging. In this wise, you will finally have a modicum of concurrence [with no-mind].

世人盡不識爾 爾亦不用教人識不識 心如頑石頭 都無縫罅 一切法透汝心不入 兀然無著 如此始有少分相應.

If your original place is obvious and you can go with the flow, you need then only let time pass. When you move, you move; when you stop, you stop. Whatever people in the world say, it's of no consequence to you.

People think that training means to go here and there learning things. However, those who arouse the aspiration for enlightenment will go visit a Seon master and, turning one thought around, will come into accord with no-mind and put everything down (*fangxiazhao*/*banghachak* 放下着).

"One who escapes the sense objects connected with the three realms of existence is said to be a buddha appearing in the world. Mentality that is not contaminated (*āsrava*) is called uncontaminated wisdom (*anāsravajñāna*). You make no karma to be reborn among heavenly beings, humans, or the denizens of the hells. When you do not give rise to any states of mind, and all conditioning is completely unproduced, your body and mind will be that of a free person.

透得三界境過名為佛出世 不漏心相名為無漏智 不作人天業 不作地獄業 不起一切心 諸緣盡不生 即此身心是自由人.

Not arousing even a single thought is what is meant by "uncontaminated." If your mind follows external phenomena, it creates defilements (*kleśa*). If you realize that even defilements are products of the sublime functioning of the self-nature, defilements will be immediately transformed into bodhi. When your every move, word, and thought clearly becomes a manifestation of the one mind, the uncontaminated wisdom is revealed.

When you are free from all characteristics, delusory thoughts no longer arise. Once you realize that the myriad dharmas are mere manifestations of the one mind, clearly there will be no hindrances at any time.

"This does not mean there is no longer any rebirth, just that you will be reborn in accord with your intention. This is what the sūtras mean when they say, 'Bodhisattvas have a mind-made body.'[161]

不是一向不生 秖是隨意而生 經云 菩薩有意生身 是也.

A *mind-made body* (*manomayakāya*) is not the body that you receive from your parents; it is the fruition of your intentional thought. Bodhisattvas have no fixed form; they stay separate from form. As they demonstrate the mind of compassion, they take a form appropriate to the situation. If you reach the bodhisattvas' level, you take rebirth in accord with your mental intention. Since bodhisattvas who cultivate the six perfections and myriad of practices possess divine power that is not tinged with unwholesome karma, they can even intentionally choose to regress.

"If suddenly you were no longer able to comprehend no-mind and acted while clinging to characteristics, then these [acts] would all be associated with Māra's karma; and even if you cultivated a buddha's activities in his pure land, these would all create karma and would then be called a buddha's hindrances.

忽若未會無心 著相而作者 皆屬魔業 乃至作淨土佛事 並皆成業 乃名佛障.

If you do not know that the mind is formless and thus generate attachments to external objects, you will be subject to the demon Māra. If you are in this situation, even though you cultivate the samādhi of reciting the Buddha's name, you just end up creating karma.

"Since you have obstructed your mind, your going and staying are bound by cause and effect, without a hint of freedom. Therefore such dharmas as bodhi are originally not existent.

障汝心故 被因果管束 去住無自由分 所以菩提等法 本不是有.

If you seek the pure land or enlightenment by holding to a conception of them, they will obstruct your nature. You will cling to external phenomena without even being aware of it. Then, entrapped by causality, you will experience suffering.

There are originally neither buddhas nor sentient beings at the place of origin, neither birth and death nor nirvāṇa. It is foolish to discriminate between existence and nonexistence.

"Everything the Tathāgata taught was a means to transform people. It is like pretending a yellow leaf is real gold to try and stop a child from crying.[162]

如來所說 皆是化人 猶如黃葉為金權止小兒啼.

In the eighty thousand pages of the Buddhist canon, the Buddha, out of his compassion, preached all sorts of sermons in response to the diverse spiritual capacities of different people, using such terms as *buddhas* and *sentient beings*, *bodhi* and *nirvāṇa*.

However well you may understand what has been said as a stratagem to help soothe a crying child, your understanding of it is intellectual, and thus you end up feeling constrained. As clouds disperse, the green mountains naturally appear. Only when the basis of intellectual understanding is overturned will the place where not a single dharma can be established be clearly made manifest. Passing through what we call "the checkpoints of the ancient Seon patriarchs and teachers" (*zushi guan / josa gwan* 祖師關) is the fastest, shortest, and most complete way to awake from "distorted views and dream-like conceptions."

"Therefore, in actuality there is no dharma named *anu[ttara-samyaksaṃ]bodhi*. Having already comprehended this meaning, what need have you now for trifling and trivial [explanations]? If you just dissolve old karma in accordance with conditions and create no further calamities for yourself, all will be brilliant and bright in your mind.

故實無有法 名阿耨菩提 如今既會此意 何用區區 但隨緣消舊業 更莫造新殃 心裏明明.

Defilements are originally false, so if they disappear, that's it. Since all is originally pristine, there is nothing to be attained. This is the state of *anuttarasamyaksaṃbodhi*, the supreme, perfect enlightenment that is unsurpassed, right, and equanimous.

"Therefore, completely discard all your outmoded views and understandings.

所以舊時見解 總須捨却

If you already know the reality that your nature is originally pristine, let go of your old wrong views and knowledge so you are no longer dragged around by your intellectual understanding. Where is there anything lighter than living with an emptied mind? You should live as a free person, frolicking playfully.

"Vimalakīrti said, 'Get rid of all your possessions!'[163] The *Lotus Sūtra* says, "For twenty years, [the wealthy father] kept [his long-lost impoverished son] shoveling manure.'[164]

淨名云 除去所有 法華云 二十年中常令除糞.

Sentient beings are attracted to characteristics. When they have something they cherish, they will not let go of it. However, those cherished objects are in fact stinking filth.

In the account in the *Lotus Sūtra*, a rich man finally finds his long-lost son after a lengthy search. This son had lived as a beggar for so long he was reluctant to enter the house of the rich man who was his father. Sentient beings cannot deal with the signless scenery of the original ground because they are so attracted to characteristics, which are actually stinking filth. That wise rich man therefore kept his beggar-son shoveling manure for some twenty years until he finally gained his trust.

"Just remove point of view from the mind. It is also said, 'Clear the manure of conceptual proliferation.'[165]

"Therefore the tathāgatagarbha is originally empty and quiescent in and of itself and does not linger on a single dharma. As a sūtra says, 'All the buddha lands are also empty.'[166]

秖是除去心中作見解處 又云 蠲除戲論之糞 所以如來藏本自空寂 并不停留一法 故經云 諸佛國土 亦復皆空.

The worst stench comes from the views in our minds. It is hardest to remove the characteristics of phenomena, which are the manure of conceptual proliferation (*prapañca*). This is because sentient beings never doubt that these characteristics are indeed the truth just as they are.

True treasure does not come from outside us. Leaving this home of the original nature, wandering around looking outside the original nature, is to be like a beggar or a non-Buddhist. You are all children of a rich man, lacking nothing. Only when you understand the idea that since it is empty, it is endowed with everything can you let go of the coarse views of non-Buddhists. Since all the buddhas and patriarchs offer the exact same sort of explanation, you have to accept these words. Only then will your practice of the Buddhadharma be headed in the right direction. Vimalakīrti said, "All the buddha lands are also empty." We have to let go of all views in order to enter a buddha land. If you can truly do so, the three realms of existence will immediately turn into a buddha land.

"You may say that the Buddha Way is attained through practice and training, but such a view or interpretation has absolutely nothing to do with it.

若言 佛道是修學而得 如此見解全無交涉.

The Way is not attained through training or learning. Since you are originally endowed with it, there is nothing you need to attain. It is like a fish for the first time becoming aware of the water in which it swims or a person realizing that his head has always been his head. Your every movement is initiated by your mind. There are no spiritual powers that are outside your mind. If just once you recognize this fact thoroughly, you can escape "distorted views and dreamlike conceptions."

If you just approach this matter intellectually, you end up becoming a puppet of your conceptual understanding and have a distorted dream. If you do so, a thousand buddhas cannot save you. Once you destroy the black-lacquer bucket of ignorance and come into accord with your original mind, you will find 'peace of mind and the correct course in life.'

"You might see someone make a particular gesture or give a certain response, maybe raise his eyebrows or shift his eyes, and since that matches your understanding, you say, 'I get it,' or 'I've had a realization-awakening (*zhengwu/jeungo* 證悟) of the principle of Seon.' Or you may happen upon a person you don't understand and say to him, 'Oh, you don't know anything.' You may think you've gained a certain principle from a person, and your mind is delighted; or you may be defeated in debate by someone and and think you are not his equal, and your mind becomes despondent and disappointed. If this is the frame of mind in which you intend to train in Seon, what relevance will it have?

或作一機一境 揚眉動目 秖對相當 便道契會也 得證悟禪理也 忽逢一人 不解便道 都無所知 對他 若得道理 心中便歡喜 若被他折伏 不如他 便即心懷惆悵 如此心意學禪 有何交涉.

Practitioners who have not yet realized their own Original Matter often learn the outward format and style of Seon dialogues, develop rational Seon (*uiri* Seon 義理禪), and imitate those who have opened their eyes. It seems there were such practitioners even during Master Huangbo's time.

In any era, false practitioners wear the Buddha's robe and sell the Buddha's sermons. Reflecting on ourselves, it is patently obvious that the great matter of birth and death—opening our eyes to the Buddhadharma—does not lie in such mimicry. We cannot deceive our own conscience. The correct attitude is to discard all dry knowledge (*ganhui/geonhye* 乾慧), all intellectual speculation, and return to our initial aspiration for enlightenment.

Master Gaofeng Yuanmiao in his *Essentials of Chan* asserted that great faith, fury, and doubt were the three essentials of Seon practice.[167] Renew your resolve by returning to that moment of your initial arousal of the aspiration for enlightenment, generate the mind of great ferocity in your practice, and keep on trying. This is more crucial than relying on conceptual understanding and wasting your time, accomplishing nothing.

Turning back to your initial aspiration for enlightenment is always the fastest shortcut to awakening. Those who are able to turn one thought around are the real noble persons.

"You may have comprehended a modicum of principle, but that is just a mental factor (*caitta*); it has nothing whatsoever to do with the Way of Seon. For this reason, Bodhidharma faced the wall [in wall contemplation] to help people free themselves from any point of view.

任汝會得少許道理 即得個心所法 禪道總沒交涉 所以達摩面壁 都不令人有見處.

Seon practice means to be free of views. If you have no views, everything will be empty in all directions, and you will be as free as a bird in the sky; but if you cling to even a hair's breadth of principle, your mind will immediately darken. In that place, not a single dharma can be established. Layman Pang 龐居士 (Pang Yun 龐蘊, 740–808) said, "I just hope that you will regard as empty all that is existent; but be careful not to consider as real all that is nonexistent."[168]

Bodhidharma's facing the wall in wall contemplation demonstrated that our minds should not scurry around outside. Avoid clinging to karmic conditions outside, and stop the mind from rushing around inside. Only when your mind becomes like a wall will you be able to enter the Way.

If you seek something outside the mind, you will still have views. Views become perceptual signs, and with your mind full of thoughts, your mind becomes the black-lacquer bucket of ignorance. The patriarchs' checkpoints are established in order to destroy this lacquer bucket. The words of all the generations of patriarchs are a sword of wisdom that severs ignorance with a single stroke. If the doubt you raise regarding the master's words settles deep within your heart, discriminating delusions will stall and begin to melt away.

"Therefore, it is said, 'Remaining oblivious to mental impulses is the Buddha's Way; discrimination is Māra's domain.'[169]

故云 忘機是佛道 分別是魔境.

Everyone is fully endowed with the intrinsic nature that is originally pristine. The Buddhadharma is clearly revealed throughout the whole world; if you simply open your eyes to it, you will see that it is nothing special. But if you give rise to one thought and begin discriminating this from that, the difference will be as huge as heaven and earth. Therefore the Seon patriarchs tell you simply to not contaminate your minds. Since those who accord with this place neither abide in nor cling to functioning, they act all day long without actually taking any action.

The fasting that Bodhidharma talked about does not mean abstaining from food. It really means that you eat all day long without actually eating anything. During or after eating, you should have no attachment to food. You are simply aware that you are eating when you are eating. This is the true appearance of one who practices Buddhism. However, since worldlings generate delusions and all sorts of thoughts, when they eat, it is not they that eat food; the food eats them.

"Even when you are deluded, this nature is not lost; even when you awaken, it is not gained.

此性縱汝迷時亦不失 悟時亦不得.

The nature is always simply thus; it is not something either gained or lost. Just as empty space brightens and darkens as the sun rises and sets, the nature brightens and darkens in accord with karma but is never tinged by that karma.

Those who practice Buddhism with unfailing zeal live undaunted, thoroughly understanding causes and effects without being affected by them.

"This immaculate self-nature is originally neither deluded nor awakened. The realm of empty space that entirely pervades the ten directions is intrinsically our one-mind essence.

天真自性 本無迷悟 盡十方虛空界 元來是我一心體.

The nature that is intrinsic to us is identical in its nonduality. It does not fall into such binaries as delusion and awakening or sentient beings and buddhas. Since the nature encloses the entire universe like empty space, there is nothing that does not contain it. However, unlike empty space, this nature is full of numinous force. The empty and numinous mind permeates the entire universe. Nonetheless, if one thought arises and discriminating delusions envelop the mind, this mind becomes dark because of the lacquer bucket of ignorance.

Master Huangbo opened the first chapter of his *Essentials of Transmitting the Mind-Dharma* by saying, "All the buddhas and sentient beings are only the one mind; there is no other dharma." He says here in the *Wanling Record*, "The realm of empty space that entirely pervades the ten directions is intrinsically our one-mind essence." The mind-dharma that the successive generations of patriarchs and teachers seek to transmit refers to this one real characteristic of things.

"Even though you engage in dynamic functioning and productive activity, how are these separate from empty space?

縱汝動用造作 豈離虛空.

The myriad dharmas adorn the dharma realms without adorning anything. Because people do not know this, they wander around, seeking the mind. If they turn one thought around and accord with the mind, everything will be fine. However, they drift far from the mind by arousing one thought and seeking the mind outside.

"Empty space is originally neither large nor small, neither contaminated nor conditioned, neither deluded nor awakened. If

you look clearly, you'll find not a single thing, no persons and no buddhas.

虛空本來無大無小 無漏無為 無迷無悟 了了見 無一物 亦無人 亦無佛.

If you thoroughly understand the nature that is originally pristine, it is certain that at that spot you will not establish even a single dharma. The nature is empty and, at the same time, full of numinous force. Thus it manifests in various forms.

It cannot be said that all these matters either exist or do not exist. Being ineffable, it is said they are inconceivable.

Since the true characteristic of the middle way means that "the pathways of words and speech are eradicated" (*yanyudao duan / eoneodo dan* 言語道斷) and "the locus of mental activity is annihilated" (*xinxingchu mie / simhaengcheo myeol* 心行處滅), it cannot be understood through conceptual understanding. It can only be confirmed through "authentic contemplation and authentic cultivation" (*shican shixiu / silcham silsu* 實參實修) under the guidance of a Seon master.

"Bringing an end to even a hair's breadth of conceptualization means not relying on or being attached to anything. A clear stream flowing in one direction is the self-nature's acquiescence to the nonproduction of dharmas. What hesitation can there be?

絕纖毫的量 是無依倚 無粘綴 一道清流 是自性無生法忍 何有擬議

The acquiescence to the nonproduction of dharmas (*anutpattikadharmakṣānti*) is the Buddha's teaching that can solve the great matter of birth and death. While our physical body and our mental defilements and delusions are reborn through the cycle of birth and death, our intrinsic nature is neither created nor destroyed. Although the Buddha said that "all compounded things are impermanent" (*zhuxing wuchang / jehaeng musang* 諸行無常), the place where those things arise and cease is "quiescent and unmoving" (*jiran budong / jeog-yeon budong* 寂然不動) and flowing freely. You should resolve at its very root this matter of birth and death by awakening to this reality.

If you realize the acquiescence to the nonproduction of dharmas, you cannot die, even though you might want to, because you were never actually born. Since you have encountered this affinity with the great perfection of wisdom that leads to the acquiescence to the nonproduction of dharmas, take full advantage of this opportunity and thoroughly resolve this issue of birth and death by entering into authentic practice. If you just memorize this precious teaching on the acquiescence to the nonproduction of dharmas and do not realize it through practice, on your deathbed, your regrets will be too late.

> **"Since the authentic buddha has no mouth, he does not know how to preach the dharma. Since authentic listening does not involve ears, who is it who hears? Take care!"**
>
> 真佛無口 不解說法 真聽無耳 其誰聞乎 珍重.

Although Master Huangbo preached all day long, there was nothing that he preached. Although those who understood his words listened to him all day long, there was nothing that they heard. All the myriad phenomena in the universe preach without actually preaching anything. Although those who have the power to hear listen to a long speech, there is nothing that they hear.

A swift horse breaks into a gallop the moment it sees the mere shadow of the whip. Those whose eyes have illuminated the gist of Seon respond with silence when a Seon master ascends the dharma seat, hits the seat with his staff, and steps down.

If you cling to any of Master Huangbo's compassionate teachings and cling to them in your mind, they will immediately turn into Māra's instructions. Just as a bird in flight leaves no traces, just as there is no trace of a snowflake that has fallen onto a red-hot brazier, the obligation later generations of students have to Master Huangbo's compassion is, as he says above, to be "a clear stream flowing in one direction."

The Account of Activities

(*Xingzhuang* 行狀)

17. On Mount Tiantai

The master originally came from the province of Min. As a youth, he left the household life [to ordain as a monk] on Mount Huangbo in this prefecture [of Hongzhou]. On his forehead was a lump shaped like a pearl. His speech was sonorous and fluid, his temperament sublime and placid.

師本是閩中人 幼於本州黃蘗山出家 額間隆起如珠 音辭朗潤 志意沖澹.

This is a story from the time when Master Huangbo was traveling around to study Seon. Seon adepts call such travel *youxing*/*yuhaeng* 遊行, which means to wander as an itinerant monk, seeking instruction from various spiritual mentors. Min province is in present-day Fujian province, in the south of China. It seems that there was a lump shaped like a pearl on the master's forehead, which gave him a quite unusual appearance.

Later, when he journeyed to Mount Tiantai, he met a monk who felt like an old friend, and they ended up traveling together. They came upon a mountain torrent that was overflowing its banks, so the master halted, leaning on his staff. The monk entreated the master to cross with him, but the master said, "Please, my brother, you cross first." The monk made his way to the other side of the stream by floating on his bamboo rain-hat. The master said, "How did I let such a loser be my traveling companion? I regret that I did not strike him dead with a single blow of my staff."

後遊天台 逢一僧如舊識 乃同行 屬澗水暴漲 師倚杖而止 其僧率師同過 師云 請兄先過 其僧即浮笠於水上便過 師云 我卻共箇稍子作隊 悔不一棒打殺.

Guoqingsi 國清寺 in present-day Chejiang province was the monastery founded by the master Tiantai Zhiyi 天台智顗 (538–97). During the Tang dynasty, it was the residence of the "three hermits of Guoqing," referring to the three famous poet-recluses Hanshan 寒山 (fl. mid-eighth century), Shide 拾得 (d.u.), and Fenggan 豊干 (d.u.).

It seems that when Master Huangbo was traveling around Mount Tiantai, where Guoqingsi was located, he met a monk who seemed like a long-lost acquaince. As the master and the monk reached a mountain stream that was flooding, he saw the monk demonstrate supernatural powers by crossing the stream on his bamboo rain-hat. The master regretted traveling with him, saying he wished he had hit the monk.

Everyday mind is the Way. As Layman Pang said, "Drawing water and chopping firewood are my supernatural powers and sublime functions."[170] But if you seek to display such powers, you are following a deviant or non-Buddhist way. All such actions are useless.

18. The Single-Flavor Seon of Guizong

A monk bid farewell to Guizong.

Guizong asked, "Where are you going?"

The monk said, "I am going to go everywhere to study five-flavor Seon."

Guizong said, "You can find five-flavor Seon anywhere. Only I, right here, have single-flavor Seon."

The monk asked, "What is single-flavor Seon?" Guizong then hit him.

The monk said, "I get it! I get it!"

Guizong said, "So tell me! Tell me!"

As the monk was about to open his mouth, Guizong hit him again.

Later, the monk arrived at Master Huangbo's residence. The master asked, "Where are you coming from?"

The monk answered, "I come from seeing Guizong."

The master asked, "What words did Guizong have for you?"

The monk told the master about this previous exchange.

The master ascended the hall and brought up this episode, saying, "Great Master Ma produced eighty-four Seon masters, but if they're asked anything, each and every one of them shits his pants. Only Guizong is worth a little something."

有僧辭歸宗 宗云 往甚處去 云 諸方學五味禪去 宗云 諸方有五味禪 我這裡祇是一味禪 云 如何是一味禪 宗便打 僧云 會也會也 宗云 道道 僧擬開口 宗又打 其僧後到師處。師問 問甚麼處來 云 歸宗來 師云 歸宗有何言句 僧遂舉前話 師乃上堂舉此因緣云 馬大師出八十四人善知識 問著箇箇屙漉漉地 祇有歸宗較些子.

Guizong Zhichang 歸宗智常, who resided at the monastery of Guizongsi 歸宗寺 on Mount Lu, was a senior dharma-successor of Master Mazu Daoyi. He was often called "red-eyed Guizong" (赤眼歸宗). It is said that Xitang Zhizang, Baizhang Huaihai, Nanquan Puyuan, and Guizong were the most outstanding of Mazu's many disciples. Huangbo was a student of Baizhang. Zhaozhou Congshen was a student of Nanquan's. Xitang's dharma was transmitted to Korea through the Silla state preceptor Doui. Guizong's teaching was called "single-flavor Seon" because it was so direct and immediate. Master Huangbo also respected his dharma-uncle Guizong.

Another episode involving the master Guizong appears in *Secrets on Cultivating the Mind* by the Goryeo state preceptor Bojo Jinul 普照知訥 (1158–1210).

> A monk asked the master Guizong, "What is the buddha?"
>
> The master answered, "I'll tell you, but I'm afraid you won't believe me."
>
> "How would I dare not believe the sincere words of the master?"
>
> "It's you!"
>
> "How can you prove it?"
>
> "If there's the slightest bit of dust in your eyes, flowers in the sky will fall profusely."
>
> The monk heard this and understood.[171]

19. Repeatedly Slapping a Novice

The master was at Yanguan's for a ceremony together with the emperor of the Dazhong era, who was then a *śramaṇera* [novice monk]. The master entered the main shrine hall and prostrated himself before the Buddha.

The śramaṇera asked, "Do not seek with attachment to the buddha, the dharma, or the saṅgha. What are you seeking, elder, by making these prostrations?"

The master replied, "I'm not seeking with attachment to the buddha, the dharma, or the saṅgha. I customarily prostrate myself in this manner."

The śramaṇera asked, "What's the use of such an act?" The master then slapped him.

The śramaṇera said, "What a coarse lout you are!"

The master replied, "Where do you get off talking about coarse and refined?" and slapped him again from behind. The śramaṇera then fled.

師在鹽官會裡 大中帝為沙彌 師於佛殿上禮佛 沙彌云 不著佛求 不著法求 不著眾求

長老禮拜 當何所求 師云 不著佛求 不著法求 不著眾求 常禮如是事 沙彌云 用禮何為 師便掌 沙彌云 太麤生 師云 這裡是什麼所在 說麤說細 隨後又掌 沙彌便走.

This is a story from when Master Huangbo was staying with Mazu's disciple Yanguan Qi'an 鹽官齊安 (d. 842), who was Huangbo's dharma uncle. Li Chen 李忱 (810–59), the future Emperor Xuanzong 宣宗 of the Tang dynasty (r. 846–59), whose reign period was known as Dazhong 大中

(The Great Mean), was hiding in the monastery as a novice monk to escape a political purge.

The novice taunted Master Huangbo, who was prostrating himself before the Buddha image. However, the novice was no match for the master. He was repeatedly slapped and knocked around.

After the end of the Huichang persecution of Buddhism 會昌法難 (843–45), this novice monk was escorted back to the Chinese imperial court to ascend the throne. The emperor then recounted this previous event with the master and was about to label Master Huangbo a "śramaṇa of coarse practice" (*chuxing shamen / chokhaeng samun* 麤行沙門), that is, a fake monk. At that time, Grand Councilor Pei Xiu defended the master, arguing that the master had repeatedly struck the emperor because he was trying to keep the emperor from cycling through rebirth over past, present, and future. The emperor accepted the minister's petition and granted the master the title Duanchu 斷除 ("Eradicator").

20. Prior to the King with the Awe-Inspiring Voice

During his travels, the master visited Nanquan. One day at mealtime, he took his bowl and got up on Nanquan's seat. Nanquan came down [to the refectory] and, seeing the master, asked, "Elder, how many years have you been practicing the Way?"

The master answered, "Prior to the King with the Awe-Inspiring Voice."

Nanquan said, "It seems you are Old Master Wang's descendant!" The master then got down.

師行腳時 到南泉 一日齋時 捧鉢向南泉位上坐 南泉下來見便問 長老什麼年中行道 師云 威音王巳前 南泉云 猶是王老師孫在 師便下去.

Nanquan Puyuan was a dharma-brother of Baizhang, who was Huangbo's teacher; Nanquan was therefore Huangbo's dharma uncle. While Huangbo was traveling around on pilgrimage, he paid a visit to Nanquan to test his dharma uncle.

Weiyin Wang 威音王, "King with the Awe-Inspiring Voice," refers to Bhīṣmagarjitaghoṣasvararāja, the first buddha of the past auspicious eon. "Before the time of Weiyin Wang" is therefore the same as the Seon topic "before your parents conceived you." Nanquan, who always gave sharp responses, responded to Huangbo's words, saying "It seems you are Old Master Wang's [i.e., Nanquan] descendant," meaning that Nanquan now recognized Huangbo as his legitimate successor. Huangbo then went back to his place without saying a word.

Do you hear the two masters' peals of thunder?

21. A Bamboo Hat

One day, when Master Huangbo was leaving, Nanquan asked, "Why would such a large man wear such a tiny bamboo hat?"

The master replied, "The trichiliocosm is completely contained within it."

Nanquan responded, "Am I also?"

The master put on his hat and left.

師一日出次 南泉云 如許大身材 戴箇些子大笠 師云 三千大千世界 總在裡許 南泉云 王老師你 師戴笠便行.

The dialogue between Master Huangbo and his dharma uncle Nanquan continued. It seems that the master's bamboo hat was too small for his large body. Nanquan deliberately provoked Huangbo because he thought the master looked funny. Then the master replied with a straight face that the entire universe was contained within his hat. Nanquan's sword was sharp when he responded to the master, "Am I also?"

Where on earth is Nanquan's original face?

What do you think of Huangbo's technique for immediately removing all traces?

22. Do Not Rely on Even a Single Thing

One day, when the master was sitting in the tea hall, Nanquan came down and asked, "'Training concurrently in concentration and wisdom, one clearly sees the buddha nature.'[172] What does this mean?"

The master answered, "During the twenty-four hours of the day, do not rely on even a single thing."

Nanquan asked, "Is that your view, Elder?"

The master replied, "I wouldn't dare [say so]!"

Nanquan asked, "Along with the payment for your tea, whom should I tell to receive the payment for your straw sandals?" The master said nothing further.

Later, Weishan brought up this episode with Yangshan and asked, "Didn't Huangbo try to trap him but Nanquan wouldn't let him?"

Yangshan answered, "Not so. You should know that Huangbo had the ingenuity to entrap a tiger."

Weishan said, "Your perspective has really grown!"

師一日在茶堂內坐 南泉下來問 定慧等學 明見佛性 此理如何 師云 十二時中不依倚一物 泉云 莫便是長老見處麼 師云 不敢 泉云 漿水錢且置 草鞋錢 教什麼人還 師便休. 後溈山舉此因緣問仰山 莫是黃蘗搆他 南泉不得麼 仰山云 不然 須知黃蘗有陷虎之機 溈山云 子見處得與麼長

Nanquan tested his dharma nephew Huangbo, who in turn responded splendidly. They were well matched. Later, Huangbo's dharma brother Weishan Lingyou tested the level of his favorite disciple, Yangshan Huiji

仰山慧寂 (807–83), by bringing up this episode. The bright-eyed Yangshan penetrated the essence of the episode and delighted his master.

Weishan and Yangshan enhanced the Seon style of the Weiyang school, which was like the eldest brother of the Five Houses and Seven Schools of Chinese Chan Buddhism during the Song dynasty. Master Huangbo's time was worthy of being called "The golden age of Chan," when a galaxy of sages appeared in the world.

23. The Role of a Master

On the day of communal labor, Nanquan asked the master, "Where are you going?"

The master replied, "I am going to harvest some vegetables."

Nanquan asked, "What are you going to cut them with?"

The master held up a knife.

Nanquan said, "You only know how to be the guest, not the host."

The master tapped the knife three times.

一日普請 泉問什麼處去 師云 擇菜去 泉云 將什麼擇 師豎起刀子 泉云 只解作賓 不解作主 師扣三下.

Here, Nanquan is again testing the master: "What are you going to cut them with?" If you understand the gist of these words, you simply need to reveal that directly. If when you hear such words, however, you give a rambling response like a drunkard, or you are so confounded you cannot respond at all, you're just an inanimate marionette.

As Huangbo held up his knife, Nanquan checked him once more. "You only know how to be the guest, not the host." Huangbo tapped his knife three times at Nanquan's words. If you say you can guess what was happening, then tell me what it meant!

24. Tracking an Antelope

One day, five people arrived and together presented themselves to [Master Huangbo]. One of them did not prostrate and remained standing, drawing a circle with his hand. The master asked, "Do you know how to be a good hunting dog?"

[The monk] answered, "I tracked the antelope's scent here."

The master asked, "If the antelope has no scent, how would you track him?"

[The monk] replied, "I would follow the antelope's hoofprints here."

The master asked, "If the antelope leaves no tracks, how would you track him?"

[The monk] replied, "But I did track the antelope's tracks here."

The master asked, "But the antelope left no hoofprints, so to where would you track him?"

[The monk] answered, "In that case, it's a dead antelope."

The master remained silent.

The next day, after finishing his formal sermon, the master said, "Would the monk who was tracking antelopes yesterday come forward!" The monk then came forward.

The master asked, "At the end of our exchange yesterday, this old monk had nothing more to say. Why was that?" The monk was speechless.

The master said, "I thought you were a genuine patched-robed monk, but you're really just a śramaṇa who's studied doctrine!"

一日五人新到 同時相看 一人不禮拜 以手畫一圓相而立 師云 還知道好隻獵犬麼 云 尋羚羊氣來 師云 羚羊無氣 汝向什麼處尋 云 尋羚羊蹤來 師云 羚羊無蹤 汝向什麼處尋 云 尋羚羊跡來 師云 羚羊無跡汝向什麼處尋 云 與麼則死羚羊也 師便休 來日陞座退 問 昨日尋羚羊僧出來 其僧便出 師云 老僧昨日後頭未有語在 作麼生 其僧無語 師云 將謂是本色衲僧 元來祇是義學沙門.

When an antelope sleeps, it leans its antlers against tree branches so that it leaves no hoofprints on the ground. Inspired by this, the Seon school often compares the signless state to that of an antelope, so tracking an antelope is like attempting to track signlessness. In this anecdote, we see clearly how Master Huangbo struck down a monk who came to him for instruction.

So why do we refer to "tracking an antelope"?

25. An Encounter Dialogue with Pei Xiu

The master dismissed his congregation and was staying in the monastery of Kaiyuansi 開元寺 in Hongzhou. One day, Grand Councilor Pei Xiu was walking around the monastery and saw a wall painting. He then asked the monastery's proctor, "What is this painting?"

The proctor answered, "It's a painting of an eminent monk."

The Grand Councilor asked, "This may be his likeness, but where is that eminent monk?" The proctor could not respond.

The Grand Councilor asked, "Isn't there a Seon monk here?"

The proctor answered, "There is one."

The Grand Councilor immediately requested an audience with the master and asked him about his earlier exchange.

The master called to him, "Pei Xiu!"

Pei Xiu responded, "Yes?"

The master asked, "Where are you?"

The Grand Councilor gained some understanding through these words, and again requested that the master deliver a formal sermon.

師曾散衆在洪州開元寺 裴相公一日入寺行次 見壁畫 乃問寺主 這畫是什麼 寺主云 畫高僧 相公云 形影在這裡 高僧在什麼處 寺主無對 相公云 此間莫有禪僧麼 寺主云 有一人 相公遂請師相見 乃舉前話問師 師召云 裴休 休應諾 師云 在什麼處 相公於言下有省 乃再請師開堂.

Since the narrator of this exchange several times refers to Pei Xiu as Grand Councilor, it is obvious that this section of the text could not have been recorded by Pei Xiu himself. This exchange occurred during the ninth-century Huichang persecution of Buddhism, when Huangbo hid out among the people. This was a harsh period for Buddhism because Emperor Wuzong 武宗 (r. 840–46) of the Tang dynasty persecuted the Buddhadharma, looting the monasteries and disrobing monks. Master Huangbo also dismissed his congregation and secretly stayed at Kaiyuansi, the only official monastery in the region. There, he happened to meet Pei Xiu, who was captivated by Buddhism. The master laid the foundation for the thriving of the Seon school after the persecution ended.

Based on his questions, we can see that although Pei Xiu had some understanding of the Buddhadharma, his mind was disturbed by that understanding so he couldn't truly rest. But you need to have doubts like Pei Xiu's to open your eyes. Thanks to Pei Xiu's encounter with the master, the precious teachings of Master Huangbo have been transmitted to us today. How fortunate this is!

Where are the pupils of Layman Pei Xiu's eyes?

26. The Goose King

The master ascended the hall and said, "You guys are all drunkards. This sort of itinerancy is ridiculed by others. If it's all so easy, how on earth did we end up like this today? Do you know that there are no Seon masters in the great Tang empire?"

At that time, a monk asked, "But we see masters appearing right now in all directions, ministering to their followers and guiding congregations. How can you say there are no Seon masters?"

The master answered, "I didn't say there is no Seon. I just said there are no masters."

Later, Weishan related this episode to Yangshan and asked, "What do you think?"

Yangshan answered, "The goose king extracts the pure milk [from a milky solution]; he's not your average duck."

Weishan said, "This is really hard to discern!"

上堂云 汝等諸人盡是酒糟漢 與麼行腳 笑殺他人 總似與麼容易 何處更有今日 汝還知大唐國裡 無禪師麼 時有僧問 祇如諸方 見今出世 匡徒領衆 為什麼卻道無禪師 師云 不道無禪 祇道無師 後潙山舉此因緣問仰山云 意作麼生 仰山云 鵝王擇乳 素非鴨類 潙山云 此實難辨.

Master Huangbo ascended the hall and preached the dharma at Pei Xiu's request. From his very first words, the master provoked the audience. This was a time of disruption, immediately following the Huichang persecution of Buddhism. The master gave many admonitions, keenly aware that he had to get people back on the true Buddhist path. "Drunkards" means people who try to practice Buddhism but are still full of intellectual understanding; he criticizes them for not yet opening their eyes.

The story of the goose king appears in the Buddhist scriptures.[173] This king is said to be able to extract just the pure milk from a solution of milk and water. The goose king is an analogy for the buddha, who has the clear dharma eye. Yangshan agreed with Huangbo's reflection on the reality of the time: that although there was Seon, there were few Seon masters.

Have you met the goose king yourself?

27. Bestowing a Name

One day, Grand Councilor Pei brought along a buddha-image and, kneeling in Hun fashion [*hugui/hogwe* 胡跪] before the master, said, "Please, master, bestow on me a name!"

The master called out, "Pei Xiu!"

Pei Xiu responded, "Yes?"

The master said, "I've given you a name."

The Grand Councilor then prostrated.

裴相一日 托一尊佛於師前胡跪云 請師安名 師召云 裴休休應諾 師云 與汝安名竟 相公便禮拜.

Master Huangbo thought highly of Pei Xiu and gave him a great name. If Pei Xiu had been the kind of person who did not understand the master's words at all, the master would have responded accordingly. However, since Pei Xiu knew what it all came down to, the master gave him a name appropriate to his level.

This was an unbearable sight to watch with their eyes open. Which buddha's name is this? It's a rabbit's horns and a turtle's fur. *Bah* [*duo/dol* 咄]!

28. Pei Xiu's Poem Dedicated to the Master

Once, the grand councilor offered the master a poem he had written. The master accepted it, sat down, and asked, "Do you get it?"

The grand councilor answered, "I don't get it."

The master replied, "It may be a little better if you don't get it. If you try to describe it with paper and ink, what would that have to do with our school?"

[Pei Xiu's] poem said:

Since the great master transmitted the mind seal,
his seven-foot body has had a pearl in his forehead.
Ten years have passed since I have roosted by the river in Shu;
a floating cup crossed to the far bank of the Zhang River today.
A thousand dragons and elephants [great monks] follow his exalted steps;
a flower whose scent wafts for ten thousand leagues bears excellent fruits.
We wish to serve the master as his disciple;
we know not to whom he will entrust his dharma.

The master responded:

The mind is like a boundless sea;
the mouth spouts red lotuses that revive ailing bodies.

Although I have a pair of hands with nothing to do,
I have never used them to salute idle people.

相公一日上詩一章 師接得便坐卻 乃問 會麼 相公云 不會 師云 與麼不會 猶較些子 若形紙墨 何有吾宗.

詩曰 自從大士傳心印 額有圓珠七尺身 掛錫十年棲蜀水 浮杯今日渡漳濱 千徒龍象隨高步 萬里香花結勝因 願欲事師為弟子 不知將法付何人.

師答曰 心如大海無邊際 口吐紅蓮養病身 雖有一雙無事手 不曾祇揖等閑人.

Pei Xiu opened his eyes thanks to Master Huangbo, so Pei Xiu offered a poem to him, a custom of elite society. Although the master looked coarse, he was infinitely delicate. Coarse and refined simultaneously, his words struck a chord in the hearts of people and made a precious connection with them, pointing them toward the right path.

The master's compassion knew no boundaries. What is the greatest meaning of the Buddhadharma?

29. The Pure Seon of the Tathāgata

"Now, practitioners of the Way, first release all affinities you have for particular trainings. Neither seek them nor cling to them. When you hear a profound teaching, do not follow it; treat it as a fresh breeze that brushes past your ears but is gone in the blink of an eye. To enter Tathāgata Seon deeply, don't generate even the merest conception of Seon. From the very beginning, the patriarchs and teachers have transmitted only the one mind. Since there are not two such dharmas, they point to the fact that the mind is buddha.

夫學道者 先須屏卻 雜學諸緣 決定不求 決定不著 聞其深法 恰似清風屆耳 瞥然而過 更不追尋 是為甚深入如來禪 離生禪想 從上祖師唯傳一心 更無二法 指心是佛.

Practitioners of the Way should think and act from a proper perspective. If you waste your time on useless pursuits, you will be divorced from the Way. Focus only on resolving the great matter of birth and death, devoting yourself to matters of real consequence. True practitioners do not use their mind like ordinary beings. They do not develop such concepts as good and evil or liking and disliking. Their outward appearances are rather plain and not especially sacred or splendid. However, when true practitioners use their minds with no-thought, even ghosts cannot see them.

Tathāgata Seon (*rulai chan / yeorae seon* 如來禪)is typically contrasted to the superior Patriarchal Seon (*zushi chan / chosa seon* 祖師禪). But here, Huangbo seems to be identifying the two with one another, without positing any hierarchy.

Later, when Yangshan tested Xiangyan 香嚴 (d. 898), he distinguished Tathāgata Seon from Patriarchal Seon. However, those with the correct eye of the dharma can digest both terms without either obstructing the other. Those without such an eye cling to these terms and attempt to analyze them. This only intensifies the discriminative mind, making them even more ignorant, and their practice yields no benefits.

A particular word is used in a certain way in a specific time and situation. If those who have not yet opened their eyes study the words alone and act carelessly, they are far removed from true practice.

"Transcending suddenly the signifiers of virtual and sublime enlightenment, allow absolutely no second thoughts whatsoever. Only then will it be akin to entering our school. How would you preoccupied people engage in such training here?

頓超等妙二覺之表 決定不流至第二念 始似入我宗門 如斯之法 汝取次人 到這裡 擬作麼生學.

Tathāgata Seon does not involve such ranks or stages as "virtual enlightenment" or "sublime enlightenment"; it establishes something that is completely perfect, without anything in front of or behind it.

Master Huangbo gave his thorough instruction from the standpoint of sweeping away every defilement all at once without uttering a word.

When a Seon master encounters other monks, he should evoke in them such a conviction.

"Therefore it is said that when you discriminate with your mind, you are bound by the Māra of that very same discriminative mind. When you do not discriminate with your mind, you are bound by the Māra of your undiscriminating mind. When you are not undiscriminating with your mind, you are bound by the Māra of the non-undiscriminative mind. Māra does not come from outside; he issues forth from your own mind. Only the footsteps of bodhisattvas with no supernatural powers cannot be tracked.

所以道擬心時 被擬心魔縛 非擬心時 又被非擬心魔縛 非非擬心時 又被非非擬心魔縛 魔非外來 出自你心 唯有無神通菩薩 足跡不可尋.

Saying that you should be neither discriminating nor undiscriminating means that you should attain awakening so that you are finished with such suppositions. Those with understanding accord with the dharma in whatever they say or do; those without understanding are far removed from the dharma, whether they are discriminating or undiscriminating.

If the Buddha appears, he gets thirty blows. If Māra appears, he gets thirty blows. Who can avoid being struck?

"If at all times you believe in eternalism, then you are a non-Buddhist holding eternalist views. If you are one who observes the emptiness of all dharmas and generates a view of annihilationism, then you are a non-Buddhist holding annihilationist views. Therefore, 'The three realms of existence are mind only. The myriad dharmas are consciousness only': these explanations are given in response to the deviant views of non-Buddhists. If it is said, 'The dharma body is the ultimate fruition,' this statement is made in response to people on the three levels of sagacity and the ten stages of sanctity.[174]

若以一切時中心有常見 即是常見外道 若觀一切法空作空見者 即是斷見外道 所以三界唯心 萬法唯識 此猶是對外道邪見人說 若說法身以為極果 此對三賢十聖人言.

Eternalism (*śāsvatadṛṣṭi*) is the view that everything exists forever. According to this view, for example, even though people die, the self never disappears, and the five aggregates exist forever without ever changing. This is a mistaken view. Annihilationism (*ucchedadṛṣṭi*) is the opposite of eternalism. It is the view that everything is impermanent and nothing exists in reality. Annihilationists cling to the mistaken view that when people die, nothing is left because everything, including mind and matter, disappears. They are prone to the nihilistic denial of causality and thus make no effort to be moral in their conduct. Eternalism and annihilationism are called the "two extreme views"; they are included in a list of six heterodox views.[175]

The Buddhadharma does not deviate from the middle way. In particular, from the standpoint of the original scene in which there is originally no matter, all views, including eternalism, annihilationism, and idealism, as well as such ideas as the three levels sagacity and the ten stages of sanctity, are given as provisional instructions to help people who are one-sided or biased.

Whenever the Seon master Juzhi was asked about the dharma, he would just hold up one finger.[176] While doing so, he would say, "Even though I use this dharma my entire life, I will never be able to use it up."

Therefore the nondual dharma that the Buddha and patriarchs transmitted from mind to mind is truly precious. Only those who have real eyes and ears can experience this dharma.

"Therefore the Buddha eradicated these two types of foolishness: first, the foolishness of subtle conceptual understanding, and second, the foolishness of extremely subtle conceptual understanding.

故佛斷二愚 一者微細所知愚 二者極微細所知愚.

During practice, when you have a certain type of experience or have some resolution to your *hwadu* meditative topic, be especially careful. If you cling to an external object, mistaking it for the dharma, you will get stuck there, unable to go any further. For this reason, agreeable objects are to be feared even more than disagreeable objects.

"Subtle conceptual understanding" refers to the characteristics of dharmas, because it makes practitioners cling to them unconsciously.

Pay no attention even to something great that occurs in an extremely tranquil state, for you can get stuck there if you are not careful. If just once you clearly come into conformity with enlightenment, then although you live like a fool without clinging to conceptual understanding, everything will eventually be clearly revealed to you.

"This is how it was for the Buddha, so why would he say anything about virtual enlightenment and sublime enlightenment? You people are all just drawn toward the light and want nothing to do with the darkness. You seek awakening and try to avoid defilements and ignorance. You then say that a buddha is awakened but sentient beings are deluded. With such a perspective, you may cycle through the six rebirth destinies for a hundred kalpas or a thousand lifetimes, but you will never reach an end to it. Why? Because you slander the intrinsic self-nature of all the buddhas.

佛既如是 更說什麼等妙二覺來 所以一切人但欲向明 不欲向闇 但欲求悟 不受煩惱無明 便道佛是覺 衆生是妄 若作如是見解 百劫千生輪迴六道 更無斷絕 何以故 為謗諸佛本源自性故.

There is a reason the doctrinal traditions of Buddhism lay out a series of stages to practice. Those stages serve as provisional methods for sentient beings to arouse faith, deepen that faith, and eventually open their dharma eyes. However, what stages are there in the original place? To bring about a greater breakthrough, "relinquish doctrine and enter Seon." Leave behind all extreme views at once and realize that all sentient beings are originally buddhas.

"He [the Buddha] clearly told you that buddhas are not light and sentient beings are not dark, for the dharma is neither light nor dark. Buddhas are not strong and sentient beings are not weak, for the dharma is neither strong nor weak. Buddhas are not wise and sentient beings are not foolish, for the dharma is neither wise nor foolish.

他分明向你道 佛且不明 衆生且不闇 法無明闇故 佛且不彊 衆生且不弱 法無彊弱故 佛且不智 衆生且不愚 法無愚智 故.

The perspective on dharma taken here by Master Huangbo is that of the Supreme Vehicle. It will be easy for those without ears to hear it incorrectly.

The Buddha provided expedient means so that we could follow a training that will lead us step by step to enlightenment. Why do Seon masters confuse us by denying all such steps? If you misunderstand their approach and ask such a naïve and superficial question, you will be unable to practice the dharma of the Supreme Vehicle.

Therefore Patriarchal Seon focuses on those with the appropriate capacity. It is like an angler who can cast a rod over the water and hook a jumping fish without using any bait; he need not place a weir in the stream to trap his prey.

Master Huangbo here is firm and resolute in his attitude toward the Buddhadharma; he takes the middle way of nonduality, where no distinction is made between buddhas and sentient beings, between wisdom and foolishness.

"You stick out your heads and claim you understand Seon. But as soon as you open your mouths, an illness strikes. You speak not of the root but only of branches. You speak not of delusion but only of awakening. You speak not of the essence but only of implementation. This is utterly worthless talk.

是你出頭總道解禪 開著口便病發 不說本 祇說末 不說迷 祇說悟 不說體 祇說用 總無你話論處.

Without thoroughly understanding the fundamental root, people nonetheless claim to understand Seon and offer explanations. Those explanations are nothing but delusions. When bright-eyed Seon masters were asked about the dharma, they would just hold up a finger or say, "The cypress tree in the courtyard." Had they tried to explain it, the moment they opened their mouths, they would have been estranged from the essence. Therefore, it is said, "prolix verbal explanations are arsenic powder."[177] If you penetrate the meaning right away, as soon as you hear the master's words, you will have a breakthrough; but if you do not, it will then be like "adding frost to snow,"[178] and you will be left with an even bigger question.

A truly compassionate Seon master does not give exhaustive explanations about the dharma. Rather, he helps his students develop their sense of doubt. As this doubt grows larger, it becomes a ball of doubt that fills the entire universe. When you explode such a ball of doubt, you will be a hero who has resolved the great matter of birth and death.

"All dharmas may originally be not existent, but neither are they now nonexistent. Although conditionally generated, they are also not existent; although those conditions disappear, they are not nonexistent. The root is also not existent, because the root is not a 'root.' The mind is not the mind, because the mind is not a 'mind.' Signs are also not a sign, because a sign is not a 'sign.' Therefore it is said that once there are neither dharmas nor the original mind, you will understand the mind that is the 'mind-dharma.' That dharma is in fact not-dharma, and not-dharma is in fact that dharma. Because it is neither dharma nor not-dharma, this mind is the mind-dharma.

他一切法且本不有 今亦不無 緣起不有 緣滅不無 本亦不有 本非本故 心亦不心 心非心故 相亦非相 相非相故 所以道 無法無本心 始解心心法 法即非法 非法即法 無法無非法 故是心心法.

What we call "root" is just the word *root*. It is exactly the same with mind or dharma. Since they are free from appearances, there is no basis to say, "This is the root; this is the mind; this is the dharma." Nonetheless, were there no root, how would the myriad things in Mother Nature be revealed? They are revealed because something is in fact there. Thus the word *root* is used to refer to that "something," since there is no other way to describe it.

Even so, there is no real basis for calling it a "root." Why is this so? It is because we cannot find it, no matter how hard we try. However, since it is true that all dharmas are revealed, it cannot be said that there is no root. How can we make this claim? Do we have to say that it either exists or does not exist?

Since you practitioners cannot solve this question, you cannot but ask a Seon master if you are earnest. At the end of your exchange with a master, if the conditions are right, you will come into accord with the root. Then everything will be clear.

All these matters are inconceivable and ineffable. However, there can be no dispute, since everything is perfect and delightful.

"When suddenly a thought arises,[179] and you understand clearly that all is like an illusion or a conjurer's trick, you will then match the buddhas of the past, but those 'buddhas of the past' do not exist. The buddhas of the future, for their part, do not not exist, and moreover, there is nothing that can be called 'buddhas of the future.' And since present thoughts do not abide, we also cannot refer to 'buddhas of the present.' When 'buddha' arises, do not regard him as awakened or deluded, good or evil. Do not, even for a moment, cling to him or discard him.

忽然瞥起一念 了知如幻如化 即流入過去佛 過去佛且不有 未來佛且不無 又且不喚作未來佛 現在念念不住 不喚作現在佛 佛若起時 即不擬他是覺是迷 是善是惡 輒不得執滯他 斷絕他.

According to the *Diamond Sūtra*, "Past thoughts are unascertainable, present thoughts are unascertainable, and future thoughts are unascertainable."[180] Whatever illusory forms appear, they are all illusory transformations, with no reality of their own. When you clearly understand that everything is unascertainable, you no longer discriminate among things.

"If one thought suddenly arises, you can neither lock it up with a thousand locks nor tie it down with ten thousand feet of rope. How, then, can you strive to extinguish it or bring it to an end? Let me explain this clearly. Say you want to shut off this blazing consciousness, which is like a mirage. You may say it is close, but you'll never discover it anywhere in all the worlds of the ten directions. You may presume it is distant, but you find it right before your eyes. If you follow it, it just gets

further away. If you try to avoid it, it keeps following you. You can neither grab hold of it nor let go of it. If you know this, you will know that it is the same for the nature of all dharmas. There's no use being worried or anxious about it.

如一念瞥起 千重關鎖鎖不得 萬丈繩索索他不住 既若如是 爭合便擬滅他止他 分明向你道 爾啖識 你作麼生擬斷他 喻 如陽啖 你道近 十方世界求不可得 始道遠 看時祇在目前 你擬趁他 他又轉遠去 你始避他 他又來逐你 取又不得 捨 又不得 既若如此 故知一切法性自爾 即不用愁他慮他.

You may try to lock up that one thought that has arisen, but you cannot. You may try to rid yourself of it, but you cannot. The very thought to get rid of a deluded thought is itself a deluded thought, and a thought cannot remove a thought.

By simply realizing that it is originally a mirage, it naturally disappears. A thought fundamentally is not something you either should or should not remove. Therefore, the *Diamond Sūtra* says, "Arouse a thought that does not abide anywhere."[181]

"As the saying goes, 'For a prior thought to be ordinary and a subsequent thought noble is the same as flipping over your hand.'[182] This [statement] is the pinnacle of the three vehicles. In our Seon school, a prior thought is not ordinary and a subsequent thought is not noble; a prior thought is not a buddha and a subsequent thought is not a sentient being. All forms are a buddha's form and all sounds are a buddha's sounds.

如言 前念是凡 後念是聖 如手翻覆一般 此是三乘教之極也 據我禪宗中 前念且不是凡 後念且不是聖 前念不是佛 後念 不是衆生 所以一切色是佛色 一切聲是佛聲.

In teachings that convey sequential steps of practice, quickly moving upward step by step is considered the best approach. Seon, as the dharma gate of sudden awakening, makes people realize that there is no such sequence.

When you realize that even though clouds come and go in accord with causes and conditions, the sky remains unchanging and unmoving, you do not cling to the appearance and disappearance of clouds. When you thoroughly understand that even though changes occur outwardly, the original root never changes, you remain unshaken. Arousing thoughts in response to changing external phenomena, however, you become ignorant.

> **"If you raise one principle, you raise all principles. If you see one thing, you see all things. If you see one mind, you see all minds. If you see one way, you see all ways. There is nowhere that is not the Way. If you see one mote of dust, you see the mountains, streams, and lands of all the worlds in the ten directions. If you see one drop of water, you see all the moisture of all the worlds in the ten directions. Furthermore, seeing all dharmas is seeing all states of mind. Since all dharmas are originally empty, the mind is not nonexistent. The lack of nonexistence is sublime existence. Existence is nonexistence; nonexistence is existence: this is the sublime existence of true emptiness.**
>
> 舉著一理 一切理皆然 見一事 見一切事 見一心 見一切心 見一道 見一切道 一切處無不是道 見一塵 十方世界山河大地皆然 見一滴水 即見十方世界一切性水 又見一切法 即見一切心 一切法本空 心即不無 不無即妙有 有亦不有 不有即有 即真空妙有.

To give an analogy for the "sublime existence of true emptiness," although in true emptiness there is no past, present, or future, no north, south, east, or west, every diverse appearance, including blue, yellow, red, and white, appear in this true emptiness. All dharmas appear, mature, decay, and vanish in true emptiness. However, whatever happens, true emptiness remains, unchanging and unmoving. Since there is numinous vitality or sublime existence in true emptiness, the myriad dharmas come to be produced.

Such words belong to the third statement.[183] However well you understand them, you cannot save yourselves with these words. You must sweep away even such words as the "sublime existence of true emptiness" in order to be truly free and unfettered.

"This being the case, all the worlds of the ten directions are not separated from our one mind. Lands as numerous as tiny motes of dust are not separate from our one thought. Since this is so, how can we speak of what is inside and outside? It is like the nature of honey: if honey is sweet by nature, then all honey is sweet—you cannot say that a specific honey is sweet while the rest is bitter. Where would such a thing be possible? Therefore, it is said, 'Empty space has neither inside nor outside';[184] so too is it with the dharma nature. Empty space has no middle; so too is it with the dharma nature. Therefore sentient beings are buddhas and buddhas are sentient beings.

既若如是 十方世界 不出我之一心 一切微塵國土 不出我之一念 若然 說什麼內之與外 如蜜性甜 一切蜜皆然 不可道這箇蜜甜 餘底苦也 何處有與麼事 所以道 虛空無內外 法性自爾 虛空無中間 法性自爾 故衆生即佛 佛即衆生.

Distinguishing subject from object or inside from outside derives from external appearances that are created in accord with causes and conditions. Therefore there are no distinctions in the original nature, which is free from causes and conditions. From the standpoint of the original essence in which no relative forms are made manifest, there are no buddhas who save sentient beings and no sentient beings saved by the buddhas.

"Sentient beings and buddhas are intrinsically one in their essence. Saṃsāra and nirvāṇa, conditioned and unconditioned, are intrinsically one in their essence. Mundane and supramundane, the six rebirth destinies and the four modes of birth, the mountains, streams, and lands, and the nature and its lack are also the same one essence. By calling them the 'same,' we mean that their designations are empty, their existence is empty, and their nonexistence is empty. Worlds as numerous as the sands of the Ganges are inherently this one emptiness.

眾生與佛 元同一體 生死涅槃 有為無為 元同一體 世間出世間 乃至六道四生 山河大地 有性無性 亦同一體 言同者名相亦空 有亦空 無亦空 盡恒沙世界 元是一空.

The outward appearances of the myriad things in this world are endlessly diverse, but the fundamental reality of those things is that they are nondual. Sentient beings and buddhas, saṃsāra and nirvāṇa, conditioned and unconditioned, the mountains, streams, and lands, and sentient beings and insentient things may all be different in terms of their outward appearances, but their fundamental essence is emptiness. Sentient beings that are born from egg, womb, moisture, or metamorphosis in the six rebirth destinies of heavenly beings, humans, demigods, animals, hungry ghosts, and the denizens of the hells are nondual in terms of their natures.

"This being the case, where are the buddhas who save sentient beings? Where are the sentient beings saved by the buddhas? Why is it this way? Because the nature of all dharmas is just as it is. If you generate a view that this all occurs naturally, you fall into a non-Buddhist view of naturalism.[185] If you generate a view that there is no 'I' or 'mine,' you drop into one of the three levels of sagacity or ten stages of sanctity.

既若如此 何處有佛度眾生 何處有眾生受佛度 何故如此 萬法之性自爾故 若作自然見 即落自然外道 若作無我無我所見 墮在三賢十聖位中.

Just as emptiness includes everything, so too is it with the nature. If you look into all external phenomena, you will see that the myriad dharmas are manifestations of the original essence and thus can neither be augmented nor diminished. Since they are all unchanging, they are unascertainable.

Even though the three levels of sagacity and the ten stages of sanctity are advanced levels attained by bodhisattvas, do not cling even to such illustrious outward appearances.

"Why do you now try to measure empty space foot by foot or inch by inch? You have been clearly told that dharmas do not complete each other, because dharmas are quiescent in and of themselves. They abide themselves exactly where they should be and are authentic themselves exactly as they should be.

你如今 云何將一尺一寸 便擬量度虛空 他分明向汝道 法法不相到 法自寂故 當處自住 當處自真.

Dharma can't be sought; it is always present. All the myriad dharmas do not depart from that very spot. Dharma has no past, present, or future; it is neither redundant nor deficient. In accord with causes and conditions that originate from this very place of the dharma, the distinctions of red and yellow, long and short, large and small, complete and incomplete all appear. However unnatural or unharmonious they may be, all these distinctive appearances are not separate from the dharma because they are nondual. They all may look different, but from the standpoint of the true reality of the dharma, they are not different.

"Since the body is empty, we designate dharmas as empty; since the mind is empty, we designate the nature as empty. Since body and mind are both empty, we designate the dharma nature as empty. Even were we to supply thousands of distinct designations, none would be separate from your original mind. Such designations as bodhi, nirvāṇa, true suchness, buddha nature, the two vehicles, and bodhisattvas are like 'placing a leaf in [a child's] palm and pretending it is real gold.'[186]

以身空故名法空 以心空故名性空 身心總空 故名法性空 乃至千途異說 皆不離你之本心 如今說菩提涅槃真如佛性二乘菩薩者 皆指葉為黃金 拳掌之說.

Everything, seen and unseen, is the functioning of this mind. There can be no appearances outside this mind. Therefore, however many different designations there may be, such as dharma, mind, nature, dharma nature, bodhi, nirvāṇa, true suchness, buddha nature, two vehicles, bodhisattva, and so forth, all are just fingers pointing to this one mind. All these are expedient means, like giving candy to console a crying child.

It is therefore foolish to satisfy your intellectual curiosity by clinging to these expedients, saying this provisional description is right but all the others are wrong. All these fingers are pointing to the same one thing. If this thing appears clearly right before your eyes, all these countless designations and discriminative thoughts that have thus far caused subtle delusions will instantly disappear.

This is what is meant by the phrase, "when a lion roars, foxes' brains are ripped to shreds."

"When you open your hand, the entire congregation, whether divinities or humans, all see that there is not a single thing in your palm. Therefore, it is said, 'Originally there is not a single thing,/ so where can dust alight?'[187] Since originally there is nothing, the three time periods are originally unascertainable.

若也展手之時 一切大眾若天若人 皆見掌中都無一物 所以道本來無一物 何處有塵埃 本既無物 三際本無所有.

Hearing such phrases as "clearly penetrating both inside and out" (*neiwai mingche / naeoe myeongcheol* 內外明徹) or an "expansive great awakening" (*kuoche dawu / hwakcheol daeo* 廓徹大悟), people presume that must be something numinous, like "mind" or "dharma." They assume there must be some profound principle in the Seon masters' words.

However, the dharma is "expansive and free from sanctity" and "originally not a single thing"; enlightenment is "unascertainable." Since the original face is wide open like empty space, it has no north, south, east, or west, no past, present, or future.

However much intellectual smarts you may have, you will never be able to figure this out; you simply have to suddenly come into accord with it. This is why bright-eyed Seon masters do not try to explain it. Instead they lead students to raise a doubt so they can eventually penetrate to the truth by exploding that ball of doubt.

"Therefore practitioners of the Way should seek direct access with a single slice of their swords (*dandao zhiru / dando jigip* 單刀直入). They must cognize this meaning and then they will get it. The great master Bodhidharma came to this land from India in the west. Although he journeyed through several lands, he found only a single person, the great master Huike, to whom he secretly transmitted the mind seal. This was the seal of your original mind. He stamped the dharma with this mind and stamped the mind with this dharma. Since the mind is like this, so too is the dharma. This state is identical to the apex of reality and equivalent to the dharma nature. Within the emptiness of the dharma nature, who is it that gives the prophecy [of future enlightenment]? Who is it that attains buddhahood? Who is it that gains the dharma?

故學道人 單刀直入 須見這箇意始得 故達摩大師 從西天來至此土 經多少國土 祇覓得可大師一人 密傳心印 印你本心以心印法 以法印心 心既如此 法亦如此 同真際 等法性 法性空中 誰是授記人 誰是成佛人 誰是得法人.

The dharma is what you practitioners of the Way transmit from mind to mind without transmitting anything and receive without receiving anything. Although the great master Bodhidharma had several students, ultimately it was Huike who received the dharma by obtaining the marrow of his teachings.

Although the buddhas and patriarchs transmit the dharma from generation to generation, since the nature of that dharma is empty, those who transmit it, those who receive it, and the dharma that is transmitted and received are all empty. You practitioners of the Way should experience this inconceivable dharma for yourself. Without this experience, any words you may use to describe it are nothing but conceptual proliferation.

"You have been clearly told that bodhi cannot be achieved by the body because the body is signless. It cannot be achieved by the mind because the mind is signless. It cannot be achieved

by the nature because the nature is the impeccable buddha of the original self-nature.

他分明向你道 菩提者不可以身得 身無相故 不可以心得 心無相故 不可以性得 性即便是本源自性天真佛故.

Bodhi is not something achieved. It is not subject to the law of causality. It has nothing to do with whether this universe is created or destroyed. The impeccable buddha of the original self-nature is always such, whether Buddhism exists or not. It was such before Buddhism began; it was such when Buddhism was at its height and people throughout the world believed in the religion; it will be such even when people no longer follow Buddhism. It will remain unchanging even after this whole universe is destroyed. Even this word "unchanging" is used in vain.

"You cannot use the buddha to achieve buddhahood. You cannot use the signless to achieve signlessness. You cannot use emptiness to achieve emptiness. You cannot use the Way to achieve the Way. Since there is originally nothing to be attained, nonattainment also cannot be attained. Therefore, it is said, 'There is not a single dharma that can be ascertained.'[188]

不可以佛更得佛 不可以無相更得無相 不可以空更得空 不可以道更得道 本無所得 無得亦不可得 所以道 無一法可得.

You may think, "If there were no dharma, then why would you tell us to realize the dharma? Isn't it because the dharma does in fact exist that you tell us to realize it?"

If you realize the dharma, you will clearly understand this principle that "there is not a single dharma that can be ascertained." If not, you will remain deluded, no matter how much you hear about this principle.

"I simply teach you to comprehend your original mind. The moment you comprehend it, you will find no sign of compre-

hension. There is no sign of either comprehending it or not comprehending it, for those are unascertainable. Those who get it just get it, without thinking that they have done so, just as those who don't get it also don't think that they have done so, either. How many people thus far have understood this sort of dharma? As the question goes, 'How many people in this world have forgotten themselves?'

祇教你了取本心 當下了時 不得了相 無了無不了相 亦不可得 如此之法 得者即得 得者不自覺知 不得者亦不自覺知 如此之法 從上已來 有幾人得知 所以道 天下忘己者 有幾人.

The Way is already fully revealed. Whether practitioners realize it or not, it is always present. Since those who clearly understand it are in accord with the law of causality, they receive it without receiving anything. Since those who do not understand it ignore the law of causality, they create even greater karma for themselves.

Such a teaching is a provisional means by which those who have realized the true reality of the original mind guide their students to attain awakening. This teaching is not something that students should approach intellectually. Practitioners who digest these words should not cling to anything or abide anywhere.

"If now you try to comprehend it through one faculty, one sense object, one scripture, one doctrine, one realm, one time, one name, or one word that is presented to your six sense organs, how would you be any different from a wooden marionette? You might presume that a person could suddenly appear who generates no understanding with regard to one name or one characteristic, but I say that you could search for such a person throughout every world in the ten directions and never succeed in finding one.

如今於一機一境一經一教一世一時一名一字 六根門前領得 與機關木人何別 忽有一人出來 不於一名一相上作解者 我說此人盡十方世界覓 這箇人不可得.

Since the physical body is an insentient thing, it is no different from a wooden marionette. However, what you see, hear, sense, and know is clearly revealed right before you. If you name it buddha nature, fundamental essence, or dharma body, you will be as foolish as the simpleton who, thinking he has lost his head, looks for another head to put on top of his existing head.[189]

Every one of you makes use of your original face to see, hear, sense, and know. But if you are not yet sure about what it is, you must use your doubt about your fundamental origin to collapse your mental wall.

> **"Since that person would be second to none, he would succeed to the status of a patriarch; pristine and free from anything extraneous, he would be considered a member of the Śākya clan. It is said that when the king attains buddhahood, his princes follow him in going forth into homelessness. This idea is extremely difficult to understand.**
>
> 以無第二人故 繼於祖位 亦云釋種 無雜純一故言 王若成佛時 王子亦隨出家 此意大難知

The moment you attain awakening, this one mind alone is clearly revealed. At that moment, since your mind is pure, free from any admixture, you will be worthy of being called a member of the Śākya clan. If the one mind is revealed, nothing further needs to be done, and all the myriad things will attain buddhahood simultaneously.

It is like when the king abdicates the throne and ordains as a monk, his princes and vassals must all follow him into the Buddhist order.

> **"I teach you only to stop seeking. If you seek, you will fail. This is like a simpleton who shouts out from the top of a mountain: as the echo resounds through the valley, he runs down the mountain, chasing the sound, but is unable to locate it. When he shouts from below and it echoes from the peak, he chases it back up the mountain.**

祗教你莫覓 覓便失卻 如癡人山上叫一聲 響從谷出 便走下山趁 及尋覓不得 又叫一聲 山上響又應 亦走上山上趁.

You cannot obtain the nature no matter how hard you try. The moment you open your mouth or give rise to a thought, you are off the mark. But if you just let go, it will be revealed to be right before your eyes. Practitioners know why this is so. You may not have learned this yet through practice, but if you have affinities with this practice, investigate the point of such words.

Those who only study the words generate intellectual understanding and do not try to find a way out of it. They wander around their entire lives with no prospect of attaining awakening, not knowing that they are being deceived by mirages. Therefore, bright-eyed Seon masters seek not to offer explanations but to guide their students to generate the sense of doubt.

"Those who, like this, follow the echo in search of its source for a thousand lifetimes and ten thousand kalpas are folks who are born in vain and die for naught. If you make no sound, there will be no echo. Nirvāṇa has nothing to be heard, nothing to be known, nothing that resounds; it leaves no tracks and no traces. If you can be thus, you will draw nigh to the abode of the patriarchs."

如是千生萬劫 祗是尋聲逐響人 虛生浪死漢 汝若無聲 即無響 涅槃者 無聞無知無聲 絕跡絕蹤 若得如是 稍與祖師鄰房也.

To seek nirvāṇa does not mean to cease thinking. Rather, no matter how many thoughts you generate, you accord with the real characteristic of things that generates not a single thought. Those who clearly realize this know how to distinguish between right and wrong. They are untarnished in every motion they make. Though moving all day long, they move without actually being in motion. Those who do not realize this may practice all their lives but will remain far from awakening.

If you happen to encounter the Buddha's teachings and enter the Buddhist Way, go a step further and open your eyes to the Buddhadharma. Stand at the spot where the teachings and the dharma are nondual. Open your eyes to the fact that there is originally nothing to be let go of. Know how to empty your mind by living in accord with the causes and conditions of the mundane world.

Master Huangbo must have thoroughly studied Buddhist doctrine before he attained awakening. His teachings reveal the fruits of the strenuous efforts he made even after he opened his eyes. Accordingly, his encounter with Linji demonstrates his supreme level, transcending words and letters. Had Huangbo simply offered explanations to Linji, the latter would never have seen even a shadow of the truth. As an extreme tactic, Huangbo hit Linji three times with his staff. He beat him without mercy, frightening Linji. After opening his eyes during his visit with the monk Dayu 大愚 (d.u.), Linji thanked Huangbo for his beating, realizing Huangbo's compassionate action had led him to awakening.

Pei Xiu was not so different. When Pei Xiu first met Huangbo and asked him about the truth, Huangbo flung him to the ground, like a dog taking a bite out of something. This jolted Pei Xiu to wake up from his dream. Huangbo's action was not merciless; it was in fact a truly merciful act.

30. A Ram's Horns

[Pei Xiu] inquired, "I humbly request your instruction on the passage 'There is no such sword in my armory.'"[190]

The master replied, "The royal armory has the nature of empty space. It is able to contain the worlds throughout empty space in all the ten directions, none of which are separate from your mind. We also can call this Ākāśagarbha Bodhisattva. If you say that it either exists or does not exist, or that it neither exists nor does not exist, then these all turn into a ram's horns. A ram's horns are what you are seeking."

[Pei Xiu] asked, "Is there an actual sword in the royal armory then or not?"

The master answered, "This is also a ram's horns."

[Pei Xiu] asked again, "If originally there is no actual sword in the royal armory, then why is it said that the prince took a sword from the royal armory and left for another kingdom? Why do you alone say there is no sword?"

The master replied, "'Leaving with a sword' is an analogy for an emissary of the Tathāgata. If you say that the prince left with an actual sword from the royal armory, you imply that he took something from the armory. No one can carry off anything that, at its original source, has the nature of empty space. What does this statement mean? Even though you presume you get it, it is a ram's horns."

問 如王庫藏內 都無如是刀 伏願誨示 師云 王庫藏者 即虛空性也 能攝十方虛空世界 皆總 不出你心 亦謂之虛空藏菩薩 你若道是有是無 非有非無 總成羊角 羊角者 即你求覓者也. 問 王庫藏中有真刀否 師云 此亦是羊角 云 若王庫藏

中本無真刀 何故云 王子持王庫中真刀 出至異國 何獨言無
師云 持刀出者 此喻如來使者 你若言 王子持王庫中 真刀
出去者 庫中應空去也 本源虛空性 不可被異人將去 是什麼
語 設你有者 皆名羊角.

According to the *Mahāparinirvāṇa Sūtra*, a prince had a poor friend. The friend saw the prince's marvelous sword and coveted it. One day, the prince left for another country. Talking in his sleep, the friend kept saying, "The sword! The sword!" People thought he had stolen the sword, so they captured him and took him to the palace. The king asked him about the sword, but the friend answered that, since he had just seen the sword and hadn't stolen it, he could be cut open and the king still wouldn't find the sword either on or inside his body. When the king interrogated him about the shape of the sword, the friend answered that it was shaped like a ram's horns. The king laughed, saying, "There is no such sword in my armory, so how could the prince display such a sword?"

The Buddha offered this simile: a bodhisattva-mahāsattva, who was like an emissary for the Tathāgata, appeared in the world, preached the dharma, and left the world, just like that prince who showed his friend a marvelous sword for just a moment and then left for another land. He added that people talking this and that about the dharma was like the friend talking in his sleep, "The sword! The sword!" and saying that the sword looked like a ram's horns. To remove the discriminative delusions of such people, the Buddha said, "There is no such a sword in my armory."

Every one of us is the king of the six countries that rule over our eyes, ears, nose, tongue, body, and mind. The royal armory, which refers to our original mind, is of the nature of empty space. If we are compelled to name it, all we can say is that it is called Bodhisattva Ākāśagarbha (Womb of Empty Space). Saying that empty space is either existent, nonexistent, or neither existent nor nonexistent is nothing but conceptual proliferation. To cure sentient beings' chronic disease of clinging to something that does not originally exist, the Buddha said, "There is no such a sword in my armory." We should keep in mind here the Buddha's intent.

The final, and most difficult, task in Buddhist practice is to eliminate the subtle delusions, the ram's horns in this simile.

31. Kāśyapa and Ānanda

[Pei Xiu] asked, "Kāśyapa received the mind seal of the Buddha and became a person who transmitted words, didn't he?"

The master answered, "Yes."

[Pei Xiu] replied, "If he transmitted words, he must not have escaped from being a ram's horns."

The master answered, "Kāśyapa comprehended his original mind for himself, so he was not associated with ram's horns. If you comprehend the Tathāgata's mind, you will perceive the Tathāgata's intent. One who then perceives the Tathāgata's physical characteristics belongs to the Tathāgata's emissaries and becomes a person who transmits words. Consequently Ānanda, who served as the Buddha's attendant for twenty years, only perceived the Tathāgata's physical characteristics, so the Buddha scolded him, saying, 'If you view me only as being the savior of the world, you cannot escape being a ram's horns.'"

問 迦葉受佛心印 得為傳語人否 師云是 云若是傳語人 應不離得羊角 師云 迦葉自領得本心 所以不是羊角 若以領得如來心 見如來意 見如來色相者 即屬如來使 為傳語人 所以阿難為侍者二十年 但見如來色相 所以被佛訶云 唯觀救世者 不能離得羊角.

Those who awaken to the mind and illuminate the nature have the power to rule the entire world while seated on a bejeweled throne. However, those who cling to such externalities are nothing but emissaries. If you turn one thought around, you will become a host, but if you follow one thought, you cannot avoid being an emissary.

A stupid dog chases a dirt clod someone throws, but a bright-eyed lion bites the person who threw it. Those who perceive only the outward appearance of the Tathāgata cannot escape characteristics. But if they awaken to the Tathāgata's original mind, they perceive the Tathāgata's intent and live as a master of the world.

Ānanda served as the personal attendant of the Buddha for twenty-five years and listened to many of the Buddha's sermons. However, he was unable to open his eyes while the Buddha was alive. Only after the Buddha's death was Ānanda finally able to attain awakening and receive the dharma, thanks to Kāśyapa.

In later generations, Xianglin Chengyuan 香林澄遠 (908–87) served for a long time as the personal attendant for Master Yunmen Wenyan. Yunmen frequently called him, saying, "Attendant Yuan!" When Chengyuan would answer, Yunmen would teach him by asking him, "What is it [that's answering]?" Despite Yunmen's persistent instruction, Chengyuan was unable to gain any spiritual breakthrough. Eighteen years later, when Chengyuan finally attained awakening, Yunmen said to him, "I will not call you any longer." Chengyuan's disciple was Zhimen Guangzuo 智門光祚 (d. 1031), whose disciple was Xuedou Zhongxian. Xuedou compiled the *Hundred Old Cases with Verse Commentary* (*Baize songgu* 百則頌古), which provided the Chan cases that were was incorporated into the *Blue Cliff Record*. Therefore no small merit accrued from Master Yunmen asking "What is it?" for eighteen years.

32. *Cutting through Wisdom with Wisdom*

[Pei Xiu] asked, "What does it mean that 'Mañjuśrī brandished his sword in front of Gautama'?"[191]

The master replied, "Five hundred bodhisattvas attained the knowledge of their previous lifetimes and perceived the karmic obstructions created during their past lives. 'Five hundred' refers to your body, which consists of the five aggregates. Since they perceived the obstructions created during their past lives, they sought out the Buddha and sought out the bodhisattvas and nirvāṇa. Consequently, Mañjuśrī raised his sword of wisdom and slayed this view that posits a buddha mind that is existent.[192] Therefore he was told, "You have slayed it well."

[Pei Xiu] asked, "What is this sword?"

The master answered, "The liberated mind is this sword."

[Pei Xiu] asked, "Since the liberated mind is this sword, [Mañjuśrī] cut through the view that the buddha mind exists. How then will we be able to eliminate the mind that is so easily able to eradicate views?"

The master answered, "You can use nondiscriminative wisdom (*nirvikalpajñāna*) to eradicate the discriminative mind that posits the view of existence."

[Pei Xiu] asked, "If I have the view of existence and seek out the buddha mind, I can eradicate [this view] with nondiscriminative wisdom. How then does the sword of wisdom exist?"

The master answered, "If nondiscriminative wisdom cuts through the views of existence (*asti*) and nonexistence (*nāsti*), then nondiscriminative wisdom would also be unascertainable."

[Pei Xiu] said, "I cannot cut through wisdom with wisdom or cut through a sword with a sword."

The master said, "If a sword cuts through a sword, each sword cuts through the other; therefore those swords are also unascertainable. If wisdom cuts through wisdom, each type of wisdom cuts through the other; therefore those wisdoms are also unascertainable. This is exactly the same as when 'doe and fawn died together.'"[193]

問 文殊執劍於瞿曇前者 如何 師云 五百菩薩得宿命智 見過去生業障 五百者即你五陰身是 以見此夙命障故 求佛求菩薩涅槃 所以文殊將智解劍 害此有見佛心故 故言你善害 云 何者是劍 師云 解心是劍 云 解心既是劍 斷此有見佛心 祇如能斷見心 何能除得 師云 還將你無分別智 斷此有見分別心 云 如作有見有求佛心 將無分別智劍斷 爭奈有智劍在何 師云 若無分別智 害有見無見 無分別智亦不可得 云 不可以智更斷智 不可以劍更斷劍 師云 劍自害劍 劍劍相害 即劍亦不可得 智自害智 智智相害 即智亦不可得 母子俱喪 亦復如是.

According to *Sources of the Five Lamplights* [of Chan],[194] when the Buddha preached the dharma to the congregation on Vulture Peak, there were five hundred bhikṣus in attendance. Through the superknowledge of recollecting their past lives (*pūrvanivāsānusmṛti*), these bhikṣus all saw the heinous deeds they had performed in their past lives, such as killing their fathers and mothers, and were concerned that they would not be able to attain awakening in these very bodies. At that moment, Mañjuśrī perceived their doubt, so he appeared brandishing a sword and, relying on the Buddha's awesome power, harassed the Buddha. The five hundred bhikṣus then praised Mañjuśrī, realizing that the Buddha and the sword both had the same identical characteristic, since there was no sword that could be used to kill and no Buddha that could be killed.

Our bodies that consist of the five aggregates of material form, sensations, perception, volitional factors, and consciousness can never be free from karmic obstructions. Therefore those who misunderstand that their bodies are what will be liberated try hard to remove their karmic obstructions. Over many years, they make every effort to remove defilements. However, the dharma of nonduality means that "form is emptiness." If you realize this principle, then "defilements are bodhi" and "karmic obstructions are sublime functions." It is like the principle by which a lotus flower blooms in the mud. When defilements and bodhi are unified in the middle way, karmic obstructions and nirvāṇa are nondual.

Therefore Mañjuśrī removes the cause of discrimination by slashing through these views of the existence of karmic obstructions and the buddha mind with his sword of wisdom.

At this moment, Pei Xiu, who had become quite clever, asks, "How can he sever the very mind that cuts through views?" His question, in fact, is profound, essentially asking, "How can we discover the causes and conditions that will remove even wisdom?" If you cling to this sword of wisdom, you must be really careful because, unawares, it can change into a subtle delusion.

Huangbo explains that, even though nondiscriminative wisdom eradicates the views of existence and nonexistence, this nondiscriminative wisdom is also unascertainable. Pei Xiu then asks him another incisive question, pointing out that people can neither remove wisdom with wisdom nor cut through a sword with a sword.

Huangbo then reveals the inconceivable, sublime dharma—which comes alive as the everyday mind after the one great death—by quoting the line, "Doe and fawn died together."

33. Seeing the Nature

[Pei Xiu] asked, "What is 'seeing the nature'?"

The master answered, "The nature is seeing and seeing is the nature; you cannot see the nature with the nature. Hearing is the nature; you cannot hear the nature with the nature. If you generate a view of the nature and presume that the nature is something that can be heard or can be seen, you immediate produce dharmas that are either identical or different. It has been clearly stated that that which perceives cannot itself be perceived. How can you add a head atop your head? Also clearly stated is that it is akin to loose pearls scattered on a tray: large ones have a large round shape and small ones have a small round shape. None is aware of the other and none impedes the other. When one is produced, it does not say, 'I am produced'; when one ceases, it does not say, 'I cease.' Therefore there has never been a time when this was not so for the four modes of birth and the six rebirth destinies.

問 如何是見性 師云 性即是見 見即是性 不可以性更見性 聞即是性 不可以性更聞性 祇你作性見能聞能見性 便有一異法生 他分明道 所可見者 不可更見 你云何頭上更著頭 他分明道如盤中散珠 大者大圓 小者小圓 各各不相知 各各不相礙 起時不言我起滅時 不言我滅 所以四生六道 未有不如時.

The nature is not an object to be perceived. It is so completely revealed in the world that everyone is constantly perceiving it, so it would be foolish to try to find it again. "The Buddha cannot see the Buddha; the Buddha does not worship the Buddha."

All big and small matters in the world are not estranged from the nature. They appear, change, and disappear in accord with causes and conditions. It is a natural law that the interplay of causes and conditions inevitably entail change. The fundamental reality of the self-nature cannot be explained through such words as "changing" or "unchanging." Expedient descriptions are offered to help sentient beings understand—"things change without actually changing" or "things change but are in fact unchanging." But there is a limit in taking such words as a golden rule. Only when you transcend all limitations and realize the actual self-nature can you remove all traces and extinguish all illusory sounds.

In *Vimalakīrti's Instructions*, when Mañjuśrī asks Vimalakīrti about his illness, Vimalakīrti greets the bodhisattva, saying, "Mañjuśrī! Do you come without any sign of coming and see without any sign of seeing?" Mañjuśrī answers,

> Yes! If I've come, there is no more coming; if I've gone, there is no more going. Why is this so? I may come, but there is nowhere from which I've come; I may go, but there is nowhere to which I go. I may see, but there is nothing I perceive.[195]

If there were any signs of coming, going, and seeing, the dharma would be far removed from the nonduality that *Vimalakīrti's Instructions* emphasizes. The myriad dharmas have no independent natures of their own; at their root, they are nondual. Therefore, even though they blossom in all kinds of forms and shapes, they do not interact haphazardly but coexist harmoniously.

> **"By the same token, sentient beings do not perceive buddhas and buddhas do not perceive sentient beings. The four fruitions do not perceive the four candidacies [for that fruition]; the four candidacies do not perceive the four fruitions. The three levels of sagacity and the ten stages of sanctity do not perceive virtual enlightenment and sublime enlightenment; virtual enlightenment and sublime enlightenment do not perceive the three levels of sagacity and the ten stages of sanctity. This remains the case even up to the fact that water does**

> **not perceive fire and fire does not perceive water. Earth does not perceive wind and wind does not perceive earth. Sentient beings do not access the dharma realm and buddhas do not leave the dharma realm. Therefore the dharma nature is free from going and coming; there is no perception of subject or object. This being so, how can you say that I see or I hear?**
>
> 且眾生不見佛 佛不見眾生 四果不見四向 四向不見四果 三賢十聖不見等妙二覺 等妙二覺不見三賢十聖 乃至水不見火 火不見水 地不見風 風不見地 眾生不入法界 佛不出法界 所以法性無去來 無能所見 能如此 因什麼道我見我聞.

If you mistake an expedient description for truth, you will cling to that account and become foolish. Understanding this, you will come to know that even the phrase "seeing the nature" is illusory, because no sentient being has not already seen that nature. But they see it without realizing they see it, so they lose the fundamental root.

To give an example, all things associated with the self-nature are associated with the six perfections. You should know that the six perfections are established in order to lead sentient beings to attain awakening through practice when the time is right, so that they will not be separated from the real characteristic of things.

The *four fruitions* refer to the four ārya stages in the Hīnayāna path: stream-enterer, once-returner, nonreturner, and arhat. The *four candidacies* (*pratipannaka*) refer to the four candidates for these four fruitions. The *three levels of sagacity* refer to bodhisattvas on the three preliminary levels of the Mahāyāna path: the ten abidings, ten practices, and ten dedications. The *ten stages of sanctity* refer to advanced bodhisattvas on the ten "grounds," or *bhūmi*. *Virtual enlightenment* indicates the fifty-first of the fifty-two stages of the bodhisattva path, while *sublime enlightenment* is the fifty-second. The bodhisattva who has reached the stage of virtual enlightenment enters this stage after eradicating all ignorance. Sublime enlightenment is the realm of the buddhas, who have eradicated all types of defilements.

Gradual advancement in practice involves a series of stages. However, since there are originally no stages in the dharma nature, you may practice all you want, but there is nothing actually to practice and there is neither coming nor going.

"We gain awakening where there is a spiritual mentor. A spiritual mentor preaches the dharma to us. All the buddhas appear in the world in order to preach the dharma to sentient beings. Since Kātyāyana transmitted the dharma of the real characteristic of things with only the mind that is subject to production and cessation, he was reprimanded by Vimalakīrti.

於善知識處 得契悟 善知識與我說法 諸佛出世 與衆生說法 迦旃延祇為以生滅心 傳實相法 被淨名呵責.

Mahākātyāyana came from South India. He was one of the ten chief disciples of the Buddha and famous for his skill in explicating the meaning of the Buddha's sermons. In *Vimalakīrti's Instructions*, when the Buddha asked him to visit Vimalakīrti and inquire about his illness, Kātyāyana replied,

> World Honored One, I am not qualified to visit him and inquire about his illness. Why? Because I recall how in the past the Buddha had briefly addressed all the bhikṣus on the essentials of the dharma. Later, I elaborated on the meaning of what he had said, discussing the meaning of impermanence, suffering, emptiness, nonself, and tranquil extinction. At that time, Vimalakīrti approached me and said, "Ah, Kātyāyana! You must not expound on the dharma of the real characteristics of things with mental factors that are associated with production and cessation. Kātyāyana! Utimately, all dharmas are not produced and do not cease; this is the meaning of impermanence. The five aggregates are utterly empty, without anything arising; this is the meaning of suffering. All dharmas ultimately involve nothing that exists; this is the meaning of emptiness. Self and nonself are not two; this is the meaning of nonself. Dharmas originally are not burning and now are unextinguished; this is the meaning of tranquil extinction." When he expounded this teaching, the minds of all the bhikṣus gained liberation. This is why I say I am not qualified to visit him and inquire about his illness.[196]

"I say as clearly as I can that all dharmas are originally unbound, so what need is there to free them? They are originally immaculate, so what need is there to purify them? Therefore, it is said, 'The real characteristic of things is just so.'[197] How then can it be expressed? Currently, you simply master states of mind that involve right and wrong or stains and purity, or gain knowledge of this and understanding of that, or travel all over the world, watching people and trying to determine who has the mind's eye, or who is strong and who weak. If this is what you are doing, the difference will be as huge as that between heaven and earth. What then is all this talk about 'seeing the nature'?"

分明道 一切法本來無縛 何用解他 本來不染 何用淨他 故云 實相如是 豈可說乎 汝今祇成是非心染淨心 學得一知一解 遶天下行 見人 便擬定當取 誰有心眼 誰彊誰弱 若也如此 天地懸殊 更說什麼見性.

The original real characteristic of things cannot be sullied, divided up, burned, or augmented. It is originally just so. All sorts of mirages are created in accord with causes and conditions. The mirages that have been so created include all types of distinctions, such as right and wrong or pure and defiled. However, the real characteristic of things is always the same, being neither produced nor extinguished. Without according with this original source, you cannot overcome conceptual understanding, and you will find yourself weighing the spiritual level and strength of every person you meet. And once you generate such distinctions, you will be as far from the original ground as heaven is from earth. Therefore Seon masters seek to awaken their students by saying, "Do not choose between this and that," or "Do not allow yourself to become tainted."

If you attain a penetrating, great awakening, then all distinctions and discriminations will disappear. Once even subtle delusions vanish, all delusions will be revealed to be the mind's sublime functions, not stained by any mirages.

[Pei Xiu] asked, "You've noted that 'the nature is seeing and seeing is the nature,' which means that the nature itself is free

from obstructions and restrictions. Why is it, then, that if something is blocking our view, we can't see beyond it; or if something in the sky is close, we can see it, but if it is distant, we can't?"

[The master] replied, "This [question] derives from a view of differentiation that you have mistakenly raised. 'If something is blocking our view, we can't see beyond it' means that, if nothing were there, you would say you could see. But you would then presume that the nature can be blocked or obstructed when there is actually no connection at all between them. The nature neither sees nor does not see. The dharma also neither sees nor does not see. For those who have seen the nature, where wouldn't their original nature be? Consequently, the six rebirth destinies and the four modes of birth, as well as mountains, streams, and lands, are all the pristine, luminous essence of our natures. Therefore, it is said, 'Seeing a visual object is seeing the mind,'[198] for a visual object and the mind are not different.

問 既言性即見 見即性 祇如性自無障礙無劑限 云何隔物即不見 又於虛空中近即見 遠即不見者 如何 師云 此是你妄生異見 若言隔物不見 無物言見 便謂性有隔礙者 全無交涉 性且非見非不見 法亦非見非不見 若見性人 何處不是我之本性 所以六道四生山河大地 總是我之性淨明體 故云見色便見心 色心不異故.

Seeing everything is ultimately the mind seeing everything, because without the mind, you wouldn't see anything. You are able to see everything else because you have already seen the mind. Believe, therefore, that you are seeing the mind. This is not easy to believe, because sentient beings do not realize the reality that they are seeing the nature. Before being told to believe in this prospect, you should believe that you are in fact already seeing the nature.

The nature originally is free from obstructions or restrictions. In that case, if you aroused the views of "identity" or "difference," then those views would become obstructions and would create false forms. No one is separate from the nature, so everyone is able to see, hear, sense, and know.

The cognizing mind creates illusory mirages, doing useless things that in turn are deceiving and deceptive. If you illuminate the nature, it's enough just to put it all down. However, Layman Pei Xiu gave rise to intellectual views and interpretations and created unnecessary troubles for himself by trying to apply reason.

There is originally no discrimination among the five types of eyes—physical eye, divine eye, wisdom eye, dharma eye, and buddha eye—that the Buddha mentions in the *Diamond Sūtra*.[199] Discrimination appeared because of false views. Since the real characteristic of things is nondual, everything is identical from the standpoint of the origin. The physical eye is the divine eye and is also the buddha eye.

Pei Xiu misunderstood because, as Vimalakīrti said above, he expounded the dharma of the real characteristic of things while using the discriminating mind that is associated with production and cessation. If you thoroughly accord with original reality, all doubts will naturally disappear, like a snowflake falling onto a red-hot brazier.

"If you are one who sees, hears, senses, and knows only by grasping at sensory characteristics, and you presume you will be able to gain a vision [of the mind] only by removing the things before your eyes, you fall into two-vehicle adherents' intellectual understanding, which derives from dependent power.[200] You presume you can only see something nearby in the sky but not far away—this [view] is associated with the non-Buddhists. I say as clearly as I can that it is neither inside nor outside; it is neither nearby nor far away. The nature of the myriad things is nearby but invisible. If we can't see it even when it's nearby, what's the point of saying that you can't see it when it's far away?"

祇為取相作見聞覺知 去卻前物 始擬得見者 即墮二乘人中依通見解也 虛空中 近則見 遠則不見 此是外道中收 分明道 非內亦非外 非近亦非遠 近而不可見者 萬物之性也 近尚不可見 更道遠而不可見 有什麼意旨.

Since most people only see, hear, sense, and know things that belong to the world of appearances, those who can see things that are behind other things are presumed to have "dependent power." People also say that they can see things that are nearby but not things that are far away, because their perception of visual forms is dependent on their physical eyes. Such sensory perception has nothing to do with whether they can see the nature.

Similarly, people think that they cannot see the nature because it is obscured by defilements and false thoughts, so they just try to remove those defilements in order to see it. Bear in mind that the sky remains the same whether clouds appear or disappear.

Although buddhas and sentient beings both make use of the nature, this nature cannot be seen by their physical eyes; it can be seen only by their dharma eyes. This nature is neither nearby nor far away. Even though it is always clearly present right before your eyes, you are called a "blind fool," because you let it slip away.

34. If One Thought Does Not Arise, That Is Bodhi

[A monk] asked, "How will you instruct practitioners who do not comprehend what you've said, master?"

The master replied, "I do not have a single thing and have never conveyed a single thing to anyone else. Since time immemorial, you have received others' instructions and sought insight and understanding. Does this mean that both master and disciple have fallen into royal difficulties? This is all you need to know: if you do not sense even a single thought, you will be free from the body of sensation (*vedanākāya*); if you do not perceive even a single thought, you will be free from the body of perception (*saṃjñākāya*); if you absolutely do not move and act, you will be free from the body of volitional factors (*saṃskārakāya*); if you do not conceptualize, conjecture, and discriminate, you will be free from the body of consciousness (*vijñānakāya*).

問 學人不會 和尚如何指示 師云 我無一物 從來不曾將一物與人 你無始已來 祇為被人指示 覓契覓會 此可不是弟子與師俱陷王難 你但知 一念不受即是無受身 一念不想 即是無想身 決定不遷流造作 即是無行身 莫思量卜度分別 即是無識身.

The true meaning of "leaving the household life" to become a monk has nothing to do with leaving the house. If you are awakened, you have left the household life, even if you are a layperson; if you are not awakened, then you are still living in the household, even if you are a monk. The real meaning of "leaving the household life" is to stay separate from characteristics. If you just follow others' teachings, there is no chance for you to escape the house of the five aggregates. If you do not stay separate from characteristics, whatever it is you are doing, you are not free from the fetters of your body.

If you open your eyes to the Buddhadharma and stay separate from characteristics, then notions of both freedom and restraint are irrelevant. These words are a severe instruction and, at the same time, a primary phrase (*yiju/ ilgu* 一句) that directly reveals the real characteristic of things.

"When, like now, you discretely give rise to a single thought, you enter back into the twelvefold chain of dependent origination (*pratītyasamutpāda*): with ignorance (*avidyā*) as condition, there are predispositions (*saṃskāra*), which serve as both a cause and an effect. This chain continues on up to old age and death, which also serves as both a cause and an effect. Therefore Sudhana may have [traveled on pilgrimage] to 110 places seeking a spiritual mentor, but he was only searching within the twelvefold chain of dependent origination. At the end, he met Maitreya, who instructed Sudhana to go back and visit Mañjuśrī [his very first mentor]. 'Mañjuśrī' refers to the ignorance of your original ground.

你如今纔別起一念 即入十二因緣 無明緣行亦因亦果 乃至老死亦因亦果 故善財童子一百一十處求善知識 祗向十二因緣中求 最後見彌勒 彌勒卻指見文殊 文殊者即汝本地無明.

If you are not in accord with your original mind and just give rise to thoughts, you cannot escape the twelvefold chain of dependent origination. The twelvefold chain refers to the twelve links of ignorance, predispositions, consciousness, materiality and mentality, six sense bases, sense contact, sensation, craving, clinging, existence, birth, and old age and death, in that order.

Sudhana is a practitioner of the Way who goes on an extensive pilgrimage in search of the dharma in "Entering the Dharma Realm," the lengthy final chapter of the *Flower Garland Sūtra*. After visiting fifty-three spiritual mentors, he entered the realm of enlightenment.

Huangbo, however, offers this astonishing statement, "'Mañjuśrī' refers to the ignorance of your original ground." In doctrinal studies, practitioners go through a sequence of steps one by one, symbolized by these fifty-three teachers, to access the dharma realm. In Seon, regardless of ignorance, the true essence remains simply such and unmoving (*ruru budong / yeoyeo budong* 如如不動).

There is an expression, "When Maitreya snapped his fingers, Sudhana suddenly forgot all about birth and death."[201] Maitreya made Sudhana suddenly forget what he learned from his fifty-three teachers and sent him back to Mañjuśrī. From the standpoint of the original ground, all Sudhana had learned from his previous teachers was the mind still subject to production and cessation, which remained part of the twelvefold chain of dependent origination.

This question was asked from the standpoint of the mind that remained subject to production and cessation. Master Huangbo repeatedly instructs the questioner to turn around that mind that is subject to production and cessation and accord directly with the real characteristic of things.

Do not try to distinguish what is right and what is wrong in this world of birth and death, where all kinds of distinctions and discriminations arise, such as the twelvefold chain and the three poisons of greed, hatred, and delusion. Instead turn one thought around and realize the mind clearly.

"If you seek outside for a spiritual mentor as one thought succeeds another, then as soon as a thought arises, it ceases, and as soon as it ceases, another thought arises. Therefore you bhikṣus also experience birth, old age, sickness, and death. Since you continue to reciprocate with a cause and to respond with an effect, you are subject to the production and cessation of the five groupings [of factors]. The five groupings are the five aggregates. But when one thought does not arise, the eighteen cognitive elements (*dhātu*) become empty. This is the flower and fruit of bodhi. This state of mind is then numinous wisdom and the numinous terrace. But if you abide in or cling to anything, your body will become a corpse, which is also called 'a ghost guarding a corpse.'[202]

> 若心心別異向外求善知識者 一念纔生即滅 纔滅又生 所以汝等比丘 亦生亦老亦病亦死 酬因答果已來 即五聚之生滅 五聚者五陰也 一念不起 即十八界空 即是便是菩提華果 即心便是靈智 亦云靈臺 若有所住著 即身為死屍 亦云守死屍鬼.

Master Huangbo here says, "You bhikṣus," suggesting that this latter part of the "Account of Activities" in the *Wanling Record* must not have been addressed to Grand Councilor Pei Xiu. This part was probably teachings that Huangbo had given at the monastery that were later appended to the *Wanling Record*.

If you seek the dharma outside your original mind, that mind will become the five aggregates that arise and cease and that are subject to the law of cause and effect. The eighteen cognitive elements consist of the six sense faculties (eye, ear, nose, tongue, body, and mind), their six sense objects, and the corresponding six sense consciousnesses. The five aggregates and the eighteen cognitive elements are categories that are commonly used in Buddhist scripture to analyze mentality.

35. The Dharma Gate of Nonduality

[A monk] asked, "When Vimalakīrti remained silent, Mañjuśrī praised him, saying, 'This is the true entrance to the dharma gate of nonduality.' What does this mean?"

The master answered, "The dharma gate of nonduality is your original mind. Either to say or not to say something involves production and cessation. When he remained silent, he revealed nothing. Therefore Mañjuśrī praised him."

問 淨名默然 文殊讚歎云 是真入不二法門 如何 師云 不二法門 即你本心也 說與不說 即有起滅 無言說時 無所顯示 故文殊讚歎.

In the "Dharma Gate of Nonduality" chapter in *Vimalakīrti's Instructions*, Vimalakīrti asks the bodhisattvas who had come to visit him on his sickbed: "How do bodhisattvas enter the gate of nonduality?" In response, thirty-two bodhisattvas present their answers one by one. They all answer that they entered the dharma gate by unifying ultimate truth (*paramārthasatya*) and conventional truth (*saṃvṛtisatya*). Finally, Mañjuśrī says, "My understanding is that it means to be free from words, speech, and cognition and to leave behind all questions and answers. This is entering the dharma gate of nonduality." Then he asks Vimalakīrti for his response, but Vimalakīrti just stays silent, not saying anything. Mañjuśrī praises Vimalakīrti, saying, "Excellent! Excellent!"[203]

The eighty-fourth case in Yuanwu Keqin's *Blue Cliff Record* is "Vimalakīrti's Dharma Gate of Nonduality."[204] Xuedou's verse commentary to that case notes, "Since Vimalakīrti escaped by remaining silent,/ the golden-haired lion had nowhere to look for him." Vimalakīrti's silence has been praised as a clap of thunder, the loudest sound in the world.

The attendant bodhisattvas all abandoned words in order to hear the dharma gate of nonduality. Mañjuśrī abandoned words without ever using words. However, as Yuanwu pointed out, "This was a sacred tortoise dragging its tail. In wiping away his tracks, he was leaving traces." Vimalakīrti then swept away all of Mañjuśrī's remaining traces by remaining silent.

[A monk] asked, "Since Vimalakīrti did not speak, does that mean that all sound was eliminated or not?"

The master answered, "Speech is silence and silence is speech, for speech and silence are nondual. Therefore, it is said, 'The real nature of sound also never ceases.'[205] Mañjuśrī's original hearing never ceases either. Therefore the Tathāgata's speech is eternal, for there has never been a time when he has not been speaking. The Tathāgata's speech is the dharma and the dharma is his speech, for the dharma and his speech are nondual.

云 淨名不說 聲有斷滅否 師云 語即默 默即語 語默不二 故云聲之實性 亦無斷滅 文殊本聞 亦無斷滅 所以如來常說未曾有不說時 如來說即是法 法即是說 法說不二故.

The sky is the clouds and the clouds are the sky, for the sky and the clouds are nondual. In the same way, speech is silence and silence is speech.

As the forms that impinge on the eyes change, perceptual phenomena arise and discriminative states of mind appear. Due to this discrimination, sentient beings become caught in the cycle of birth and death and experience suffering. Sound is like the clouds in sky, which have no real essence. You generate various shapes through your discrimination, but none of those shapes are separate from the one great matter.

Therefore, although the Tathāgata preached his entire life, he did not preach even a single word. The Tathāgata's speech is the dharma and the dharma is his speech. Sentient beings are just the same.

An authentic patch-robed monk should sweep away even Vimalakīrti's silence.

> **"This is the case even with the reward body and the transformation body, bodhisattvas and śrāvakas, the mountains, streams, and lands, and water, birds, trees, and forests: they all simultaneously preach the dharma. Consequently, speech is preaching, but silence is also preaching. [The Tathāgata] preaches all day long without ever saying anything. If you are like the Tathāgata, you would consider silence to be the root."**
>
> 乃至報化二身 菩薩聲聞 山河大地 水鳥樹林 一時說法 所以語亦說 默亦說 終日說而未嘗說 既若如來 但以默為本.

The myriad things appear without ever leaving this very place. All the myriad dharmas are displayed in myriad different ways in accordance with causes and conditions, along with the dharma body.

Just as a bird in flight all day long leaves no traces, in the same way, if you accord with this principle, though you may preach the dharma all day long, there is nothing you preach. Thanks to your wise power that can accept changes, you live freely without abiding anywhere or clinging to anything. You can preach the dharma in accord with the capacities of your audience and deploy the dharma while remaining silent.

Listeners also should open their wisdom eyes so they can listen to the teaching of the dharma from both sentient beings and insentient things. This practice is wide, profound, and limitless. Although you are always close to it, it is inconceivable.

Huangbo's words here are intended to help the practitioners who have tasted the flavor of the practice but are still trying to understand the true quality of nonduality with their discriminative mind. These people still have a lingering propensity to discriminate between right and wrong.

However, it will not be easy for those who have not properly entered the path to understand and digest his words. If you try always to remain close to the dharma, you will have a chance to receive it more extensively and profoundly. If you take his precious teachings as a means to arouse your aspiration for enlightenment, then, transcending space and time, you will become an intimate friend of Master Huangbo and enjoy great freedom in this human realm.

36. No Traces

[A monk] asked, "How is it that śrāvakas hide their bodies away in the three realms of existence but cannot hide away in bodhi?"

The master answered, "The body is matter. Śrāvakas are only able to eradicate the views and conduct associated with the three realms of existence; they remain far removed from defilements, but they still cannot hide away in bodhi, so they may still be plucked out of bodhi by King Māra. Therefore they sit serenely in the forest and instead have only the slightest perception of the bodhi mind.

問 聲聞人藏形於三界 不能藏於菩提者 如何 師云 形者質也 聲聞人但能斷三界見修 已離煩惱 不能藏於菩提 故還被魔王於菩提中捉得 於林中宴坐 還成微細見菩提心也.

Disturbances (*huo/hok* 惑) is an early Chinese equivalency for the Buddhist technical term *defilements* (*kleśa, fannao/beonnoe* 煩惱), referring to deluded states of mind. Disturbances are of two types. The disturbances deriving from wrong views (*jianhuo/gyeonhok* 見惑) refers to the defilements that the sixth mental consciousness creates in response to mental objects. The disturbances deriving from conduct (*xiuhuo/suhok* 修惑) refer to the defilements of greed, hatred, and delusion that the first five sense consciousnesses of eye, ear, nose, tongue, and body generate due to clinging to sense objects. It is said that if you overcome these two types of disturbances, you will attain nirvāṇa and escape continued birth and death in the three realms of existence.

If you overcome the disturbances deriving from wrong views, you will reach the stage of the path of vision (*darśanamārga*; *jiandaowei*/*gyeondowi* 見道位); if you remove the disturbances deriving from conduct, you will reach the stage of the path of cultivation (*bhāvanāmārga*; *xiudaowei*/*sudowi* 修道位). Those who overcome these two disturbances hide their bodies away in the three realms of existence—sensuality, subtle materiality, and immateriality—because they have left behind defilements. However, they still retain the subtle delusion that they must cultivate the Way. Therefore they continue their meditation practice in the forest and enjoy just doing that. Those who cultivate the Way should completely sweep away all traces of enlightenment and, without settling even for no-mind, live in a state of everyday mind.

"Bodhisattvas absolutely neither abandon nor cling to either the three realms of existence or bodhi. Since they do not cling to anything, they cannot be found among the seven elements. Since they do not abandon anything, non-Buddhists and Māra will never be able to locate them either. If you are disposed to clinging to a single dharma, imprints will already have been already created. If you imprint 'clinging to existence,' the imprints of the six rebirth destinies and the four modes of birth will be displayed. If you imprint 'clinging to emptiness,' the imprint of signlessness will appear. Now, you just need to know that if you absolutely do not imprint a single thing, that imprint will be neither identical to nor different from the void. Voidness is originally not void; the imprint is originally not existent.

菩薩人 已於三界菩提 決定不捨不取 不取故 七大中覓他不得 不捨故 外魔亦覓他不得 汝但擬著一法 印子早成也 印著有 即六道四生文出 印著空 即無相文現 如今但知 決定不印一切物 此印為虛空不一不二 空本不空 印本不有.

Since bodhisattvas act without doing anything, you cannot find them though you may try to locate them in the seven great elements of earth, water, fire, wind, space, sight, and consciousness. Since they do not fall into emptiness either, non-Buddhists and Māra cannot find them either, however much they try. If you try to reveal, realize, or cultivate something, that will always leave behind traces, because it is like printing something with a stamp.

If you do not cling to anything you do, then "wherever you are, you will be your own master, and wherever you stand, all will be just right."[206]

> **"The appearance of all the buddhas of the worlds as vast as space in the ten directions is like the sight of a flash of lightning. All the numinous wriggling creatures appear like an echo. Lands as numerous as tiny motes of dust in the ten directions appear like a drop of water in the ocean. All the profound teachings sound like an illusion or a conjurer's trick. Each and every mind is not different; each and every dharma is not different. It is the same as a thousand sūtras and ten thousand treatises being just your one mind. If you can avoid clinging to a single sign, then it is said,**
>
> **In this way, the one mind,**
> **is assiduously adorned with skillful means.**[207]
>
> 十方虚空世界諸佛出世 如見電光一般 觀一切蠢動含靈 如響一般 見十方微塵國土 恰似海中一滴水相似 聞一切甚深法 如幻如化 心心不異 法法不異 乃至千經萬論 祇為你之一心 若能不取一切相 故言如是一心中 方便勤莊嚴.

Although it is said that all the buddhas in the worlds of the ten directions save sentient beings with their skillful means, there are in fact no sentient beings to be saved.

Therefore, although the buddhas appear in the world, they in fact never appear. Appearance and disappearance, birth and death, are just illusions. Even though the Buddha provided all sorts of steps and provisional means in order to help suffering sentient beings, in fact not even once did he provide them. However, like Master Huangbo, if you thoroughly understand the one mind, you will live a life in the middle way, which will be "assiduously adorned with skillful means."

If you listen repeatedly to Master Huangbo's teachings, you can understand them to some degree. Just like Pei Xiu, those who have an experience will obtain the gist of Seon. But even if you do not, you will gain a great benefit if you arouse your aspiration for enlightenment. If you come to have an ear for Seon teachings, you will gradually be able to let things go. You will gain the strength to listen without actually listening to anything.

Even so, be careful to not just study the words alone.

37. The Sage Kṣāntivādin

[A monk] asked, "What is the meaning of 'long ago, my body [of the sage Kṣāntivādin] was dismembered by King Kaliṅga'?"[208]

The master replied, "The sage is your mind and Kaliṅga is the penchant to seek out something. Not guarding the throne [and instead going out hunting] is called craving for gains. Practitioners these days do not accumulate merit or amass blessings; instead they choose to study whatever it is that they see. How are they any different from Kaliṅga? Seeing visual objects is like poking out the sage's eyes; hearing sounds is like cutting off the sage's ears; it is the same whenever they perceive or sense anything. This is why he said that his body was torn limb from limb.'"

問 如我昔為歌利王 割截身體 如何 師云 仙人者即是你心 歌利王好求也 不守王位 謂之貪利 如今學人 不積功累德 見者便擬學 與歌利王何別 如見色時 壞卻仙人眼 聞聲時 壞卻仙人耳 乃至覺知時 亦復如是 喚作節節支解.

Master Huangbo is referring here to the *Diamond Sūtra*'s story of King Kaliṅga, which he discussed above in chapter 13 of the *Wanling Record*. As the sūtra relates, King Kaliṅga was jealous of the ascetic Kṣāntivādin ("Endurer"), who was Śākyamuni Buddha in a former life, and dismembered his body. Master Huangbo here reveals the deeper meaning of this story. The sage Kṣāntivādin is our original mind while King Kaliṅga symbolizes the three poisons of greed, hatred, and delusion. The king going out hunting and neglecting his royal duties refers to forgetting our original mind because of our craving for material possessions. According to the master, practitioners who ignorantly look outside for learning, without staying in accord with their own original minds, are just like King Kaliṅga. We see, hear, sense, know, conceive, and discriminate; we look outside when we generate thoughts to chase external phenomena. Master Huangbo compares this tendency of ours to the king who went out hunting and dismembered the sage's body.

When we practice holding a hwadu, we sometimes feel unwittingly the violence of explosive energy welling up inside. In the story, the more the king tears the sage's body apart, the brighter his body becomes; in the same way, the more we overcome all sorts of conflicts and tensions welling up inside us by relying on the hwadu's power, the clearer and brighter our minds and bodies become.

Therefore, just as the king finally repented of his actions before the sage and threw down his sword, when we overcome the meditative hindrances (*nīvaraṇa*) of lethargy and torpor (*styāna-middha*) and restlessness and worry (*auddhatya-kaukṛtya*), the original pristine mind is revealed.

[A monk] stated, "Only when the sage practiced forbearance was he then not torn limb from limb. Thus it cannot be claimed that it is the one mind that endures or does not endure."

The master responded, "You have created the view that nothing is produced, the notion that there is something to endure, and the understanding that there is nothing to seek. These are all damaging."

[A monk] asked, "When the sage was being dismembered, did he experience pain or not?" He added, "If he didn't feel anything during this event, then who felt that pain?"

The master answered, "Seeing as you're not in pain, what could you be looking for here?"

云 祇如仙人忍時 不合更有節節支解 不可一心忍 一心不忍也 師云 你作無生見 忍辱解 無求解 總是傷損 云 仙人被割時 還知痛否 又云 此中無受者 是誰受痛 師云 你既不痛出頭來 覓箇甚麼.

The questioner here still clings to the routines of practice, so he asks: if we keep building our forbearance to avoid generating the mind that discriminates among things, won't we be in accord with the one mind? Such a perspective would generate an attachment to the act of forbearance.

Master Huangbo responds tersely (*dandao zhiru/dando jigip* 單刀直入) from the standpoint of the origin: if you're not in pain now, then that's it! Why go through the motions of enduring something?

38. Past, Present, and Future Are Unascertainable

[A monk] asked, "Did Dīpaṃkara Buddha prophecize that [the sage Kṣāntivādin's eventual attainment of enlightenment, when he would become Śākyamuni Buddha,] would take place within five hundred years or would take longer than five hundred years?"

The master replied, "He could not have prophecized that it would take place within five hundred years. 'Prophecizing' means you must never forget your root, abandon the conditioned realm, or cling to bodhi; you need only understand that time is timeless. Thus he could not have prophecized that [Kṣāntivādin's attainment of buddhahood] would take place within five hundred years or would take longer than five hundred years."

[A monk] asked, "Has he already understood that the three time periods are unascertainable or not?"

The master replied, "There is not a single dharma that can be ascertained."

[A monk] asked, "Then why is it said, 'We pass repeatedly through five-hundred-year periods;/ the extremes of both past and future are long?'"[209]

The master replied, "A five-hundred-year period is long and far away. Remember that [Kṣāntivādin] was then still a sage. Therefore, when Dīpaṃkara Buddha offered him this prophecy, there was in fact not even the slightest dharma to be ascertained."

問 然燈佛授記 為在五百歲中 五百歲外 師云 五百歲中不得授記 所言授記者 你本決定不忘 不失有為 不取菩提 但

以了世非世 亦不出五百歲外別得授記 亦不於五百歲中得授記 云 了世三際相不可得已否 師云 無一法可得 云 何故言 頻經五百世 前後極時長 師云 五百世長遠 當知猶是仙人 故然燈授記時 實無少法可得.

To prophecize someone's future attainment of enlightenment is a worldly prophecy; a genuine prophecy is "not even a single dharma is ascertainable." You should be able to completely understand such a principle and put it to use. Of course, the word "use" here means to use without using anything. Worldlings presume that time consists of past, present, and future. In fact, since even a single dharma cannot be ascertained, time is also nothing but an illusion revealed in accordance with causes and conditions. Dīpaṃkara Buddha's prophecy is made not from a temporal standpoint in which time flows from the past through the present to the future but from the standpoint that not even a single dharma can be ascertained.

In genuine almsgiving, the giver, the recipient, and the gift are all empty. Since a buddha acts without doing anything, prophecizing is also like this: since the giver and recipient of a prophecy and the prophecy itself are each originally empty and pristine, they leave no traces.

The measuring unit of time in this episode, "within five hundred years or longer than five hundred years," is also an illusion. At that juncture where you turn one thought around and all delusions disappear, there is no room for the slightest sense of time. Therefore the master said, "You need only understand that time is timeless."

Here, the questioner asks his questions from the standpoint of understanding the meaning of "prophecize" with his discriminating mind, wherein all sorts of mirages are created. However, since Master Huangbo stood at the spot where mirages have not yet been created, he clearly instructs that prophecy means there is not the slightest dharma to be ascertained.

39. The Dharma Body Is Unascertainable

[A monk] asked, "In the scriptural teachings it is said,

> **By dissipating the distorted views (*viparyāsa*) I have created over countless kalpas,**
> **I obtain the dharma body without passing through incalculable kalpas.[210]**

"What does this mean?"

The master replied, "If you presume you attain realization by practicing for three incalculable kalpas, you will have no success even after kalpas as numerous as the sands of the Ganges. But if in a single *kṣaṇa* [instant] you obtain the dharma body and directly see the nature, this is the culminating discourse of the three-vehicle teachings. Why is this so? Seeing the dharma body as something that can be obtained is a view associated with the provisional (*neyartha*) teachings."

問 教中云 銷我億劫顛倒想 不歷僧祇獲法身者 如何 師云 若以三無數劫修行 有所證得者 盡恒沙劫不得 若於一剎那 中獲得法身 直了見性者 猶是三乘教之極談也 何以故 以見 法身可獲故 皆屬不了義教中收.

Since the dharma body is formless, it can be neither gained nor lost. Originally, there is not a single dharma. Forms just appear in accordance with causes and conditions. However many eons you may practice, if you abide in or cling to anything, it will be impossible to attain buddhahood. Striving to attain realization brings suffering instead.

If you perceive a pure, calm, and clear place during your practice, it is easy to cling to that place and strive to preserve it and teach others to do the same. Being bound by such a goal is not true practice. If you turn one thought around and attain awakening, you will know that even that awakening is false.

The dharma body is unobtainable. Wake up from your dream and gain the strength you need to digest the principle that is not a dream. If you keep thinking about escaping the dream, you will have great difficulty actually waking from the dream.

Since awakening is universally valid, it is not available only to special people. The definitive teaching that can open someone's eyes is not something approached gradually over time. To practice by waiting for the mud to sink below the water is a provisional teaching.

Seon is a dharma gate premised on the prospect of sudden awakening. It is a definitive teaching.

40. All Relativity Is Eradicated

[A monk] asked, "Do those who see the dharma and have sudden understanding perceive the patriarch's intent?"

The master answered, "The patriarch's mind transcends empty space."

[A monk] asked, "Does it have limits?"

The master answered, "Limited and limitless are dharmas that involve counting and measuring. The patriarch said, 'It is neither limited nor limitless, neither non-limited nor non-limitless, because it severs all relativity.' If you practitioners are still not able get beyond even these three-vehicle teachings, how can you call yourselves Seon adepts? Let me state this as clearly as I can: first-class trainees in Seon should not heedlessly and mistakenly generate discriminative views. 'A person who has drunk water knows for himself whether it is cold or warm.'[211] In that kṣaṇa when you are walking or standing, thought-moment after thought-moment will remain undifferentiated. If this is not the case, you will not escape the cycle of rebirth."

問 見法頓了者 見祖師意否 師云 祖師心出虛空外 云 有限劑否 師云 有無限劑 此皆數量對待之法 祖師云 且非有限量 非無限量 非非有無限量 以絕待故 你如今學者 未能出得三乘教外 爭喚作禪師 分明向汝道 一等學禪 莫取次妄生異見 如人飲水 冷煖自知 一行一住一刹那間 念念不異 若不如是 不免輪回.

Counting and measuring depend on thinking and discriminating. The original real characteristic of things cannot be fathomed through such means. Because the patriarch's intent, the gist of his teachings, always lies in the origin, it cannot be approached by counting and measuring. It also does not leave any traces.

Since the three vehicles of śrāvakas, pratyekabuddhas, and bodhisattvas are teachings that involve sequential stages, you cannot understand through them the patriarch's intent, which severs all relativity. It is only proper that a real Seon master not only digests the relative teachings of the three vehicles but also penetrates via the mind-to-mind transmission the original real characteristic of things, wherein the ways of words and speech are eradicated and the locus of mental functioning is annihilated.

41. It Is Hard to See the Genuine Relics of the Buddha

[A monk] asked, "The Buddha's body is unconditioned, so it doesn't involve anything that can be counted. Why is it, then, that his body yielded eight bushels and four pecks of *śarīra* [relics]?"

The master replied, "If you have such a view, you're just seeing fake śarīra, not genuine śarīra.

[A monk] asked, "Do śarīra inherently exist or are they created through the virtue derived from the Buddha's practice?"

The master answered, "They don't inherently exist, but they're also not created through the virtue of his practice."

[A monk] asked, "If they neither inherently exist nor are created through the virtue of his practice, then why are the Tathāgata's śarīra so thoroughly tempered and refined that his golden bones survive eternally?"

The master scolded him, saying, "With this sort of view, how can you be called a Seon practitioner? Have you ever seen bones in empty space? All the buddhas' minds are the same as the great void. What bones are you going to find there?"

[A monk] asked, "What are these śarīra I've seen today, then?"

The master answered, "You have produced these from your own delusional mind and perceived that they are śarīra."

問 佛身無為 不墮諸數 何故佛身舍利八斛四斗 師云 你作如是見 祇見假舍利 不見真舍利 云 舍利為是本有 為復功勳 師云 非是本有 亦非功勳 云若非本有 又非功勳 何故如來舍利 唯鍊唯精 金骨常存 師乃呵云 你作如此見解 爭喚

作學禪人 你見虛空曾有骨否 諸佛心同太虛 覓什麼骨 云 如今見有舍利 此是何法 師云 此從你妄想心生 即見舍利.

The questioner here directly asks the kind of compelling question ordinary people might want badly to ask, like an itch they want to scratch: the Buddha's body is unconditioned and therefore formless, so how could it leave relics?

Master Huangbo says that since this question comes from the level of one who just sees relics' external form, the questioner cannot see genuine relics. Those who open their dharma eyes, which see the real characteristic of all things, clearly know that all sentient beings without exception possess the buddha nature. Those who do not open the dharma eye do useless things, seeking the buddha by chasing forms. Master Huangbo here points out how wrong it is for people to arouse a discriminative mind regarding these material relics and not be able to reflect back on themselves.

Whatever has form, including the relics of the Buddha, is false. Those who cling to forms ask, "Since the Buddha's relics are obviously present, why do you, Master, deny their existence?" Since genuine relics of the Buddha transcend forms, ordinary people cannot see them.

Although he chastised the questioner, Master Huangbo compassionately instructed practitioners to turn one thought around and accord with the original root and not allow themselves to be dragged around by the delusional mind. Clinging to relics that can be seen by our physical eyes is the delusional mind.

[A monk] asked, "Do you, Master, have śarīra or not? Please show them to us!"

The master replied, "Genuine śarīra are hard to see. Only if you completely pulverize Mount Sumeru into tiny dust motes with your bare hands will you see genuine śarīra. Those who practice Seon and train on the Way must not produce a mind that is grounded anywhere. If you just forget conceptualization, the Buddha's Way will flourish; but if you discriminate, Māra's minions will thrive. Ultimately not the slightest bit of dharma, not even as small as a hair, can be ascertained.

云 和尚還有舍利否 請將出來看 師云 真舍利難見 你但以十指 撮盡妙高峰為微塵 即見真舍利 夫參禪學道 須得一切處不生心 祇論忘機即佛道隆 分別即魔軍盛 畢竟無毛頭許少法可得.

Since the questioner, with a discriminative mind, requests Master Huangbo to display his relics, the master engages in a Seon exchange with him.

Long ago, Layman Pang asked Mazu Daoyi, "Who is it who does not keep company with all the dharmas?"

Master Mazu replied, "Wait till you've swallowed in one swig all the water of the West River, then I'll tell you."[212] Through these words, Layman Pang realized the gist of Master Mazu's teachings.

Although Master Huangbo directly instructs him here, the questioner does not understand. If you arouse even a hair's breadth of discrimination in the mind, you will be as far from the original root as heaven is from earth. Seon practitioners should immediately overcome the discriminative mind by opening their eyes to the fact that there is no dharma to be ascertained. However, it is also true that it is difficult for ordinary people not to arouse the discriminative mind while immersed in the sense fields, because they are not yet free from the functioning of karmic cause and effect. A discriminative mind may arise in Seon practitioners because of karma, but they should build their strength to see through external phenomena by accepting those phenomena just as they are. If you empty your mind and believe in causality, you will always penetrate to the truth.

42. There Is No Dharma to Be Transmitted

[A monk] asked, "To whom did the [First] Patriarch transmit the dharma?"

The master replied, "He had no dharma to transmit to anyone."

[A monk] asked, "Why then did the Second Patriarch ask the master to pacify his mind?"

The master replied, "If you say it exists, then the Second Patriarch would have gained the mind by seeking it. However, since he looked for the mind but couldn't find it, [Bodhidharma] told him, 'I have already pacified it for you.' If there were something to gain, you would end up back in production and cessation."

問祖傳法付與何人 師云 無法與人 云 云何二祖請師安心 師云 你若道有 二祖即合覓得心 覓心不可得故 所以道 與你安心竟 若有所得 全歸生滅.

Master Huangbo clearly points out that since the dharma cannot be seen, it is not something to be given or received. Nonetheless, the questioner persists: "If there is no dharma to be transmitted, then why did Master Huike, the Second Patriarch, ask Bodhidharma to pacify his mind for him?" Master Huangbo then answers that, since the dharma is formless, it is not an object that can be gained or lost. Whenever somebody says that he or she gains something, that is false. What is false belongs to dharmas that involve production and cessation. It is nothing but a mirage created in accordance with causes and conditions.

Since there is nothing to be gained, the mind can be pacified.

43. Unobstructed Wisdom

[A monk] asked, "Did the Buddha bring an end to ignorance or not?"

The master replied, "Ignorance is the very site where all buddhas attain the Way.

問 佛窮得無明否 師云 無明即是一切諸佛得道之處.

In the history of humankind, Śākyamuni Buddha was the one who discovered a method for illuminating wisdom, which he then transmitted to the mundane world. Was there anyone before Śākyamuni Buddha who transmitted this method for revealing the wisdom that can remove ignorance? Once the great saint Śākyamuni Buddha showed the causal conditions through which the bright wisdom that had been covered by ignorance could be revealed, changes began to occur. Therefore, there is a huge difference in the quality of life before and after the Buddha appeared in the world.

If you attain realization, you will know that ignorance is the very locus of enlightenment.

"Therefore dependent origination is the site of enlightenment. Every single dust mote and visual object that you see accords with the ideal nature that has no boundaries. Wherever you lift and put down your feet is not separate from the site of enlightenment. The site of enlightenment is unascertainable. I tell you that this quality of being unascertainable is what is called 'sitting at the site of enlightenment.'"

所以緣起是道場 所見一塵一色 便合無邊理性 舉足下足不離道場 道場者無所得也 我向你道 祇無所得 名為坐道場.

The prospect of the Buddha's enlightenment occurs only at his enlightenment site (*bodhimaṇḍa*) and nowhere else. Therefore, whether ignorant or wise, material or immaterial, everything arises and changes here without disappearing there.

When you cling to conditioned external appearances, you suffer. But if you turn one thought around and penetrate to the fact that they are illusory fictions—and go even further to see that truth exists in those illusions—it can be said that you have opened your eyes and tasted the truth. Whether walking, standing, sitting, or reclining, whether speaking or keeping silence, whether active or still, you do not depart from the enlightenment site. Neither do wriggling creatures or invisible things.

The enlightenment site is neither brought from somewhere nor created. It is always present throughout past, present, and future. Although it is never separate from the myriad things, there is nothing that cannot be accomplished there. Therefore it is said that the real nature of ignorance is the nature's true form.

[A monk] asked, "Is ignorance [*wuming/mumyeong* 無明; lit. "absence of brightness"] bright or dark?"

The master replied, "It is neither bright nor dark. Brightness and darkness are alternating dharmas. Ignorance is not bright, but it is also not dark. Not being bright is just the original brightness. This one phrase 'not bright but not dark' confuses the eyes of the people of this world.

云 無明者 為明為暗 師云 非明非暗 明暗是代謝之法 無明且不明亦不暗 不明祇是本明 不明不暗 祇這一句子 亂卻天下人眼.

The true form of ignorance is neither bright nor dark. If you just learn the words without opening your eyes to the Buddhadharma, you will be unable to figure out what ignorance really is. Therefore the practice that leads students to experience the Buddhadharma is most precious of all.

What is truly bright is bright because it is free from all notions of brightness. It does not fall into the relative concepts of brightness or darkness. Since it brightens the myriad things, we may force on it the name "brightness," but by this we don't mean the brightness that is the opposite of darkness.

Since the original real characteristic of things stays separate from forms, it is infinite. It cannot be said that it exists from here to there. If this is illuminated, all discrimination will be ended.

"Therefore, it is said,

Even if this world were filled
with [śrāvakas] like Śāriputra,
and all of them together tried to comprehend it,
they still could not fathom the Buddha's wisdom.[213]

"His unobstructed wisdom extends throughout empty space;
there is no prospect of you being able to explain it verbally.

所以道 假使滿世間 皆如舍利弗 盡思共度量 不能測佛智
其無礙慧 出過虛空 無你語論處.

As the *Lotus Sūtra* states, even smart persons like Śāriputra cannot measure the great wisdom of the Buddha. There is a difference between these people and the Buddha that is as huge as that between the material and immaterial realms. Therefore, it is said, "If there is a hair's breadth of difference,/ heaven and earth are rent asunder."[214]

We may have a form subject to limitations, but shouldn't there be a way to fathom the true form that the Buddha himself realized? The Buddha appeared in this world and revealed teachings by which sentient beings could remove ignorance and be endowed with wisdom. We are fortunate that a path has been opened whereby we can attain awakening through Patriarchal Seon. We have to be grateful to the Buddha and patriarchs for their kindness in teaching us.

"Śākyamuni Buddha is as vast as the trichiliocosm. A bodhisattva suddenly appeared and stepped over him in a single stride. But even though he stepped over the entire trichiliocosm, he could not escape from a single hair follicle of Samantabhadra. Now what innate talent can help you study that?"

釋迦量等三千大千世界 忽有一菩薩出來一跨 跨卻三千大千世界 不出普賢一毛孔 你如今把什麼本領擬學他.

No matter how hard the monkey king Sun Wukong 孫悟空 tried, he could not escape the Buddha's palm;[215] so too, we cannot escape from a single hair follicle of Samantabhadra, the bodhisattva who sits at the Buddha's right side. What else is there to say?

The Buddha's enlightenment is this immense! Since it transcends all words and thoughts, we cannot reach it by applying some special skill.

[A monk] asked, "If it cannot be obtained by studying, then why is it said,

> **Returning to the source, the nature is nondual,**
> **but expedients involve many gates."[216]**

云 既是學不得 為什麼道 歸源性無二 方便有多門 如之何.

If there is nothing to be attained because of this original nonduality, then why should we practice, and why are there so many expedient gates?

Only those who are awakened have the capacity to help sentient beings open their eyes to wisdom. You must be able to realize your original nature through actual practice, not just by believing in and following the Buddha's teachings.

The master answered, "'Returning to the source, the nature is nondual' means that the real nature of ignorance is the nature of all the buddhas. 'But expedients involve many gates' refers to the following. Śrāvakas see the production of ignorance

and the extinction of ignorance. Pratyekabuddhas see only the extinction of ignorance but not the production of ignorance, so they realize tranquil extinction thought after thought. All the buddhas see sentient beings produced all day long without ever being produced and extinguished all day long without ever being extinguished. To be free from both production and extinction is the fruition of the Mahāyāna. Therefore, it is said,

> **When fruit ripens, enlightenment is complete;**
> **when flowers blossom, the whole world appears.**[217]

師云 歸源性無二者 無明實性 即諸佛性 方便有多門者 聲聞人見無明生 見無明滅 緣覺人但見無明滅 不見無明生 念念證寂滅 諸佛見眾生終日生而無生 終日滅而無滅 無生無滅 即大乘果 所以道 果滿菩提圓 華開世界起.

Since the original nature is nondual, the real nature of ignorance is in fact the buddha nature. Śrāvakas aim to realize impermanence by observing the production and cessation of ignorance. Pratyekabuddhas pay attention only to the cessation of ignorance, not its production, and thereby enjoy tranquil extinction; but this is also suffering. The buddhas realize that all phenomena that are produced, decay, and disappear are illusions and awaken to the fact that there are originally neither causes nor effects; therefore they are not subject to the law of causality.

Since originally there is no birth and death, it is said that the real nature of ignorance is the true nature.

Huangbo is quoting Prajñātāra, the twenty-seventh Indian patriarch, who conferred on Bodhidharma the following dharma-transmission verse:

> In the mind-ground sprouts all the seeds;
> it is from phenomena that the principle arises.
> When fruit ripens, enlightenment is complete;
> when flowers blossom, the whole world appears.

"'Lifting one's foot' is to be a buddha; 'putting down one's foot' is to be a sentient being. All the buddhas are 'foremost

among the bipeds' (*dvipadottama*), for they have the foot of principle and the foot of phenomena, the foot of sentient beings and the foot of birth and death, as well as all other kinds of feet. Since they are endowed with these feet, they need not seek them out.

舉足即佛 下足即衆生 諸佛兩足尊者 即理足 事足 衆生足 生死足 一切等足 足故不求.

Since the original place is complete in and of itself, it is neither redundant nor deficient. That is where there are no distinctions of either time or space.

Since there is no way adequately to explain this matter, there is nothing else we can say except that "the buddhas are endowed with all these kinds of feet." This is the true form of nirvāṇa. To try to explain such matters through doctrinal understanding will always reveal the limitations of language. We must never forget the greatness of the Buddha, who experienced the truth for himself and opened a way forward for sentient beings. As bipeds ourselves, we should strive to emulate the Buddha and also become foremost among the bipeds.

"Nowadays, when you emulate the Buddha thought after thought, you are despising sentient beings. If you despise sentient beings, you slander all the buddhas of the ten directions.

是你如今 念念學佛 即嫌著衆生 若嫌著衆生 即是謗他十方諸佛.

Ignorance is the collection of defilements and illusions. Everyone tries to abandon ignorance and to stay in the pure, quiescent, and clear place of the nature. However, all phenomena, whether good or evil, are not separate from that place and arise from there. Do not delude yourself into believing that good and evil come from some other source. They arise from there in accordance with causes and conditions. Therefore, to emulate the buddhas but despise sentient beings is as foolish as slandering all the buddhas of the three time periods.

> **"Consequently, when a buddha appears in the world, he picks up a shit pail and hauls away all the shit of conceptual proliferation. He just teaches you to get rid of the ideas of training the mind and seeing the mind that you have developed thus far. By completely removing them, you will not be swept away by conceptual proliferation. This can also be called 'hauling away shit.'**
>
> 所以佛出世來 執除糞器 蠲除戲論之糞 祇教你除卻從來學心見心 除得盡 即不墮戲論 亦云 搬糞出.

As a matter of fact, it is foolish to use the verb "to appear" in describing the manifestation of the buddhas. We simply use the expression "a buddha appears in the world" to make it easier for sentient beings to understand. "Picks up a shit pail and hauls away all the shit of conceptual proliferation" means that a buddha removes all traces of various types of ignorant thoughts. If you do not depart from the original true reality of the middle way, then whatever words you say will be like "hauling away shit."

> **"[A buddha] just teaches you not to produce states of mind. If states of mind are not produced, you will naturally be one of great wisdom. You must never discriminate between buddhas and sentient beings. Only by not engaging in any kind of discrimination can you finally enter our Caoxi gate [that is, the Southern school of the Sixth Patriarch].**
>
> 祇教你不生心 心若不生 自然成大智者 決定不分別佛與衆生 一切盡不分別 始得入我曹溪門下.

If you do not arouse the mind, then even though you hear loud noises all day long, you accept them without showing the slightest sign of being annoyed or bothered. This is because liking and disliking both belong to the functioning of the mind; they are like images reflected on the surface of a mirror. Whether things are illusory or real, how would their reflections ever be different from one other?

> **"Therefore, since ancient times, the previous saints have said, 'There is just a modicum of practice involved in my dharma gate.' Consequently, nonpractice is my dharma gate; there is only the gate of the one mind. Everyone arrives there, but no one dares to enter. But do not say no one does, for there are a few people who will succeed—those are the buddhas. Take care!"**
>
> 故自古先聖云 少行我法門 所以無行為我法門 祇是一心門 一切人到這裡盡不敢入 不道全無 祇是少人得 得者即是佛 珍重.

The phrase "a modicum of practice" refers to the state in which you practice without practicing. Since practice and nonpractice are nondual, it is like a bird flying through the sky all day long that leaves no traces. That empty sky contains neither ignorance nor enlightenment. You may work hard to enter the gate, but after you have entered it, there will remain neither the gate nor the person who entered it. Even though you entered the gate, you actually never entered anything.

The buddha is not somewhere else. When you turn your mind around, you will know.

44. How Not To Fall into Practice Ranks[218]

[A monk] asked, "How may we ensure that we don't fall into practice ranks [i.e., the fifty-two stages of the bodhisattva path]?"

The master replied, "'I eat all day, but without ever chewing even a single grain of rice.'[219] I walk all day, but without ever stepping on a single spot of ground. In these instances, there are no such characteristics as 'self' and 'others.' Without staying far removed from worldly affairs the whole day long, you are nonetheless not deceived by any sensory phenomena. Only then are you called an autonomous person.

問 如何得不落階級 師云 終日喫飯 未曾咬著一粒米 終日行 未曾踏著一片地 與麼時 無人我等相 終日不離一切事 不被諸境惑 方名自在人.

There are, in fact, no ranks in practice. Those who encounter the opportunity to attain sudden awakening immediately leave behind all characteristics and leap directly to the Tathāgata's realm. Such people chew without chewing anything and walk without walking anywhere. Their physical mouths may chew rice, but it is not their physical mouths that know how to chew. You should learn to emulate this principle of chewing without chewing anything. If you know what makes your mouth chew, you will be able to digest the meaning of these words. But if you don't, you will face a sheer precipice. It is not the mouth that chews; it is not I that chews; it is not that there is no chewing. You must directly awaken to this matter yourself. If you approach it only intellectually, you will never be able to escape the endless cycle of birth and death.

Seon is not something that exists outside this world. Know that thing that is unmoving when you move. In other words, digest what it means "to be unmoving while moving." This was already explained over a thousand years ago. If you still haven't digested it, then shame on you.

> **"At each and every moment, do not discern characteristics. Do not discern the three time-periods from the past into the future. The past has not vanished; the present does not remain; the future will not arrive. If you can comfortably sit upright and remain insouciant, without being bound by anything—only that is called liberation. Make every effort! Make every effort! Of the thousands or tens of thousands of people in this school, only three or five of them have gotten it. If you do not apply yourself to this matter, the day will come when calamity will strike. Therefore, it is said, 'If you work at taking care of this lifetime, who will suffer any lingering calamities in successive kalpas to come?'"**
>
> 念念不見一切相 莫認前後三際 前際無去 今際無住 後際無來 安然端坐 任運不拘 方名解脫 努力努力 此門中千人萬人 祇得三箇五箇 若不將為事 受殃有日在 故云 著力今生須了卻 誰能累劫受餘殃.

"Do not discern characteristics." The master may exhort you in this way, but you should be able to demonstrate that you originally discern nothing.

Although the master says to "comfortably sit upright," you should not just follow his words, misunderstanding that that's what you're supposed to be doing. If you want to demonstrate that you always sit without ever leaving the seat of enlightenment, you should be able to go with the flow and live in the state of nonaction.

Because it is not easy to cultivate the Way, only one or two among many are able to cultivate this practice. Since you are fortunate to have been born human and to have encountered the Buddhadharma in this lifetime, you should complete this great matter right now.

> **The master passed away on this mountain in this year [850] during the Dazhong era of the Tang dynasty. Emperor Xuanzong granted him the posthumous title Seon Master Duanji 斷際 ["Breaking all Limits"]. His stūpa was called Guangye 廣業 ["Expansive Action"].**
>
> 師於唐大中年中 終於本山 宣宗敕謚 斷際禪師 塔曰廣業.

After the Huichang persecution of Buddhism (842–45) during the Tang dynasty, Emperor Xuanzong ascended to the throne. His reign was called Dazhong ["The Great Mean"]. During this reign period, Master Huangbo passed away on Mount Huangbo in Gao'an province.

Master Duanji Huangbo's reliquary stūpa still stands today in the bamboo grove on Mount Huangbo.

Notes

1 This description derives from a verse attributed retrospectively to the founder of the Chan tradition, Bodhidharma 菩提達磨 (ca. late-fourth to early-fifth centuries). This first line of the verse initially appears in the *Anthology of the Patriarchs' Hall* (*Zutang ji*祖堂集) compiled in 952, and the complete verse in the *Garden of Matters from the Patriarchs' Hall* (*Zuting shiyuan* 祖庭事苑), compiled in 1108; see Robert E. Buswell, Jr., and Donald S. Lopez, Jr., *The Princeton Dictionary of Buddhism* (Princeton, NJ: Princeton University Press, 2014), 385, s.v. "jiaowai biechuan." For background on the importance of lineage in justifying Chan's sense of its own unique pedigree within Buddhism, see Seong-Uk Kim, "Three Places of Mind-Transmission: The Polemical Application of Mind-Transmission Stories in Korean Sŏn Buddhism," *Journal of the American Oriental Society* 133.4 (2013): 635–50.

2 This term is also seen transcribed in Western literature on Korean Buddhism as *kanhwa* Sŏn and in Chinese as *kanhua* Chan or *kan-hua* Ch'an. For an overview of traditional *ganhwa* Seon practice in Korea, see Robert E. Buswell, Jr., *The Zen Monastic Experience: Buddhist Practice in Contemporary Korea* (Princeton, NJ: Princeton University Press, 1992), and Robert E. Buswell, Jr., "The Short-Cut Approach of *K'an-hua* Meditation: The Evolution of a Practical Subitism in Chinese Ch'an Buddhism," in Peter N. Gregory, ed., *Sudden and Gradual Approaches to Enlightenment in Chinese Thought,* Kuroda Institute Studies in East Asian Buddhism 5 (Honolulu: University of Hawaii Press 1987), 321–77. For historical background on the development of *kanhua* Chan in China, see Morten Schlütter, *How Zen Became Zen: The Dispute over Enlightenment and the Formation of Chan Buddhism in Song-Dynasty China*, Kuroda Institute Studies in East Asian Buddhism 22 (Honolulu: University of Hawaii Press 2008). For a brief overview of this meditative technique, see Buswell and Lopez, *Princeton Dictionary*, 415–16 s.v. "kanhua Chan."

3 Hereafter, we will separate the Chinese and Korean transcriptions of Sinographs with a virgule or slash: e.g., *gong'an/gongan*, with the Chinese appearing first, the Korean second.

4 For a brief, but compelling, overview of Subul Sunim's approach to ganwha Seon practice, see Ryan Bongseok Joo (Haemin Sunim), "Gradual Experiences of Sudden Enlightenment: The Varieties of Ganhwa Seon Teachings in Contemporary Korea," in *Ganhwa Seon, Segye-reul bichuda*, Proceedings of the First International Conference on Ganhwa Seon (Seoul: Dongguk Daehakgyo Bulgyo Haksulwon, 2010), 2: 231–39. For this "what is it?" hwadu, see the account in Buswell and Lopez, *Princeton Dictionary*, 372, s.v. "imwŏtko."

5 Subul Sunim adopts both these metaphors from the *Essentials of Chan* (*Chanyao* / *Seonyo* 禪要), by the Yuan-dynasty master Gaofeng Yuanmiao 高峰原妙 (1238–95). For "silver mountain and iron wall" (*yinshan tiebi* / *eunsan cheolpyeok* 銀山鐵壁), see *Gaofeng Chanyao* 高峰禪要, Xuzangjing 1401:70.705a17, 707c10; for the "spiky burr of a chestnut" (*li jipeng* / *yul geukbong* 栗棘蓬), see 704c18, 707c19. Gaofeng also uses in this same context the metaphor of being trapped inside an "adamantine cage" (*jingang juan* / *geumgang gwon* 金剛圈), 704c18, 707c19. The *Essentials of Chan* is used in Korean Buddhism as a primer on ganhwa Seon practice and is included in the *Fourfold Collection* (*Sajip* 四集), the Seon strand of the traditional seminary curriculum. For a discussion of this text and its place in the Korean monastic curriculum, see Robert E. Buswell, Jr., *Numinous Awareness Is Never Dark: The Korean Master Chinul's "Excerpts" on Zen Practice*, Korean Classics Library: Philosophy and Religion (Honolulu: University of Hawaii Press, 2016), 83–91. Robert Buswell is currently preparing a complete, annotated translation of the *Essentials of Chan*.

6 From Subul Seunim, *Hwanggeumbit bonghwang-i* (Seoul: Yeose-A-Mun, 2005), 301; quoted in Joo, "Gradual Experiences of Sudden Enlightenment," 16.

7 Subul Seunim, *Heunjeok eopsi naneun sae: Jeonsimbeopyo, Subul Seonsa Seonhae* (Seoul: Gimm-Young Publishers, 2014).

8 Subul Sunim's Chinese text of Huangbo's *Chuanxinfayao* reproduces an edition included in the *Discourse Records of Four Houses of Chan* (*Sijia yulu* 四家語錄; Xuzangjing 1320:69), which was compiled in 1085 (the eighth year of the Yuanfeng 元豊 reign-era) during the Song dynasty and reprinted in 1589 (Wanli 萬曆 reign-era, year 17) during the Ming dynasty; the *Huangbo Duanji chanshi Chuanxinfayao* 黃檗斷際禪師傳心法要 is the fourth fascicle of that collection (Xuzangjing 1324:69), and the *Huangbo Duanji chanshi Wanling lu* 黃檗斷際禪師宛陵錄 is the fifth fascicle (Xuzangjing 1325:69). Subul Sunim's Korean rendering of the text is indebted to a modern Korean translation by Baengnyeon Seonseo Ganhaenghoe, *Seollim bojeon*, in Seollim gogyeong chongseo, vol. 1 (Seoul: Janggyeonggak Chulpansa, 1988).

9 In the longer editions of the *Chuanxinfayao*, part I is sometimes given the title *Zhunzhou Record* in distinction to the *Wanling Record* (part II) in order to distinguish it from the title of the complete collection. For an exhaustive account of the various editions of the *Chuanxinfayao*, done by a very young Albert Welter, see his "Huang-po's Notion of Mind" (MA Thesis, McMaster University, 1978), 1–9 (http://digitalcommons.mcmaster.ca/opendissertations/2815). For a valuable overview of the text and its content, see Dale S. Wright, "The Huang-po Literature," in Dale S. Wright and Steven Heine, eds., *The Zen Canon: Understanding the Classic Zen Texts* (London and New York: Oxford University Press, 2004), 107–35.

10 *The Zen Teaching of Huang Po on the Transmission of Mind* (New York: Grove Press, 1958); Blofeld's translation has been frequently reprinted. There are also two other early English translations of portions of the text. D. T. Suzuki translated excerpts from part I; D. T. Suzuki, *Manual of Zen Buddhism* (New York: Grove Press, 1994 [orig. pub. 1935]), 112–19. Charles Luk (Lu K'uan Yu) translated sections of the *Wanling lu* in *The Transmission of the Mind: Outside the Teaching* (London: Rider, 1974), 1: 139–83.

11 *Essentials of the Transmission of Mind*, in *Zen Texts*, BDK English Tripiṭaka 73-III

(Berkeley: Numata Center for Buddhist Translation and Research, 2005), 1–42. Iriya Yoshitaka, ed. and trans., *Denshin hōyō—Enryōroku*, Zen no goroku 8 (Tokyo: Chikuma Shobō, 1969).

12 The *Recorded Sayings of the Four Houses*, *Sijia yulu* 四家語錄, in Yanagida Seizan, ed., *Shike goroku, Goke goroku* (Kyoto: Chūbun Shuppansha, 1983). The text is attributed to Huanglong Huinan 黃龍慧南 (1002–69). The current edition dates from 1607 with a preface dated to 1085.

13 *Jiangxi Mazu Daoyi chanshi yulu* 江西馬祖道一禪師語錄, Xuzangjing 1321:69.3c2–4.

14 "Silver mountain and iron wall" (*yinshan tiebi* / *eunsan cheolpyeok* 銀山鐵壁) are metaphors Subul Sunim adopts from Gaofeng Yuanmiao's *Essentials of Chan*, *Chanyao* 高峰禪要, Xuzangjing 1401:70.705a17, 707c10. See note 5 above.

15 心佛及衆生 是三無差別. See the *Flower Garland Sūtra* (*Buddhāvataṃsakasūtra*), *Dafangguang fo huayan jing* 大方廣佛華嚴經, Taishō 278:9.465c29.

16 Although this precise line does not appear in the *Diamond Sūtra*, both Huangbo and Subul Sunim are alluding here to that scripture's frequent reference to making offerings to myriad buddhas: e.g., "I encountered 84 trillion *nayutas* of buddhas to whom I made offerings" (得値八百四千萬億那由他諸佛 悉皆供養). However, the usual comparison is that such offerings pale next to the merit that derives from learning the *Diamond Sūtra*: "If there were a person in the subsequent degenerate age [of the dharma] who is able to accept, keep, read, and recite this sūtra, the merit he will gain will be a hundred, thousand, ten-thousand, or a million times greater than the merit I gained from making offerings to all those buddhas; it is so much greater that it exceeds any possible analogy for its computation" (若復有人於後末世 能受持讀誦此經 所得功德 於我所供養 諸佛功德 百分不及一 千萬億分乃至算數譬喩所不能及). See *Diamond Sūtra* (*Vajracchedikāsūtra*), *Jingang bore boluomi jing* 金剛般若波羅蜜經, Taishō 235:8.750c28–751a4.

17 *Pingchangxin shi dao* / *pyeongsangsim si do* 平常心是道. *Mazu's Recorded Sayings*, *Mazu yulu* 馬祖語錄, Xuzangjing 1321:69.3a13.

18 Huangbo alludes here to two renowned lines from the *Heart Sūtra*, "There is nothing to be attained. . . . This is true, not false" (以無所得故...眞實不虛); *Heart Sūtra* (*Prajñāpāramitāhṛdayasūtra*) *Bore boluomiduo xin jing* 般若波羅蜜多心經, Taishō 251:8.848c13–14, 19.

19 This passage appears widely throughout a whole panoply of primarily Buddhist commentarial literature. Perhaps the *locus classicus* is the *Treatise on the Great Perfection of Wisdom*, *Dazhidu lun* 大智度論, Taishō 1509:25.71c07–8.

20 The prophecy of Śākyamuni's future attainment of buddhahood. This passage is adapted from the *Diamond Sūtra*, *Jingang bore boluomi jing* 金剛般若波羅蜜經, Taishō 237:8.764c24–25. See also Taishō 236:8.753c26–27; Taishō 236:8.753c26–27; and cf. Taishō 239:8.774a27.

21 Adapted from the *Diamond Sūtra*, *Jingang bore boluomi jing* 金剛般若波羅蜜經, Taishō 235:8.751c24–25.

22 Literally, "vertically and horizontally" (*zongheng* / *jonghoeng* 縱橫). For the broader connotation of this compound, cf. Robert E. Buswell, Jr., trans., *Cultivating*

Original Enlightenment: Wŏnhyo's Exposition of the Vajrasamādhi-Sūtra (Kŭmgang sammaegyŏng Non), The International Association of Wŏnhyo Studies' Collected Works of Wŏnhyo 1 (Honolulu: University of Hawaii Press, 2007), 346n7.

23 *Da banniepan jing* 大般涅槃經 chap. 7, Taishō 374:12.408a.

24 The perfection of the vow (*praṇidhānapāramitā*) refers to the perfection of the bodhisattva's aspiration to save all sentient beings from suffering. It is one of the ten perfections, which include the core six (generosity, morality, forebearance, vigor, meditative absorption, and wisdom), plus an additional four (skillful means, vow/aspiration, powers, and knowledge/omniscience). See Buswell and Lopez, *Princeton Dictionary*, 1084, s.v. "ten perfections."

25 Cf. *Diamond Sūtra*, *Jingang bore boluomi jing* 金剛般若波羅蜜經, Taishō 235:8.749c17–18: 如來 在然燈佛所 於法實無所得.

26 For these five types of eyes, see *Diamond Sūtra*, *Jingang bore boluomi jing* 金剛般若波羅蜜經. Taishō 235:8.751b13–20; for these five types of speech, see 750b27–28.

27 The "three phrases" here refers to Linji Yixuan's well-known teaching of the "three mysterious gates" (*san xuanmen / sam hyeonmun* 三玄門): the mystery in the essence, mystery in the word, and mystery in the mystery. See discussion in Robert E. Buswell, Jr., *Chinul: Selected Works*, Collected Works of Korean Buddhism 2 (Seoul: Jogye Order of Korean Buddhism 2012), 84–88; see also the treatment of these three mysterious gates in Robert E. Buswell, Jr., "Ch'an Hermeneutics: A Korean View," in Donald S. Lopez, Jr., ed., *Buddhist Hermeneutics*, Kuroda Institute Studies in East Asian Buddhism 6 (Honolulu: University of Hawaii Press, 1988), 231–56.

28 The most common list of four types of nutriment (*āhāra*) includes food (which nourishes the physical body), sense contact (which nourishes sensation), intention (which nourishes action), and consciousness (which nourishes materiality-and-mentality, viz., at the moment of rebirth); see Buswell and Lopez, *Princeton Dictionary,* 21, s.v. "āhāra."

29 This passage appears in the *Great Compilation* (*Mahāsaṃnipātasūtra*), *Fangdeng daji jing* 方等大集經, Taishō 397:13.95a1, and in the *Golden Light Sūtra* (*Suvarṇaprabhāsottamasūtra*), *Jinguangming jing* 金光明經, Taishō 663:16.344b3–4.

30 This analogy is used in the *Śūraṅgama Sūtra*, *Shoulengyan jing* 首楞嚴經, Taishō 945:19.108c21, 147a27.

31 This passage is specifically attributed to the Sixth Patriarch Huineng and first quoted in Guifeng Zongmi's 圭峰宗密 (780–841) contemporaneous *Chan Prolegomenon*, *Chanyuan zhuquanji duxu* 禪源諸詮集都序, Taishō 2015:48.411c8–10. As Jeffrey Broughton notes, this line has no close analog in the *Platform Sūtra of the Sixth Patriarch*, and is in fact not attributed to the Sixth Patriarch by Huangbo here; see Jeffrey Lyle Broughton, *Zongmi on Chan* (New York: Columbia University Press, 2009), 174, and discussion at 280–81n329. The verse is subsequently frequently cited in Chan literature, especially that associated with the Linji school. See, as but one of many examples, *Yuanwu's Recorded Sayings*, *Yuanwu Foguo chanshi yulu* 圓悟佛果禪師語録, Taishō 1997:47.757a4–5. The *Foshuo zaoxiang liangdu jing jie* 佛説造像量度經解 attributes this passage instead to a unnamed sūtra; see Taishō 1419:21.937a7–10.

32 Like soil for plants, the *mind ground* (*xindi/simji* 心地) is the field of cultivation, or

basis, for all phenomena, both wholesome and unwholesome. This teaching appears throughout the canon, e.g., the *Mahāyāna Contemplation of the Mind Ground Sūtra, Dasheng ben xindi guan jing*, 大乘本生心地觀經, Taishō 159:3.296c12 et passim.

33 The *Puyan pusa zhang* 普眼菩薩章 chapter in the *Consummate Enlightenment Sūtra, Yuanjue jing* 圓覺經, Taishō 842:17.914c2–4.

34 A similar passage, "I really attained nothing from that bodhi mind" (alt., "that bodhi mind in reality is unascertainable" 彼菩提心實無所得) appears in *The Great Saint Mañjuśrī Bodhisattva Adorns the Buddha Land with Merit Sūtra, Dasheng Wenshushili pusa focha gongde zhuangyan jing* 大聖文殊師利菩薩佛刹功德莊嚴經, Taishō 319:11.912a7. There are also evocations of this sentiment in the *Diamond Sūtra*, as seen below.

35 Devadatta, the Buddha's cousin, sought to usurp control of the Saṅgha from the Buddha and ended up causing the first schism in the Buddhist order. The Buddha rebuked him, which prompted Devadatta to try unsuccessfully to kill the Buddha and remove his rival. For this "act that brings immediate retribution" (*ānataryakarman*), Devadatta was swallowed up by the earth and fell into the Interminable Hell (Avīci). For his story, see Buswell and Lopez, *Princeton Dictionary*, 233–34, s.v. "Devadatta."

36 See the "Chapter on the Conjured City Simile" (化城喻品第七) of the *Miaofa lianhua jing* 妙法蓮華經. Taishō 262:9.22a18–27b9; Burton Watson, trans., *The Lotus Sutra* (New York: Columbia University Press, 1993), 117–42. The story relates that there was a treasure that was located on the other side of a vast wasteland. A group of travelers wanted to cross this wasteland to locate the treasure, but in the middle of their journey, they became so exhausted that they were about to turn back. Then the leader of the group, through his miraculous powers, conjured up a walled city with water and mansions where the travelers could take rest. Once they were rejuvenated, the travelers were able to cross the land and find the treasure.

37 *Icchantikas*, or "incorrigibles," were said to have destroyed the seed of buddhahood by disavowing the law of karma or rejecting the Mahāyāna sūtras, and their prospects for enlightenment were debated in Chinese Buddhism. For the famous passage in the *Mahāparinirvāṇa Sūtra* that makes the then-startling assertion that *icchantikas* do in fact have the capacity to attain buddhahood, see *Da banniepan jing* 大般涅槃經, Taishō 374:12:828a9.

38 A quotation attributed to Dazhu Huihai 大珠慧海 (d.u., ca. eighth century), a disciple of Mazu Daoyi; cf. the *Jingde Record of Transmitting the Lamplight, Jingde chuandeng lu*, 景德傳燈錄 6, Taishō 207:51.247b9.

39 Subul Sunim seems here to be referring to a passage in the "Skillful Means" chapter (方便品) of the *Lotus Sūtra*, where the Buddha tells Śāriputra that the śrāvakas and pratyekabuddhas are unable to fathom the profound wisdom of all the buddhas. See *Lotus Sūtra* (*Saddharmapuṇḍarīkasūtra*), *Miaofa lianhua jing* 妙法蓮華經, Taishō 262:9.5b25–27; Watson, *Lotus Sūtra*, 23.

40 *Nianhua weixiao / yeomhwa miso* 拈華微笑. *Tiansheng Expanded Lamplight Record, Tiansheng guangdenglu* 天聖廣燈錄 2, Xuzangjing 1553:78.428c2–3.

41 *Bore boluomiduo xin jing* 般若波羅蜜多心經, Taishō 251:8.848c13–14; and see note 18 above.

42 Quoting the *Diamond Sūtra, Jingang bore boluomi jing* 金剛般若波羅蜜經, Taishō 235:8.751c14–15 et passim.

43 This quotation appears frequently in commentarial and Chan materials; e.g., *Annotation to the Laṅkāvatāra Sūtra, Zhu Dasheng ru Lenqie jing* 注大乘入楞伽經, Taishō 1791:39.437b19; *Exposition of the Diamond Sūtra, Jingang bore boluomi jing lun* 金剛般若波羅蜜經論, Taishō 1511:25.784b19; the *Blue Cliff Record, Biyan lu* 碧巖録, Taishō 2003:48.222b24–25. Huangbo cites this same verse in part II, chap. 2.

44 Adapted from the *Śūraṅgama Sūtra, Shoulengyan jing* 首楞嚴經, Taishō 945:19.131b1, without minor differences.

45 This sentiment is a central theme of the *Lotus Sūtra*; see, for example, "There is only this dharma of the one vehicle./ There are not two and also not three [vehicles]" (唯有一乘法 無二亦無三); *Miaofa lianhua jing* 妙法蓮華經, Taishō 262:9.8a17–18. The last line, as cited here, appears later in the same verse summation; see 8a21; there, the text says, "All the buddhas appear in this world,/ only for this one great matter./ Any other is inauthentic." The first line as cited here appears in Sthiramati's *Nondistinction in the Mahāyāna Dharma Realm, Dasheng fajie wuchabie lun* 大乘法界無差別論, Taishō 1626:31.894a18–19.

46 This reference to Mahākāśyapa sharing Śākyamuni's seat appears in an early *avadāna* narrative collection, the *Zhongbenqi jing* 中本起經, Taishō 196:4.161a18–25. Huangbo's account of this event here is one of the earliest Chan versions of the story and links it with the school's emblematic attempts to distinguish itself from the mainstream scriptural traditions of Buddhism.

47 *Śūraṅgama Sūtra, Shoulengyan jing*, Taishō 945:19.117b6.

48 To "catch the fish and forget about the weir" (*de yu wang quan / deuk eo mang jeon* 得魚忘筌) is a native Chinese analogy widely used in Chan texts and Chinese commentarial literature. It is first found in section 13 of the "What Comes from Without" chapter of the *Zhuangzi* 莊子 (in the "Miscellaneous Chapters" division). In Chan, the analogy indicates that once practitioners have achieved enlightenment, they no longer need to rely on the conceptual descriptions to convey a sense of what enlightenment is. This follows closely the interpretation in the *Zhuangzi*: "Words are employed to convey ideas; but having understood the ideas, one may forget the words." The analogy is more commonly used in Chinese literature to refer to ingratitude—that is, now that you've caught the fish you forget how you got it. We translate here according to the Chan interpretation.

49 This passage appears in the *Mahāparinirvāṇa Sūtra, Da banniepan jing* 大般涅槃經, Taishō 374:12.412c24–25. Huangbo uses this same quote later in part II, chap. 30. The passage subsequently comes to be widely quoted in Seon materials.

50 Quoting the *Diamond Sūtra, Jingang bore boluomi jing* 金剛般若波羅蜜經, Taishō 235:8.749c17–18, with minor changes.

51 A "person without concerns" is *wushiren/musain* 無事人; see also note 53 below. The original Chinese term 無事 is also adopted in Buddhist texts to translate "forest dweller," as in the term 無事比丘 (*āraṇyaka-bhikṣu*), a forest-dwelling monk who is devoted to meditation. See *Madhyamāgama, Zhong ahan jing* 中阿含經 6, Taishō 26:1.455a4 and 455n1; as noted by Bhikkhu Anālayo in *Digital Dictionary of Buddhism*

(http://www.buddhism-dict.net/ddb/, s.v. 無事比丘). This contemplative denotation of the term is probably suggested in the usage here.

52 Yongjia Zhenjue 永嘉眞覺 (665–713), *Zhengdao ge* 證道歌, Taishō 2014:48.395c6.

53 For this "person without concerns" or "person who has nothing to do" (*wushiren/musain* 無事人), see *Record of Linji*, *Linji lu* 臨濟録, Taishō 1985:47.497b14, 497c27 et passim; cf. Ruth Fuller Sasaki, trans., *The Record of Linji*, ed. by Thomas Yuho Kirchner (Honolulu: University of Hawaii Press, 2009), 178.

54 *Jingang bore boluomi jing* 金剛般若波羅蜜經, Taishō 235:8.749b14–15.

55 *Ji/jeuk* 即, "is," the identity Huangbo drew when he said that "mind *is* the buddha."

56 As Subul Sunim notes below, this line appears in the *Lotus Sūtra*'s chapter on "The Previous Acts of the Bodhisattva Medicine King (Bhaiṣajyarāja)"; *Miaofa lianhua jing* 妙法蓮華經, Taishō 262:9.54a5.

57 *Jingde Record of Transmitting the Lamplight*, *Jingde chuandeng lu* 景德傳燈録, Taishō 2076:51.214b27–28, a transmission verse appearing in the biography of the twenty-third Indian patriarch Haklenayaśas (鶴勒那). Huangbo quotes the first stanza later in part II, chap. 4.

58 *Vimalakīrtinirdeśa*, *Weimojie suoshuo jing* 維摩詰所說經, Taishō 475:14.546a25–26.

59 The third of the four practices outlined in the text; see the citation in the *Record of the Masters and Disciples of the Laṅkāvatāra*, *Lengqie shizi ji* 楞伽師資記, Taishō 2837:85.1285a18 and 1285b1; cf. Jeffrey L. Broughton, *The Bodhidharma Anthology: The Earliest Records of Zen* (Berkeley and Los Angeles: University of California Press, 1999), 10–11.

60 *Shenglichu naishi delichu / seongnyeokcheo naesi deungnyeokcheo* 省力處乃是得力處. Subul Sunim is quoting Dahui Zonggao; see the *Recorded Sayings of Dahui*, *Dahui Pujue chanshi yulu* 大慧普覺禪師語録, Taishō 1998A:47.936c17, the similar phrase 省力便是得力處也 at 922b7–8, and many other similar phrases.

61 One of the most famous lines in all of Chinese Buddhist literature, taken from Kumārajīva's translation of the *Diamond Sūtra*, *Jingang bore boluomi jing* 金剛般若波羅蜜經, Taishō 235:8.749c22–23. This line is also quoted later in part II, chap. 16.

62 This line from Zhigong 志公 (a.k.a. Baozhi 寶誌, 418–514) does not appear in any of his extant writings; see Iriya Yoshitaka, *Denshin hōyō*, 83n and 145n. Huangbo also cites the same line below in part II, chap. 16, though there the subject is "this very body" rather than the buddha.

63 The *three levels of sagacity* refers to the three initial levels of practice on the bodhisattva path—the ten abidings, ten practices, and ten dedications. The *four fruitions* are the four levels of sanctity on the Hīnayāna path: the fruitions of stream enterer, once-returner, nonreturner, and arhat. The *ten stages* (*bhūmi*) constitute the culminating stages of the bodhisattva path.

64 *Mahāparinirvāṇa Sūtra*, *Da banniepan jing* 大般涅槃經 3, Taishō 7:1.204c23. See also *Ekottarikāgama*, *Bieyi za'ahan jing* 別譯雜阿含經, Taishō 100:2.489b2.

65 Yongjia Zhenjue, "Song of Realizing the Way," *Zhengdao ge* 證道歌, Taishō 2014:48.396a17–18.

66 These gāthās are *Seolsan ge* 雪山偈 and *Jehaeng musang ge* 諸行無常偈.

67 *Mahāparinirvāṇa Sūtra*, *Da banniepan jing* 大般涅槃經 3, Taishō 7:1.204c24. This

line is also widely found in the Āgama and Nikāya literature, e.g., *Ekottarikāgama, Bieyi Za'ahan jing* 別譯雜阿含經, Taishō 100:2.489b2–3. The full verse reads *jehaeng musang / si saengmyeolbeop / saengmyeol myeoli / jeongmyeol wirak* 諸行無常 是生滅法 生滅滅已 寂滅爲樂. This verse is still recited today at recited at Buddhist funeral services in Southeast Asia: "All compounded things are impermanent;/ they are dharmas that arise and pass away./ Having arisen, they vanish;/ their extinction is bliss." (Pāli: *aniccā vata saṅkhārā/ uppadā vaya dhammino./ Upajjhitvā nirujjhanti/ tesam vupasamo sukho.*)

68 Iriya Yoshitaka (*Denshin hōyō*, 84n) traces this this line, with slight variations, to Zongmi's *Annotations to the Great Commentary on the Consummate Enlightenment Sūtra, Yuanjue jing dashu chao* 圓覺經大疏鈔, *zhuan* 2下. Huangbo subsequently cites this same passage in part II, chap. 16.

69 Literally, "find a place where you can stick your head."

70 The story, as Subul Sunim notes, derives from the "Child's Play" chapter (*Ying'er xing pin* 嬰兒行品) of the *Mahāparinirvāṇa Sūtra*; Huangbo's quote here is a paraphrase: cf. *Da banniepan jing* 大般涅槃經, Taishō 374:12.485c11 and Taishō 375:12.729a4. The same simile is used later in part II, chaps. 16 and 29.

71 Quoting, with slight variations, the *Diamond Sūtra, Jingang bore boluomi jing* 金剛般若波羅蜜經, Taishō 235:8.751c22–23. And cf. note 188 below.

72 As Subul Sunim notes in his commentary that follows, Huangbo here is quoting Baozhi's "Verses in Praise of the Mahāyāna," *Dasheng zan* 大乘讚; see *Jingde Record of Transmitting the Lamplight, Jingde chuandeng lu* 景德傳燈録 29, Taishō 2076:51.449c10.

73 Huangbo quotes here, without attribution, Yongjia Zhenjue's "Song of Realizing the Way," *Zhengdao ge* 證道歌, Taishō 2014:48.396c23–24; and see *Jingde Record of Transmitting the Lamplight, Jingde chuandeng lu* 景德傳燈録, Taishō 2076:51.461a29–b1.

74 That is, if dust alights on the mirror of your mind. This and the following verse appear in the *Platform Sūtra, Liuzu tan jing*, Taishō 2008:48.348b, 349a, translated by Philip B. Yampolsky in *The Platform Sutra of the Sixth Patriarch* (New York: Columbia University Press, 1967), 130 and 132. This passage also appears in part II, chap. 8.

75 This passage is enigmatic in the extreme, which leaves it open to multiple interpretations. Subul Sunim's interpretation of the last line (p. 239) understands "[this] dharma" and "[that] dharma" as referring to the "dharma" and "no dharma" of the preceding lines, and "understand the dharma" as referring to "understand the true dharma"; thus, he translates, "How would you understand the true dharma to be dharma or no dharma?" or perhaps, "How can those things that are judged as being dharma or no dharma be true dharma?"

76 This famous line, which also appears as a Zen kōan or Seon hwadu, is often mistranslated as "your original face before your parents were born." The Sinograph *sheng/saeng* 生 ("to be born, produced") in this passage should be understood as a causative form—"to bring to life," "to give birth to," "to conceive." Thus the correct translation is: "bring me your original face before your parents *conceived* you." See, e.g., *Spurring Advancement through the Chan Checkpoints, Changuan cejin* 禪關策進, Taishō 2024:48.1103a18; see

Jeffrey L. Broughton with Else Yoko Watanabe, trans., *The "Chan Whip" Anthology: A Companion to Zen Practice* (New York: Oxford University Press, 2015), 114. Many variations are also found in the literature. The important Linji teacher and forerunner in *gong'an* study, Yuanwu Keqin 圓悟克勤 (1062–1135), for example, uses the similar phrase, "Where were your nostrils before your parents conceived you?" (父母未生前鼻孔在什麼處); *Yuanwu's Recorded Sayings, Yuanwu Foguo Chanshi yulu* 圓悟佛果禪師語録, Taishō 1997:47.769a11–12.

77 From the *Platform Sūtra*; *Liuzu tan jing* 六祖壇經, Taishō 2008:48.349b16–349c3; John R. McRae, trans., *The Platform Sutra of the Sixth Patriarch*, BDK English Tripiṭaka 73-II (Berkeley: Numata Center for Buddhist Translation and Research, 2000), 36–37. Huangbo uses this analogy about a person drinking water below in part II, chap. 40.

78 This story appears widely in Chan literature; see, e.g, *Fenyang's Recorded Sayings, Fenyang Wude yulu* 汾陽無徳語録, Taishō 1992:47.616a7–8. It is also used as case 32 in *Wumen's (Gateless) Checkpoint, Wumen guan*, Taishō 2005:48.295c12–15.

79 The metaphor of the difficulty in digesting even a drop of water appears widely in Chan literature; see, e.g., *Dongshan's Recorded Sayings, Dongshan Liangjie yulu* 洞山良价禪師語録, Taishō 1986B:47.522bc4; *Congrong Hermitage Record, Congrong lu* 從容録, Taishō 2004:48.249b5; *Jingde Record of Transmitting the Lamplight, Jingde chuandeng lu* 景徳傳燈録, Taishō 2076:51.256a12.

80 The term "grand councilor" (*xianggong/sanggong* 相公) is an unofficial title used generically to refer to the very highest officials in the Chinese central bureaucracy. See Charles O. Hucker, *A Dictionary of Official Titles in Imperial China* (Stanford: Stanford University Press, 1985), 232, no. 2331.

81 From the *Golden Light Sūtra, Jinguangming jing* 金光明經, Taishō 663:16.344b3–4.

82 The *Diamond Sūtra's* famous set of similes for compounded things appears at *Jingang bore boluomi jing* 金剛般若波羅蜜經, Taishō 235:8.752b28–29.

83 This quotation appears frequently in commentarial and Chan materials; e.g., *Notes to the Laṅkāvatāra Sūtra, Zhu Dasheng ru Lenqie jing* 注大乘入楞伽經, Taishō 1791:39.437b19; *Treatise on the Diamond Sūtra, Jingang bore boluomi jing lun* 金剛般若波羅蜜經論, Taishō 1511:25.784b19; the *Blue Cliff Record, Biyan lu* 碧巖録, Taishō 2003:48.222b24–25. Huangbo cites this same verse in part I, chap. 7.

84 幻翳, lit., an "illusory screen." Subul Sunim translates it as a "ghost" (*heoggaebi*).

85 From the *Śūraṅgama Sūtra, Shoulengyan jing* 首楞嚴經, Taishō 945:19.131a20. This line, with slight variations, appears as an unattributed quote toward the end of part II, chap. 16.

86 Scholars have been unable to trace the source of this quotation. This line, with slight variations, appears as an unattributed quote toward the end of part II, chap. 16.

87 心無異相 名作眞如 心不可改 名爲法性 心無所屬 名為解脱 心性無碍 名為菩提 心性寂滅 名為涅槃. See Yanagida Seizan, ed. and trans., *Daruma no goroku: Ninyū shigyō ron*, Zen no goroku, vol. 1 (Tōkyō: Chikuma Shobō, 1969), 71.

88 See, for example, the exchange in the *Diamond Sūtra, Jingang bore boluomi jing* 金剛般若波羅蜜經, Taishō 235.8.751b17ff.

89 This verse was previously quoted in part I, chap. 5. This passage is specifically attributed

to the Sixth Patriarch Huineng and first quoted in Guifeng Zongmi's 圭峰宗密 (780–841) contemporaneous *Chan Prolegomenon*, *Chanyuan zhuquanji duxu* 禪源諸詮集都序, Taishō 2015:48.411c8–10; it does not, however, appear in the *Platform Sūtra of the Sixth Patriarch*.

90 隨處作主 立處皆眞. *Record of Linji*, *Linji lu* 臨濟録, Taishō 1985:47.498a19 et passim.

91 "Expedient Means" is the second of the twenty-eight chapters of the *Lotus Sūtra*; see *Miaofa lianhua jing* 妙法蓮華經, Taishō 262:9.7b2–3.

92 Referring here to an event in the "Skillful Means" chapter of the *Lotus Sūtra*, where the "Hīnayānists" all depart when the Buddha speaks about there being only one Buddha Vehicle, leaving just the cream of the crop that was able to understand his revolutionary message. These specific lines appear at *Miaofa lianhua jing* 妙法蓮華經, Taishō 262:9.15a14–15 and 7c18.

93 Subul Sunim here rephrases Linji Yixuan's teaching of the three statements: "He who attains at the first statement becomes the teacher of patriarch-buddhas; he who attains at the second statement becomes the teacher of men and gods; he who attains at the third statement cannot save even himself." See Sasaki, *Record of Linji*, 264; 若第一句中得 與祖佛為師 若第二句中得 與人天為師 若第三句中得 自救不了, *Linji lu*, Taishō 1985:47.502a5–7. There have been a few different interpretations of this teaching in the history of Chan and Seon Buddhism. For example, just as Subul Sunim does here, the three statements have sometimes been understood as simply referring to different levels of Seon realization or to the various types of Seon rhetoric that lead to those different levels. In other cases, because of the teaching's obvious hierarchical implications, in inter-Seon/Chan polemical contexts, the three statements could be interpreted as referring to different Seon schools, each of which had achieved different levels of understanding. See also note 183 below. For further background, see Seong-Uk Kim, "The Zen Theory of Language: Linji Yixuan's Teaching of 'Three Statements, Three Mysteries, and Three Essentials' (*sanju sanxuan sanyao* 三句三玄三要)," *Journal of the International Association of Buddhist Studies* 36/37 (2013/2014): 69–90.

94 This story of Bodhidharma pacifying Huike's mind is told in Bodhidharma's biography in the *Continued Biographies of Eminent Monks*, *Xu gaoseng zhuan* 續高僧傳, Taishō 2060:50.551b–c.

95 理入者 . . . 深信含生凡聖同一真性 但為客塵妄覆 不能顯了: see Yanagida Seizan, *Daruma no goroku*, 21–22; see Broughton, *Bodhidharma Anthology*, 9.

96 *Record of Linji*, *Linji lu* 臨濟録, Taishō 1985:47.499c12.

97 From a transmission verse by the twenty-third Indian patriarch Haklena (鶴勒那) biography; see Subul Sunim's commentary and the following note.

98 From the transmission verse of the twenty-third Indian patriarch Haklena (鶴勒那) in the *Jingde Record of Transmitting the Lamplight*, *Jingde chuandeng lu* 景德傳燈録, Taishō 2076:51.214b27–28. Huangbo quotes this same verse in part I, chap. 12.

99 From Manorhita's (摩拏羅) biography in the *Jingde Record of Transmitting the Lamplight*, *Jingde chuandeng lu* 景德傳燈録, Taishō 2076:51.214a24–25.

100 This line is taken, with one minor variation, from the *Diamond Sūtra*; see *Jingang*

bore boluomi jing 金剛般若波羅蜜經, Taishō 236:8.761a22, Taishō 237:8.765c23. This exact line appears in Richeng's 日稱 (fl. ca. 1046) late Song-dynasty translation *Encounters of Fathers and Sons* (*Pitāputrasamāgamasūtra*), *Fuzi heji jing* 父子合集經, Taishō 320:11.953a23–24.

101 *Vimalakīrti's Instructions*, *Weimojie suoshuo jing* 維摩詰所說經, Taishō 475:14.551a13–14.

102 A nearly identical passage appears in the *The Ascetic Mahāsatya's Instructions* (**Mahāsatyanirgranthasūtra*), *Dasazhe niqianzi suoshuo jing* 大薩遮尼乾子所說經, Taishō 272:9.324c6–7.

103 As Subul Sunim notes in his commentary, these lines come from the *Diamond Sūtra; Jingang bore boluomi jing* 金剛般若波羅蜜經, Taishō 235:8.749a24–25.

104 Subul Sunim translates this last line as "there is also no action necessary in order to remove the defilements."

105 This line, as Subul Sunim notes in his commentary, is an unattributed citation from the *Brahmā's Net Sūtra* (*Brahmajālasūtra*), *Fanwang jing* 梵網經, Taishō 1484:24.1010a8. Huangbo quotes this line again in part II, chap. 36.

106 *Fanwang jing* 梵網經, Taishō 1484:24.1010a5–8.

107 The twelve categories of scripture include such genres as discourses, prophecies, verses, and fables. For the traditional list of these twelve, see Buswell and Lopez, *Princeton Dictionary*, 1087, s.v. "twelve categories of scripture."

108 For this passage, see *Weimojie suoshuo jing* 維摩詰所說經, Taishō 475:14.544b10–11.

109 As Subul Sunim notes in his commentary that follows, this line is quoted from *Vimalakīrti's Instructions*; *Weimojie suoshuo jing* 維摩詰所說經, Taishō 475:14.538a14.

110 This unattributed quotation is ascribed to Zhigong (Baozhi) in the literature and is frequently quoted in Seon materials. As but one of many examples, see Zongmi's *Notes to an Abbreviated Commentary on the Sūtra of Consummate Enlightenment*, *Dafangguang Yuanjue xiuduoluo liaoyi jing lüeshu zhu* 大方廣圓覺修多羅了義經略疏註, Taishō 1795:39.545a8–9.

111 As Subul Sunim notes below, this line is an unattributed quote from *Vimalakīrti's Instructions*; see *Weimojie suoshuo jing* 維摩詰所說經, Taishō 475:14.538c27–28.

112 Subul Sunim here seems to be alluding to a passage in the *Platform Sūtra*: when Emperor Wu of Liang asked Bodhidharma how much merit he had made by such pious Buddhist acts as building monasteries and making donations, Bodhidharma responded, "No merit." See *Liuzu tan jing*, Taishō 2007:48.341a24; Yampolsky, *Platform Sutra*, section 34, 155–56.

113 Adapted from the *Diamond Sūtra; Jingang bore boluomi jing* 金剛般若波羅蜜經, Taishō 235:8.751a15, 751a20–21.

114 *Diamond Sūtra, Jingang bore boluomi jing* 金剛般若波羅蜜經, Taishō 235:8.749a24, 752a17–18.

115 元來黃檗佛法無多子. See Linji Yixuan's biography in *Jingde Record of Transmitting the Lamplight, Jingde chuandeng lu* 景德傳燈錄, Taishō 2076:51.299b28–29.

116 This quote is derived, with minor differences, from the "Skillful Means" chapter of the *Lotus Sūtra*; see *Miaofa lianhua jing* 妙法蓮華經, Taishō 262:9.8a17–18.

117 See *Da banniepan jing* 大般涅槃經, Taishō 374:12.370c ff.

118 Quoting *Vimalakīrti's Instructions*, *Weimojie suoshuo jing* 維摩詰所說經, Taishō 475:14.542b12–13.

119 This line is an cited with attribution from *Vimalakīrti's Instructions*, *Weimojie suoshuo jing* 維摩詰所說經, Taishō 475:14.542a17–18.

120 As Subul Sunim notes, Huangbo is here quoting, without attribution, the putative Third Patriarch of Chan, Sengcan 僧璨 (d. 606), from his *Verses on Faith in Mind*, *Xinxin ming* 信心銘, Taishō 2010:48.376b24.

121 As Subul Sunim notes in his commentary, Huangbo quotes Layman Fu (*Fu dashi* 傅大士) (497–569) in *Liang Dynasty's Great Layman Fu's Verses on the Diamond Sūtra*, *Liangchao Fu dashi song Jingang jing* 梁朝傅大師頌金剛經, Taishō 2732:85.2c25–26. *Acquiescence to the nonproduction of dharmas* (*anutpattikadharmakṣānti*) refers to an advanced bodhisattva's receptivity to the reality that dharmas are unproduced (*anutpattika*) and thus lacking any sense of intrinsic existence (*niḥsvabhāva*); see Buswell and Lopez, *Princeton Dictonary*, 55, s.v. "anutpattikadharmakṣānti."

122 This is another unattributed quote from Sengcan's *Verses on Faith in Mind*, *Xinxin ming* 信心銘, Taishō 2010:48.376c3–4.

123 As Subul Sunim notes, these lines are taken, with minor differences, from Baozhi's *Dasheng zan* 大乘讚; see *Jingde Record of Transmitting the Lamplight*, *Jingde chuandeng lu* 景德傳燈録, Taishō 2076:51.449c10. Inside views and outside views are variously interpreted to mean the view of Buddhists and non-Buddhists, or internal fantasies and external phenomena.

124 *Recitations of the Buddhas Sūtra* (*Buddhasaṃgītisūtra*), *Zhufo yaoji jing* 諸佛要集經, Taishō 810:17.756b–770a. These lines are frequently quoted in Seon literature to refer to the danger of clinging to views.

125 心佛及衆生 是三無差別. *Dafangguang fo huayan jing* 大方廣佛華嚴經, Taishō 278:9.465c29.

126 An unattributed quote of a widely known passage from the Perfection of Wisdom literature, best known from the *Heart Sūtra*; see *Bore boluomiduo xin jing* 般若波羅蜜多心經, Taishō 251:8.848c12.

127 The *Mahāparinirvāṇa Sūtra* explains that "this 'unconditioned saṅgha' (*wuwei seng / muwi seung* 無為僧) means the Tathāgata," in contrast to the "conditioned saṅgha" (*youwei seng / yuwi seung* 有爲僧), which refers to the other members of the Buddhist order; see *Da banniepan jing* 大般涅槃經, Taishō 374:12.391b22–23.

128 Alluding to the passage from *Vimalakīrti's Instructions,* "Those who seek the dharma should have nothing that they seek regarding all dharmas"; *Weimojie suoshuo jing* 維摩詰所說經, Taishō 475:14.546a26.

129 絶學無爲閑道人 不除妄想不求眞. These are the opening lines of the *Zhengdao ge* 證道歌, Taishō 2014:48.395c9.

130 As Subul Sunim implies, Huangbo is quoting a line from a quatrain in the *Diamond Sūtra*: "Those who look for me in my physical form/ or seek me in the sound of my voice,/ such people practice a deviant path./ They will never be able to see the Tathāgata." *Jingang bore boluomi jing* 金剛般若波羅蜜經, Taishō 235:8.752a17–18.

131 As Subul Sunim notes, the first two lines appear in Śākyamuni Buddha's transmission verse to Mahākāśyapa, but replacing "mind-dharma" with "no dharma"; see *Jingde*

Record of Transmitting the Lamplight, *Jingde chuandeng lu* 景德傳燈録, Taishō 2076:51.205c2. The latter two lines appear, with variations in the first line, in the transmission verses of the fourth and sixth Indian patriarchs; see 208b6.

132 The last two lines of Huineng's famous verse posted in response to that of Shenxiu (606?–706), his rival to the patriarchal succession; see *Platform Sūtra*, Taishō 2008:48.349a8; Yampolsky, *Platform Sutra*, 132. Subul Sunim explains the significance of this verse in his commentary to part I, chap. 15, and in the following chap. 9. This same passage is also quoted below in part II, chap. 29.

133 The story is related in the *Platform Sūtra*; for this "lion's roar," see *Liuzu tan jing* 六祖壇經, Taishō 2008:48.349a19 (何期自性本自清淨); cf. McRae, *Platform Sutra*, 23.

134 This story of Nanyue Huairang's南越懷讓 (677–744) training and enlightenment under the Sixth Patriarch appears at *Platform Sūtra*, *Liuzu tan jing* 六祖壇經, Taishō 2008:48.357b; cf. McRae, *Platform Sutra*, 67.

135 This passage is often used in Korea to introduce the "what is it?" (*imwotko*) hwadu; see note 4 above. In Mazu's discourse records, the line appears as "it is neither mind nor buddha"; see *Mazu's Recorded Sayings*, *Mazu yulu* 馬祖語錄, Xuzangjing 1321:694a23 et passim. The full phrase "It is not mind, it is not buddha, it is not a thing" appears frequently in Seon materials from the Song dynasty onward; e.g., *Recorded Sayings of Yuanwu*, *Yuanwu yulu* 圓悟語錄, Taishō 1997:47.716b04–5; *Recorded Sayings of Dahui*, *Dahui yulu* 大慧語錄, Taishō 1998:47.812b19. In the *Gateless Checkpoint*, the full phrase is instead attributed to Mazu's disciple Nanquan Puyuan; see *Wumen guan* 無門關, Taishō 2005:48.296b12–13.

136 Ths story about Yunmen's response to the Buddha's birth is quoted from the *Blue Cliff Record*, *Biyan lu* 碧巖錄, Taishō 2003:48.156c16–17. For one of many possible sources on the Buddha's declaration upon his birth (a declaration made by all the buddhas), see *Dīrghāgama*, *Chang ahan jing* 長阿含經, Taishō 1:1.4c1–2; and for a specific reference to Śākyamuni's birth, see Xuanzang's Tang-dynasty travelogue, the *Da-Tang xiyu ji* 大唐西域記, Taishō 2087:51902a22–28.

137 As Subul Sunim notes in his commentary, this well-known passage is quoted from the *Awakening of Faith in Mahāyāna*; see *Dasheng qixin lun* 大乘起信論, Taishō 1666:32.577b2. The passage also appears widely in indigenous Chinese sources, such as the apocryphal *Divining the Effects of Good and Evil Actions Sūtra*, *Zhancha shan'e yebao jing* 占察善惡業報經, Taishō 839:17.907b29–907c1. The passage exactly as given here, citing an anonymous sūtra, is quoted in the *Platform Sūtra*, *Liuzu tan jing* 六祖壇經, Taishō 2008:48.362a5. This same passage is quoted later in part II, chap. 16.

138 Subul Sunim is alluding here to a famous line from the *Heart Sūtra*'s analysis of the twelvefold chain of dependent origination (*pratītyasamutpāda*), *Bore boluomiduo xin jing* 般若波羅蜜多心經, Taishō 251:8.848c12.

139 "Distorted views (*viparyāsa*) and dream-like conceptions" (*diandao mengxiang* / *jeondo mongsang* 顛倒夢想), alluding to a famous line from the *Heart Sūtra*; *Bore boluomiduo xin jing* 般若波羅蜜多心經, Taishō 251:8.848c15.

140 Adapted from the *Diamond Sūtra*; *Jingang bore boluomi jing* 金剛般若波羅蜜經, Taishō 235:8.749c17–18; Taishō 236:8.760a15–24.

141 Subul Sunim slightly paraphrases the Song edition of the *Platform Sūtra*, *Liuzu tan jing*

六祖壇經, Taishō 2008:48.349a19–21, compiled in 1290 by Deyi 德異 (1231–1308); cf. McRae, *Platform Sutra*, 34. This passage does not appear in the Dunhuang edition of the *Platform Sūtra* translated by Yampolsky.

142 From a verse attributed to the Eighth Patriarch of Seon, Buddhanandi 佛陀難提; see *Jingde Record of Transmitting the Lamplight, Jingde chuandeng lu* 景德傳燈録, Taishō 2076:51.208c16.

143 This précis of the cardinal doctrine of the Flower Garland (Huayan/Hwaeom 華嚴) school is ubiquitous in Chinese and Korean commentarial literature; see, as but one of many examples, Wonhyo's 元曉 (1158–1210) *Doctrinal Essentials of the Mahāparinirvāṇa Sūtra, Yeolban chongyo* 涅槃宗要, Taishō 1769:38.244c28–29. The exact line, however, does not appear in the *Flower Garland Sūtra* itself.

144 A common metaphor in the Āgama and Nikāya literature to suggest that, just as all seawater has the taste of salt, all the Buddha's teachings have a single taste, the taste of liberation.

145 *Diamond Sūtra, Jingang bore boluomi jing* 金剛般若波羅蜜經, Taishō 235:8.750b14. This same passage is also discussed below in part II, chap. 37.

146 *Platform Sūtra, Liuzu tan jing* 六祖壇經, Taishō 2008:48.346c7.

147 Huangbo quotes here, without attribution, a statement from the Sixth Patriarch Huineng; see *Platform Sūtra, Liuzu tan jing* 六祖壇經, Taishō 2008:48.360a13–14; McRae, *Platform Sutra*, 81.

148 This metaphor of pulverizing the world into tiny motes of dust is taken from the *Diamond Sūtra*; see *Jingang bore boluomi jing* 金剛般若波羅蜜經, Taishō 235:8.752b6–7.

149 This line appears frequently in the literature; see, as but one of many examples, the Sanlun exegete Jizang's 吉藏 (549–623) *Diamond Sūtra Commentary, Jingang bore shu* 金剛般若疏, Taishō 1699:33.119a11.

150 See *Jingde Record of Transmitting the Lamplight, Jingde chuandeng lu* 景德傳燈録, Taishō 2076:51.216a13–14.

151 This famous line from the *Diamond Sūtra* was quoted previously in part I, chap. 14; *Jingang bore boluomi jing* 金剛般若波羅蜜經, Taishō 235:8.749c22–23.

152 Huangbo here is quoting a statement found in the *Aṅgulimālīya Sūtra, Yangjuemoluo jing* 央掘魔羅經, Taishō 120:2.539b22; and the *Golden Light Sūtra, Jinguangming Zuishengwang jing* 金光明最勝王經, Taishō 665:16.419a8–9.

153 *Vimalakīrti's Instructions, Weimojie suoshuo jing* 維摩詰所說經, Taishō 475:14.553a12; see also *Annotation to Vimalakīrti's Instructions, Zhu Weimojie jing* 注維摩詰經, Taishō 1775:38.401c20–21.

154 Huangbo quoted this well-known passage from the *Awakening of Faith in Mahāyāna* previously in part II, chap. 10. For details, see note 146 above.

155 Huangbo is citing the *Flower Garland Sūtra*; *Dafangguang fo huayan jing* 大方廣佛華嚴經, Taishō 278:9.460a10–11.

156 "A snowflake falling onto a red-hot brazier" (*honglu yidian xue* / *hongno iljeom seol* 紅爐一點雪), an analogy found frequently in Seon texts to refer to the suddenness with which enlightenment may be experienced; see, for example, *Yuanwu's Recorded Sayings, Yuanwu Foguo chanshi yulu* 圓悟佛果禪師語録, Taishō 1997:47.749a9.

157 Huangbo also cites this line from Baozhi above in part I, chap. 14, though the subject there is "the Buddha" rather than this very body. Baozhi's line does not appear in any of his extant writings; see Iriya, *Denshin hōyō*, 83n and 145n.

158 In *Vimalakīrti's Instructions* (chap. 3), the layman Vimalakīrti feigns illness so he can receive various well-wishers and question them about the dharma; *Weimojie suoshuo jing* 維摩詰所説經, Taishō 475:14.539c15.

159 Quoting Bodhidharma's instruction to the Second Patriarch, Huike (外息諸緣 內心無喘); see *Jingde Record of Transmitting the Lamplight*, *Jingde chuandeng lu* 景德傳燈録, Taishō 2076:51.219c28. The term *panting* appears commonly in early Chinese translations of meditative texts and is associated with distracted thought (e.g., *Contemplation of Dharma Sūtra* (**Dharmānupaśyanāsūtra*), *Faguan jing* 法觀經, Taishō 611:15.241a24) or the rapid breathing that accompanies the onset of the dying process (*Mayi jing* 罵意經, Taishō 732:17.533b14). See discussion in Robert E. Buswell, Jr., trans., *Cultivating Original Enlightenment: Wŏnhyo's Exposition of the Vajrasamādhi-Sūtra (Kŭmgang sammaegyŏng Non)*, The International Association of Wŏnhyo Studies' Collected Works of Wŏnhyo 1 (Honolulu: University of Hawaii Press, 2007), 193 and 366n245.

160 Huangbo previously cited this quotation from Master Baozhi in part I, chap. 14.

161 Cf. *Flower Garland Sūtra*, *Dafangguang fo huayan jing* 大方廣佛華嚴經, Taishō 279:10.364c18 et passim.

162 This story is found in the "Child's Practice" chapter (Ying'er xing pin 嬰兒行品) of the *Mahāparinirvāṇa Sūtra*; *Da banniepan jing* 大般涅槃經, Taishō 374:12.485c11; and Taishō 375:12.729a4. The same simile is used earlier in part I, chap. 14, and part II, chap. 29.

163 *Vimalakīrti's Instructions*, *Weimojie suoshuo jing* 維摩詰所説經, Taishō 475:14.544b10.

164 From the *Lotus Sūtra*, chapter 4, "Belief and Understanding," where a rich man gains the trust of his long-lost impoverished son only after having him shovel manure for twenty years; see *Miaofa lianhua jing* 妙法蓮華經, Taishō 262:9.17a27.

165 In Tiantai Zhiyi's 天台智顗 (538–97) *Sublime Meaning of the Lotus Sūtra*, *Miaofa lianhua jing xuanyi* 妙法蓮華經玄義, Taishō 1716:33.703c10–11.

166 *Vimalakīrti's Instructions*, *Weimojie suoshuo jing* 維摩詰所説經, Taishō 475:14.544b29–c1.

167 These three essentials (*sanyao*/*samyo* 三要) are (1) the "faculty of great faith" (*daxin'gen*/*daesin-geun* 大信根), (2) "great fury," "ferocity," or perhaps "great passionate intent" (*dafenzhi*/*daebunji* 大憤志), and (3) the "great sensation of doubt" (*da yiqing* / *daeuijeong* 大疑情). For a discussion of these three and a translation of the relevant section in Gaofeng's *Essentials of Chan*, see Robert E. Buswell, Jr., "The Transformation of Doubt (*Yíqíng* 疑情) into a Positive Emotion in Chinese Buddhist Meditation," in *Love and Emotions in Traditional Chinese Literature*, edited by Halvor Eifring (Leiden: E. J. Brill, 2004), 225–36.

168 These are the widely quoted last words of Layman Pang (但願空諸所有 慎勿實諸所無), *Recorded Sayings of Layman Pang*, *Pang jushi yulu* 龐居士語錄, Xuzangjing 1336:69.134b11; Ruth Fuller Sasaki, Yoshitaka Iriya, and Dana R. Fraser, trans., *A Man*

of Zen: The Recorded Sayings of Layman P'ang, a Ninth-Century Zen Classic (New York and Tokyo: Weatherhill, 1971), 76.

169 Scholars have been unable to trace the source of this quotation. A close parallel of this line appears above in part II, chap. 3.

170 From the *Recorded Sayings of Layman Pang, Pang jushi yulu* 龐居士語錄, Xuzangjing 1336:69.131a17; see Sasaki et al., *Man of Zen*, 46.

171 *Susimgyeol* 修心訣, following the rendering in Buswell, *Chinul: Selected Works*, 210–11.

172 This line as cited here is attributed to the *Mahāparinirvāṇa Sūtra* in the *Mirror of the Source Record, Zongjing lu* 宗鏡録, Taishō 2016:48.679c23–24. The line is slightly different in the *Mahāparinirvāṇa Sūtra* itself (*Da banniepan jing* 大般涅槃經, Taishō 374:12.547a15–16): "All the buddhas, the world-honored ones, treat concentration and wisdom equally; therefore they clearly see the buddha nature, with full clarity and without obstruction."

173 It is a common trope in Indian folklore that the *haṃsa* (a goose or a swan) can with its beak separate out the milk from a solution of milk and water. This analogy of the king of geese (*haṃsarāja*) appears, e.g., in the *Sūtrālamkāraśāstra/Kalpanāmaṇḍitikā, Da zhuangyanlun jing* 大莊嚴論經, Taishō 201:4.319b21 and 26. The analogy of the king of geese appears also in Seon materials: e.g., the *Tiansheng Expanded Lamplight Record, Tiansheng guangdeng lu* 天聖廣燈錄, Xuzangjing 1553:78.469a22–23.

174 The three levels of sagacity (*sanxian/samhyeon* 三賢) are the initial three divisions of the fifty-two stages of the bodhisattva path—the ten abidings, ten practices, and ten dedications. The ten stages of sanctity (*shisheng/sipseong* 十聖) are the ten "grounds," or *bhūmi*, that culminate in buddhahood. See Robert E. Buswell, Jr., and Robert M. Gimello, eds., *Paths to Liberation: The Mārga and Its Transformations in Buddhist Thought*, Kuroda Institute Studies in East Asian Buddhism 7 (Honolulu: University of Hawaii Press, 1992), 9.

175 These wrong views (*dṛṣṭi*) include (1) the view of a perduring self or soul; the two extreme views of (2) eternalism and (3) annihilationism; (4) fallacious views, such as denying the efficacy of karma, rebirth, and causality; (5) attachment to speculative views; (6) attachment to the efficacy of rules and rituals. See Buswell and Lopez, *Princeton Dictionary*, 269–70, s.v. "dṛṣṭi."

176 Juzhi 俱胝 (ca. ninth century) was a fifth-generation successor in Mazu Daoyi's Hongzhou lineage. For the story of "Juzhi's one finger" (俱胝一指), see, for example, *Jingde Record of Transmitting the Lamplight, Jingde chuandeng lu* 景德傳燈錄, Taishō 2076:51.466a21 et passim.

177 *Shuopo pishuang / seolpa bisang* 說破砒霜. This comparison of conceptual explanations to powdered arsenic occasionally appears in Chan texts; see, e.g., "The two words *buddha dharma* ... are wolf poison and arsenic powder" (狼毒砒霜); *Comprehensive Records of the Five Lamplights, Wudeng quanshu* 五燈全書, Xuzangjing 1571:82.144c10.

178 *Xueshang jiashuang / seolsang gasang* 雪上加霜. A phrase widely found in Seon literature and frequently used, for example, by Yunmen Wenyan; see, e.g., *Yunmen's Extensive Records, Yunmen guanglu* 雲門廣録, Taishō 1988:47.553a03 et passim.

179 Huangbo evokes here the seminal line from the *Awakening of Faith*, which posits

that the origin of ignorance in the arising of conceptualization: "suddenly a thought arises; this is called ignorance" (忽然念起名爲無明); *Dasheng qixin lun* 大乘起信論, Taishō 1666:32.577c6–7; cf. Yoshito S. Hakeda, trans., *The Awakening of Faith Attributed to Aśvaghosha* (New York: Columbia University Press, 1967), 50.

180 *Diamond Sūtra*, *Jingang bore boluomi jing* 金剛般若波羅蜜經. Taishō 235:8.751b27–28.

181 *Jingang bore boluomi jing* 金剛般若波羅蜜經, Taishō 235:8.749c22–23.

182 This precise passage remains untraced. The *Treasure Store Treatise* attributes the first part of the line to an unidentified sūtra: "A sūtra says, 'The prior thought is ordinary, the subsequent thought is noble.'" See *Baozang lun* 寶藏論, Taishō 1857:45.148c13.

183 The third statement here refers to the third of Linji's "teaching of the three statements" which appear in the *Record of Linji*; *Linji yulu*, Taishō 1985:47.502a5–7; Sasaki, *Record of Linji*, 264. As we noted previously (note 93), there are a few different interpretations of Linji's "three statements" given in the tradition, but generally, the teaching is regarded as referring to three different levels of Seon realization or three different types of Seon rhetoric that lead to those different levels. In this sense, the third statement refers to a more basic rational and explanatory type of rhetoric, which leads only to a conceptual understanding of the Buddhist teachings. See Seong-Uk Kim, "The Zen Theory of Language: Linji Yixuan's Teaching of 'Three Statements, Three Mysteries, and Three Essentials' (*sanju sanxuan sanyao* 三句三玄三要)," *Journal of the International Association of Buddhist Studies* 36/37 (2013/2014): 69–90.

184 This line appears in the transmission verse of Buddhanandin 佛陀難提, the eighth Indian patriarch of the Chan tradition; see *Jingde Record of Transmitting the Lamplight*, *Jingde chuandeng lu* 景德傳燈録, Taishō 2076:51.208c23.

185 These "non-Buddhist naturalists" refers to such heterodox teachers as Ajita-Keśakambala, the head of the Naturalist or Materialist (Lokāyata) school of the śramaṇa strand of Indian religion, who denied the efficacy of moral cause and effect and therefore any prospect of rebirth. See Buswell and Lopez, *Princeton Dictionary*, s.v. "Ajita," "Lokāyata."

186 This simile, which derives from the *Mahāparinirvāṇa Sūtra*, describes an expedient way of distracting a child from crying; see note 70 above. Huangbo uses this simile previously in part I, chap. 14, and part II, chap. 16.

187 These are last two lines of Huineng's famous verse in the *Platform Sūtra*; see note 132. Taishō 2008:48.349a8. This same passage is quoted above in part II, chap. 8.

188 This line appears frequently in Mahāyāna scriptural literature. As but two of many examples, see the *Mahāratnakūṭa Sūtra*, *Dabaoji jing* 大寶積經, Taishō 310:11.0346c28; *Laṅkāvatāra Sūtra*, *Ru Lengqie jing* 入楞伽經, Taishō 671:16.528c28.Cf. also note 71 above for a similar line from the *Diamond Sūtra*.

189 Subul Sunim seems here to be alluding to the story of Yajñadatta in the *Śūraṅgama Sūtra*. Yajñadatta woke up one morning thinking he had lost his head and went around like a wild man trying to locate it; of course, his head was exactly where it had always been. The simile is to our state of ignorance, wherein we have always had the enlightened nature but think we have lost it and need to find it. See *Shoulengyan jing* 首楞嚴經, Taishō 945:19.121b.

190 As Subul Sunim notes, this passage appears in the *Mahāparinirvāṇa Sūtra*; *Da banniepan jing* 大般涅槃經, Taishō 374:12.412c24–25. Huangbo also quotes this same passage above in part I, chap. 9. The passage came to be widely quoted in Chan materials.

191 This episode is quoted in Yongming Yanshou's *Mirror of the Source Record*, *Zongjing lu* 宗鏡録, Taishō 2016:48.488a15 et passim. In his commentary, Subul Sunim notes that this account appears in the 1253 *Sources of the Five Lamplights* [of Chan]; for this story, see *Wudeng huiyuan* 五燈會元, Xuzangjing 1565:80.30b15–30c2.

192 "This view that posits a buddha mind that is existent" (*youjian foxin* / *yugyeon bulsim* 有見佛心): *youjian*/*yugyeon* often refers to the mistaken view that things have a perduring existence (*astidṛṣṭi*), which is how Subul Sunim interprets the compound here. But the term also refers to the "visible," or "tangible," quality of material form (*sanidarśana*), so it might more appropriately mean in the context here "the buddha mind as being something visible/tangible."

193 "Doe and fawn died together": this line is taken from a story in the *Dharmapāda*/*Udānavarga*, where a lion saw a doe suckling her newborn fawn. The lion knew that the doe would never abandon her fawn, so he attacked them, and "doe and fawn died together." See *Udānavarga*, *Chuyao jing* 出曜經, Taishō 212:4.640b14–15.

194 See note 191 above.

195 This exchange appears in chapter 5 of *Vimalakīrti's Instructions*, "Mañjuśrī Inquires About His Illness"; *Weimojie suoshuo jing* 維摩詰所説經, Taishō 475:14.544b13–17. Cf. the translation by John R. McRae, *The Vimalakīrti Sutra*, BDK English Tripiṭaka Series (Berkeley: Numata Center for Buddhist Translation and Research, 2004), 108.

196 This exchange appears in chapter 3 of *Vimalakīrti's Instructions*, "Disciples"; *Weimojie suoshuo jing* 維摩詰所説經, Taishō 475:14.541a12–23. Cf. McRae, *Vimalakīrti Sutra*, 91.

197 The two compounds ("real characteristic of things" 實相 and "just so" 如是) of this four-character phrase frequently appear juxtaposed in Mahāyāna scriptures, but they are usually are not connected semantically. For one of the few references that seems to carry a meaning similar to what Huangbo suggests here, see *Sūtra on the Samādhi of Sitting in Meditation*, *Zuochan sanmei jing* 坐禪三昧經, Taishō 624:15.278c10.

198 This phrase is quoted frequently in Chan literature and typically attributed to an anonymous past master. In the *Jingde Record of Transmitting the Lamplight* (*Jingde chuandeng lu* 景德傳燈録, Taishō 2076:51.348c22), the line is specifically attributed to Weishan/Guishan Lingyou, Huangbo's contemporary and cofounder of the Weiyang/Guiyang school of Chan.

199 For these five types of eyes, see note 26 above. Subul Sunim discusses them previously in his commentary to part I, chap. 3.

200 *Dependent power* (*yitong*/*uitong* 依通) is the third of five kinds of supernatural powers known in East Asian apocryphal materials. Iti s defined as supernatural power that is dependent on, or derived from, external agents, such as hallucinogenic drugs, talismans, or spells. See *Precious Store Treatise*, *Baozang lun* 寶藏論, Taishō 1875:45.147b5–7, and Buswell and Lopez, *Digital Dictionary*, s.v. "yitong."

201 This story about Maitreya snapping his fingers and bringing Sudhana to enlightenment

is widely cited in both Hwaeom and Seon literature; see, among many examples, the Huayan exegete Fazang's 法藏 (643–712) *Record Probing the Profundities of the Flower Garland Sūtra, Huayan jing tanxuan ji* 華嚴經探玄記, Taishō 1733:35.488c20.

202 The closest parallel passage we have found to this metaphor is a discussion in the **Buddhacarita* by the second-century CE Kashmiri monk Saṅgharakṣa, which says, "Those who are guarding nirvāṇa are like a big dog relentlessly guarding a corpse, running constantly to and fro without ever resting"; see *Sengqieluocha suoji jing* 僧伽羅刹所集經, Taishō 194:4.118a3–4.

203 This exchange appears in chapter 9 of *Vimalakīrti's Instructions*, the "Dharma Gate of Nonduality"; *Weimojie suoshuo jing* 維摩詰所説經, Taishō 475:14.550c1ff, esp. 551c22–23. Cf. McRae, *Vimalakīrti Sūtra*, 143ff., esp. 148.

204 For this case and the passages Subul Sunim discusses below, see *Blue Cliff Record*, *Biyan lu*, Taishō 2003:48.209b–210b; Thomas Cleary & J. C. Cleary, trans., *The Blue Cliff Record* (Boulder: Prajñā Press, 1978), 541–47.

205 This exact quotation remains untraced, but cf. the *Laṅkāvatāra Sūtra*'s statement, "Those deluded persons do not realize that a sound's aspects of production and of cessation are actually not produced and extinguished"; *Ru Lengqie jing* 入楞伽經, Taishō 671:16.551b16–17.

206 *Suichu zozhu lichu jie zhen / sucheo jakju ipcheo gae jin* 隨處作主 立處皆眞. Quoting the *Record of Linji*, *Linji lu* 臨濟録, Taishō 1985:47.498a19.

207 This line from the *Brahmā's Net Sūtra* appeared in part II, chap. 5. See note 105 above.

208 *Diamond Sūtra*, *Jingang bore boluomi jing* 金剛般若波羅蜜經, Taishō 235:8.750b14.

209 *Liang Dynasty's Great Layman Fu's Verses on the Diamond Sūtra*, *Liangchao Fu dashi song Jingang jing* 梁朝傅大師頌金剛經, Taishō 2732:85.5b5.

210 *Śūraṅgama Sūtra*, *Shoulengyan jing* 首楞嚴經, Taishō 945:19.119b13.

211 From the *Platform Sūtra*; *Liuzu tan jing* 六祖壇經, Taishō 2008:48.349b29. This same line was cited earlier in part I, chap. 15. This analogy of drinking water is found widely throughout Seon literature to point out the need for a personal experience of awakening. Dahui Zonggao uses it frequently: see, e.g., Jeffrey L. Broughton with Elise Yoko Watanabe, trans., *The Letters of Chan Master Dahui Pujue* (New York: Oxford University Press, 2017), 97, 104, 166, 262, 312, et passim.

212 From the *Recorded Sayings of Layman Pang*, *Pang jushi yulu* 龐居士語錄, Xuzangjing 1336:69.131a19; see Sasaki et al., *Man of Zen*, 47. This exchange also appears in case 42 in the *Blue Cliff Record*; see *Biyan lu* 碧巖録, Taishō 2003:48.179c4.

213 As Subul Sunim notes in his commentary that follows, this verse appears in the *Lotus Sūtra*; see chapter 2 "Skillful Means," *Miaofa lianhua jing* 妙法蓮華經, Taishō 262:9.6a2–3; cf. Tsugunari Kubo and Akira Yuyama, trans., *The Lotus Sutra*, BDK English Tripiṭaka Series (Berkeley: Numata Center for Buddhist Translation and Research, 2007), 24–25.

214 Sengcan, *Verses on Faith in Mind*, *Xinxin ming* 信心銘, Taishō 2010:48.376b21.

215 This story of the Buddha's wager with Sun Wukong that the monkey king could not escape from his palm appears in Wu Cheng'en's 吴承恩 (ca. 1500–1582) *Journey to the West* (*Xiyou ji* 西遊記); see the translation in Anthony Yu, ed. and trans., *The Journey to the West*, vol. 1 (Chicago: University of Chicago Press, 1977), 173–74.

216 Quoted (with the use of a homonym for "source") from the *Śūraṅgama Sūtra*; *Shoulengyan jing* 首楞嚴經, Taishō 945:19.130a24.

217 *Jingde Record of Transmitting the Lamplight*, *Jingde chuandeng lu* 景徳傳燈録, Taishō 2076:51.216b16. The full verse is given in Subul Sunim's commentary.

218 In other editions of Huangbo's text, this section appears as the final chapter of part I.

219 This is an unattributed quote from Yaoshan Weiyan 藥山惟儼 (745/753–827/828); see *Supplement to the Transmission of the Lamplight*, *Xu chuandeng lu* 續傳燈録, Taishō 2077:51.518c15–16.

Bibliography

Pre-modern Sinographic Buddhist sources are quoted from either the *Taishō Buddhist Canon* (Taishō) or the *Manji Supplement to the Canon* (Xuzangjing) and cited in the following format:

> Text Name, Taishō or Xuzangjing, sequential number:/volume number./page./register./line; for example,
> *Jingde chuandeng lu* 景德傳燈録, Taishō 2076:51.208c23.
> *Wudeng huiyuan* 五燈會元, Xuzangjing 1565:80.30b15.

Taishō shinshū daizōkyō 大正新修大藏經. Tokyo: Issaikyō Kankōkai, 1924–35. We have used the SAT digital search functions to search that canon: Saṃganīkīkṛtaṃ Taiśotripiṭakaṃ (SAT) Daizōkyō Text Database, produced by Masahiro Shimoda et al., and maintained by the Graduate School of Humanities and Sociology, University of Tokyo. http://21dzk.l.u-tokyo.ac.jp/SAT/. Accessed January 30, 2018.

Manji Shinsan Dainihon Zokuzōkyō 卍新纂大日本續藏經. Tokyo: Kokusho Kankōkai 株式會社國書刊行會, 1975–89. We have used the CBETA online edition for both text and search: CBETA Dianzi Fodian Jicheng 電子佛典集成. http://tripitaka.cbeta.org. Accessed January 30, 2018.

Secondary Sources

Baengnyeon Seonseo Ganhaenghoe 백련선서간행회, trans. *Seollim bojeon* 禪林寶典. In Seollim gogyeong chongseo 禪林古鏡叢書, vol. 1. Seoul: Janggyeonggak Chulpansa 장경각 출판사, 1988.

Blofeld, John, trans. *The Zen Teaching of Huang Po on the Transmission of Mind*. New York: Grove Press, 1958.

Broughton, Jeffrey L.. *The Bodhidharma Anthology: The Earliest Records of Zen*. Berkeley and Los Angeles: University of California Press, 1999.

———. *Zongmi on Chan*. New York: Columbia University Press, 2009.

Broughton, Jeffrey L., with Elise Yoko Watanabe, trans. *The "Chan Whip" Anthology: A Companion to Zen Practice*. New York: Oxford University Press, 2015.

———. *The Letters of Chan Master Dahui Pujue*. New York: Oxford University Press, 2017.

Buswell, Robert E., Jr. "Ch'an Hermeneutics: A Korean View." In Donald S. Lopez, Jr., ed., *Buddhist Hermeneutics*, 231–56. Kuroda Institute Studies in East Asian Buddhism 6. University of Hawaii Press, 1988.

———, trans. *Chinul: Selected Works*. Collected Works of Korean Buddhism 2. Seoul: Jogye Order of Korean Buddhism, 2012.

———, trans. *Cultivating Original Enlightenment: Wŏnhyo's Exposition of the Vajrasamādhi-Sūtra (Kŭmgang sammaegyŏng Non)*. The International Association of Wŏnhyo Studies' Collected Works of Wŏnhyo 1. Honolulu: University of Hawaii Press, 2007.

———, trans. *Numinous Awareness Is Never Dark: The Korean Master Chinul's "Excerpts" on Zen Practice*. Korean Classics Library: Philosophy and Religion. Honolulu: University of Hawaii Press, 2016.

———. "The Short-Cut Approach of *K'an-hua* Meditation: The Evolution of a Practical Subitism in Chinese Ch'an Buddhism." In *Sudden and Gradual Approaches to Enlightenment in Chinese Thought*, edited by Peter N. Gregory, 321–77. Kuroda Institute Studies in East Asian Buddhism 5. Honolulu: University of Hawaii Press, 1987.

———. "The Transformation of Doubt (*Yíqíng* 疑情) into a Positive Emotion in Chinese Buddhist Meditation." In *Love and Emotions in Traditional Chinese Literature*, edited by Halvor Eifring, 225–36. Leiden: E. J. Brill, 2004.

———. *The Zen Monastic Experience: Buddhist Practice in Contemporary Korea*. Princeton, NJ: Princeton University Press, 1992.

Buswell, Robert E. Jr., and Robert M. Gimello, eds. *Paths to Liberation: The*

Mārga and Its Transformations in Buddhist Thought. Kuroda Institute Studies in East Asian Buddhism 7. Honolulu: University of Hawaii Press, 1992.

Buswell, Robert E. Jr., and Donald S. Lopez, Jr. *The Princeton Dictionary of Buddhism*. Princeton , NJ: Princeton University Press, 2014.

Cleary, Thomas, and J. C. Cleary, trans. *The Blue Cliff Record*. Boulder: Prajñā Press, 1978.

Digital Dictionary of Buddhism. Edited by A. Charles Muller. http://www.buddhism-dict.net/ddb/. Accessed January 30, 2018.

Hakeda, Yoshito S. trans. *The Awakening of Faith Attributed to Aśvaghosha*. New York: Columbia University Press, 1967.

Hucker, Charles O. *A Dictionary of Official Titles in Imperial China*. Stanford, CA: Stanford University Press, 1985.

Iriya Yoshitaka 入矢義高, ed. and trans. *Denshin hōyō—Enryōroku* 伝心法要 : 宛陵錄. Zen no goroku 禪の語錄 8. Tokyo: Chikuma Shobō 筑摩書房, 1969.

Joo, Ryan Bongseok (Haemin Sunim). "Gradual Experiences of Sudden Enlightenment: The Varieties of Ganhwa Seon Teachings in Contemporary Korea." In *Ganhwa Seon, Segye-reul bichuda* 간화선, 세계를 비추다, Proceedings of the First International Conference on Ganhwa Seon, 2: 219–39. Seoul: Dongguk Daehakgyo Bulgyo Haksulwon 동국대학교 불교학술원, 2010. A version of this paper is available on-line at https://terebess.hu/zen/mesterek/Contemporary-Hwadu-Practice.pdf. Accessed January 30, 2018.

Kim, Seong-Uk. "Three Places of Mind-Transmission: The Polemical Application of Mind-Transmission Stories in Korean Sŏn Buddhism." *Journal of the American Oriental Society* 133.4 (2013): 635–50.

———. "The Zen Theory of Language: Linji Yixuan's Teaching of 'Three Statements, Three Mysteries, and Three Essentials' (*sanju sanxuan sanyao* 三句三玄三要)." *Journal of the International Association of Buddhist Studies* 36/37 (2013/2014): 69–90.

Kubo, Tsugunari, and Akira Yuyama, trans. *The Lotus Sutra*. BDK English Tripiṭaka Series. Berkeley: Numata Center for Buddhist Translation and Research, 2007.

Lu K'uan Yu (Charles Luk). *The Transmission of the Mind: Outside the Teaching*, vol. 1. London: Rider, 1974.

McRae, John R. trans. *Essentials of the Transmission of Mind*. In *Zen Texts*, 1–42. BDK English Tripiṭaka Series. Berkeley: Numata Center for Buddhist Translation and Research, 2005.

———. *The Platform Sutra of the Sixth Patriarch*. BDK English Tripiṭaka Series. Berkeley: Numata Center for Buddhist Translation and Research, 2000.

———. *The Vimalakīrti Sutra*. BDK English Tripiṭaka Series. Berkeley: Numata Center for Buddhist Translation and Research, 2004.

Sasaki, Ruth Fuller, trans., *The Record of Linji*. Edited by Thomas Yuho Kirchner. Honolulu: University of Hawaii Press, 2009.

Sasaki, Ruth Fuller, Yoshitaka Iriya, and Dana R. Fraser, trans. *A Man of Zen: The Recorded Sayings of Layman P'ang, a Ninth-Century Zen Classic*. New York and Tokyo: Weatherhill, 1971.

Schlütter, Morten. *How Zen Became Zen: The Dispute over Enlightenment and the Formation of Chan Buddhism in Song-Dynasty China*. Kuroda Institute Studies in East Asian Buddhism 22. Honolulu: University of Hawaii Press, 2008.

Subul Seunim 修弗. *Heunjeok eopsi naneun sae: Jeonsimbeopyo, Subul Seonsa Seonhae* 흔적 없이 나는 새: 傳心法要 修弗禪師 禪解. Seoul: Gimm-Young Publishers, Inc. 김영사, 2014. 604 pages. ISBN: 978-349-6903-7 03220.

———. *Hwanggeumbit bonghwang-i* 황금빛 봉황이. Seoul: Yeose-A-Mun 여세아문, 2005.

Suzuki, Daisetz Teitaro. *Manual of Zen Buddhism*. New York: Grove Press, 1994.

Watson, Burton. trans. *The Lotus Sutra*. New York: Columbia University Press, 1993.

Welter, Albert Franklin. "Huang-po's Notion of Mind." MA Thesis, McMaster University, 1978. *Open Access Dissertations and Theses*, Paper 2815 http://digitalcommons.mcmaster.ca/opendissertations/2815. Accessed January 30, 2018.

Wright, Dale S. "The Huang-po Literature." In *The Zen Canon: Understanding the Classic Zen Texts*, edited by Dale S. Wright and Steven Heine, 107–35. London and New York: Oxford University Press, 2004.

Yampolsky, Philip B., trans. *The Platform Sutra of the Sixth Patriarch*. New York: Columbia University Press, 1967.

Yanagida Seizan 柳田聖山, ed. and trans. *Daruma no goroku: Ninyū shigyō ron* 達摩の語録: 二入四行論, Zen no goroku 禪の語録, vol. 1. Tōkyō: Chikuma Shobō, 1969.

———, ed. *Shike goroku, Goke goroku* 四家語錄, 五家語錄. Kyoto: Chūbun Shuppansha, 1983.

Yu, Anthony, ed. and trans. *The Journey to the West*, vol. 1. Chicago: University of Chicago Press, 1977.

Index

C

E

K

L

M

N

O

P

T

About the Contributors

Seon Master Subul Sunim (b. 1953) is an influential Zen master in Korean Buddhism's Jogye Order, the largest Buddhist order in Korea. He was first ordained in 1975. He founded the organization Anguk Seonwon in Busan in 1989 and opened a branch in Seoul in 1996. Over twenty-five thousand laypeople have taken part in more than three hundred retreats with Master Subul in Korea and around the world. Recently, Subul Sunim has served as the abbot of Beomeosa Monastery and as the Seon master at the International Meditation Center at Dongguk University.

Robert E. Buswell, Jr. (b. 1953) is Distinguished Professor of Chinese and Korean Buddhist Studies at the University of California, Los Angeles, where he holds the Irving and Jean Stone Endowed Chair in Humanities.

Seong-Uk Kim is the Il Hwan and Soon Ja Cho Assistant Professor of Korean Culture and Religion at Columbia University.

What to Read Next from Wisdom Publications

The Zen Teaching of Homeless Kodo
Kodo Sawaki
Commentary by Shohaku Okumura and Kosho Uchiyama

"Kodo Sawaki was straight-to-the-point, irreverent, and deeply insightful—and one of the most influential Zen teachers for us in the West. I'm very happy to see this book."—Brad Warner, author of *Hardcore Zen*

Zen Vows for Daily Life
Robert Aitken
Foreword by Thich Nhat Hanh

A poetic classic from a major figure of American Zen.

Zen's Chinese Heritage
The Masters and Their Teachings
Andy Ferguson
Foreword by Reb Anderson and Steven Heine

"This is an indispensable reference for any student of Buddhism. Ferguson has given us an impeccable and very readable translation."
—John Daido Loori, late abbot, Zen Mountain Monastery

Wake Up and Laugh
The Dharma Teachings of Zen Master Daehaeng

Wisdom, warmth, and humor from a renowned Zen master.

About Wisdom Publications

Wisdom Publications is the leading publisher of classic and contemporary Buddhist books and practical works on mindfulness. To learn more about us or to explore our other books, please visit our website at wisdompubs.org or contact us at the address below.

Wisdom Publications
199 Elm Street
Somerville, MA 02144 USA

We are a 501(c)(3) organization, and donations in support of our mission are tax deductible.

Wisdom Publications is affiliated with the Foundation for the Preservation of the Mahayana Tradition (FPMT).